Aggressor

Tom Barker

# Aggressors in Blue

## Exposing Police Sexual Misconduct

palgrave
macmillan

Tom Barker
School of Justice Studies
Eastern Kentucky University
Richmond, KY, USA

ISBN 978-3-030-28440-4      ISBN 978-3-030-28441-1    (eBook)
https://doi.org/10.1007/978-3-030-28441-1

Cover credit: zef art/shutterstock.com

This Palgrave Macmillan imprint is published by the registered company Springer Nature Switzerland AG
The registered company address is: Gewerbestrasse 11, 6330 Cham, Switzerland

# Contents

# List of Tables

# List of Boxes

# 1

# Overview

## Introduction

Sexual misconduct—any form of *proscribed* sexual contact—by workers in the criminal justice system—courts, law enforcement, and corrections—is pervasive and has a long history in the various occupations that make up the formal systems of social control. That focus is too broad for this inquiry. Our focus is on the *policework* occupation (Barker 2011. Italics used whenever referring to the *policework* occupation). The nature of the duties makes *policework* a morally dangerous occupation wherever it has been established. Virtually every US police agency has a history of police misconduct and that includes police sexual misconduct (Klockers et al. 2000). Why? The workers, *policework* occupation, perform their discretionary duties in private settings without supervision or witness, and their coworkers are reluctant to report misconduct. The book will closely examine PSM in the United States; however, police misconduct including police sexual misconduct is not just an American problem. Police misconduct is an occupational deviance problem throughout the world. In 1915, the noted police authority Raymond Fosdick said the following,

© The Author(s) 2020
T. Barker, *Aggressors in Blue*,
https://doi.org/10.1007/978-3-030-28441-1_1

Everywhere [he was commenting on European Police Systems] there are special pitfalls for the policeman, peculiar temptations to which he is continually exposed. The prostitute who walks the street, the bookmaker who plies his trade on the sidewalk, the public-house proprietor who would keep open after hours, the prisoner on his way to a cell, in short every man or woman who would escape the operation of the penalty of law and is ready to pay [favors, money, or sex] for immunity constitutes a menace to the integrity of the policeman. (Fosdick 1915: 369–370)

Police sexual misconduct and other forms of police misconduct are present to some extent in all police agencies globally. To present a global analysis of police sexual misconduct is beyond the scope of this book. However, when possible I present evidence from other countries to make a point or demonstrate the occupational nature of police sexual misconduct. I use American and UK examples as my main sources of information.

## PSM in the UK

Police sexual misconduct examples in the UK are used repeatedly because: (1) the studies are in English, (2) there are numerous official and social media PSM accounts, (3) the London Metropolitan Public Paid Police Model is the basis for the American police model. Furthermore, police sexual misconduct in the UK police systems has a long history and is pervasive (Critchley 1967; Waddington 1999). An *Observer* study based on the UK Freedom of Information Act published in the *Guardian* found 1491 sexual misconduct complaints against police officers in England and Wales from 2012 to 2018 (Chaminda, May 18, 2019). Ten of the 33 police forces in England and Wales did not respond to the inquiry. The common police agency response in the United States and other countries is to not respond to media requests for damaging information.

The results of the *Observer* found that 371 complaints were upheld and resulted in the resignations of 197 police officers, special officers or community support officers. The largest number of complaints came from the London Metropolitan Police force with 594 complaints—119 were upheld. Among the overall complaints were: developing intimate sexual relationships with vulnerable members of the public—victims and suspects, child sexual abuse, producing and distributing child pornography, sexual harassment, and rape. The study concluded that there was a sexist culture among some officers leading to numerous complaints by colleagues of sexual harassment and sexual assault. There is a need for more empirical study of PSM in the UK and other global police agencies. The police sexual misconduct typology developed in this work will stimulate more interest and lead to more research and analysis.

## PSM in the United States

Police sexual misconduct has a long history in American police agencies (see Eschholz and Vaughn 2001). Police sexual assaults by police officers were reported in 19% of the brutality cases in New York City from 1863 to 1894 (Johnson 2003). Reiss (1971) in his study of patrolmen in three American cities concluded that in any year a substantial minority of police officers engage in behavior that violates the criminal law, misbehaves toward citizens, and violates department rules and regulations. Those criminal violations include police sexual misconduct.

* * *

We examine police sexual misconduct (PSM) as a form of occupational deviance and present a heuristic model—PSM Causal Equation—to explain PSM. The PSM Causal Equation is based on rational choice theory and has three dimensions: inclination, opportunity, and real or perceived low risk. The PSM Causal Equation Model is supported by data and theory—deterrence, self-control, social learning theories and a modified routine activities model—applied to police sexual misconduct. Finally, we develop an Empirical Typology of PSM and present Illustrative Examples of each type. Each PSM type is examined according to its "best fit" to the PSM Causal Equation.

## Occupational Deviance

Occupational deviance is deviant (rule or norm-violating) behaviors—criminal and non-criminal—that occur because of the nature of the worker's occupation (Bryant 1974). A worker with the inclination to engage in behavior proscribed by law, rules, or prescribed professional codes is presented with the opportunity because of their work duties. When the intersection of inclination and opportunity occurs under a perceived low-risk environment, the likelihood of occupational deviance is increased. This nexus—*inclination, opportunity, and low risk*—is impacted in police work settings by the unequal power relationship between the worker and his or her "client" (Barker 1977).

*Policework* is a unique occupation because law enforcement officers as representatives of the state engage in patterns of behavior not available to other citizens. Law enforcement officers (LEOs) by law stop and search other citizens and interfere with their free movement including making arrests with or without a warrant. Citizens are always in an extortionate relationship when confronted by law enforcement officers because law enforcement officers may use force, including deadly force to compel their legitimate objectives. Furthermore, the occupational subculture of police work contains a set of shared understandings—norms—as to when, why, and against whom deadly force can be used (Waegel 1984; Barker, forthcoming). In the US procedural laws restrict these powers, but these limitations do little good on the street in police-citizen encounters with illegal intentions on the part of the officer. There is ample evidence to support the allegations of unnecessary or illegal stops by American law enforcement officers. These awesome powers are frequently abused for personal and venal reasons, making police misconduct including sexual abuse possible (Barker 1977; Chappell and Piquero 2004). However, policing is only one of many occupations that are sexual abuse-prone.

# Sexual Abuse-Prone Occupations

Sexual misconduct is a pattern of deviant behavior common to occupations where workers and clients do not meet on equal terms of power and authority—sexual abuse-prone occupations. The noted British sociologist and police scholar, P.A.J. Waddington, called policing a "scandal-prone" occupation because of the numerous opportunities for misconduct, including sexual misconduct (Waddington 1999). There are numerous other "scandal prone" occupations—sexual abuse-prone occupations. Sexual abuse-prone relationships are most likely to occur in work-related settings where there is an unequal power differential between the victim and the perpetrator (Calhoun and Coleman 2002). That is, the victim is perceived to have less authority or status than the perpetrator, or conversely, the perpetrator possesses more enhanced power than the victim. States pass laws that prohibit sexual relationships between workers and clients in recognized sexual abuse occupations. Examples of such occupations that readily come to mind are priests and other religious clergy, coaches, doctors, and other medical workers or caregivers, college professors, and K-12 schoolteachers.

The current #MeToo movement has expanded the list of abuse-prone occupations exponentially including elected governmental officials—possibly the occupation with the most numerous examples of sexual abuse and cover-up. In effect, the work setting of sexual abuse-prone occupations creates an unequal power relationship between the victim and the perpetrator, increasing the likelihood of improper sexual relationships.

The *policework* occupation and its work setting exacerbate its sexual abuse-prone nature. Police/citizen encounters are for the most part unsupervised, clandestine events. The shared occupational police culture and isolated nature of off-duty contacts increase the likelihood that law enforcement officers will not report fellow officer sexual misconduct—The Blue Wall of Secrecy (Barker 1977; Maher 2007; Manning 2009, and other police scholars too numerous to list). The code of silence is an organizational culture problem present in other police systems throughout the world. Australia has a long history of police misconduct including police sexual aggression (Chan 1997). Australian Aboriginal and Islander women and girls are police targets for rape, custodial sexual abuse, and other forms of sexual violence (Chan 1997: 23). The code of silence is a factor in the occurrence of this police sexual misconduct. A recent study of a sample of Australian police found that a minority of officers—4 to 6%—in the eight police forces would not report fellow officers for crimes such as theft, perjury, and assault—real low risk (Porter and Prenzler 2016).

Our discussion of police sexual abuse as a type/category of police occupational deviance begins with the definition of *policework* as an occupation and the parameters that guide the discussion that follows.

## Law Enforcement Officers (LEO) Sexual Misconduct

*Policework* is an occupation performed by paid public law enforcement officers (LEOs) at all levels of government. In the United States, these paid public employees have general or limited arrest powers, depending on the state, federal statutes, and case law. LEOs perform one or more of the public safety services of traffic, patrol, investigation, and detention/custody. All these public officials have the power to detain, arrest, search, and use deadly force. The US LEO definition includes publicly paid law enforcement officers in local, county, state, federal, and special district agencies such as campus police agencies, park police, Indian tribal police, and airport police. Detention/custody officials in lockups, jails, and prison are included; however, private security personnel are not (see Barker et al. 1994 for an earlier definition).

Some object to the inclusion of detention/custody, correction workers in the definition of law enforcement officer, and a discussion of law enforcement sexual abuse. However, there is support for this inclusion. Detention/custody officers in jails, lockups, and prisons have been included in prior police sexual misconduct research studies. Sapp (1986) was the first academic to add detention/custody and corrections workers in his typology of police sexual misconduct. Vaughn (1999) added custody and correction workers to Kraska and Kappeler's definition of police sexual violence (PSV) and discussed their sexual misconduct as a pattern of police sexual violence. Vaughn cites several instances of PSV where jailers sexually assaulted inmates, including one case that the court stated, "it is foreseeable that sexual assault by some law enforcement officials occurs when male jailers are in charge of female inmates" (Vaughn 1999: 342). Eschholz and Vaughn (2001) stated that detention/custody officers are included in the study of police sexual violence because, "The combination of implied public trust and legal access to physical force creates a dangerous mix for victims of sexual abuse at the hands of police and correctional officers" (Eschholz and Vaughn 2001: 389).

The inclusion of detention/custody and corrections officers is a logical addition to the study of police sexual misconduct for several reasons: (1) detention/custody and corrections officers have custody of inmates awaiting trial or serving sentences—a public safety service; (2) local police officers and deputy sheriffs act as detention/custody workers in lockups and jails; and (3) most states and the federal government recognize correctional officers as law enforcement or peace officers with limited or general police powers. We also include federal law enforcement officers in our discussion because their sexual misconduct is pervasive and expanding.

## Federal Law Enforcement Office Sexual Misconduct

Previous LEO sexual misconduct research has predominately examined non-federal officers; however, sexual misconduct by federal law enforcement officers is a recurring and expanding form of LEO occupational deviance. Recent sexual misconduct events in federal law enforcement agencies reported in the social media include: (1) in 2010, a DEA (US Drug Enforcement Administration) agent in Bogota, Columbia, who was known to frequent prostitutes, assaulted a sex worker, and left her "bloody." The agent was suspended for 14 days; (2) in 2011, a DEA agent solicited sex from an undercover police officer. He was suspended for eight days; (3) in 2012, ten DEA agents engaged in sex parties with prostitutes supplied by drug cartels. Two received letters of reprimand. One retired. The remaining seven agents received suspension ranging from 1 to 8 days (Committee on the Judiciary-House of Representatives, April 15, 2015). The committee chairman called the disciplinary actions an example of "under discipline" by the DEA, creating a real or perceived low risk for sexual misconduct. The same hearing discussed the highly publicized 2012 incident where thirteen US Secret Service officers engaged in sexual misconduct with prostitutes during President Obama's trip to Cartagena, Columbia. Three agents returned to duty with a memorandum of counseling. Five had their security clearances revoked, and five resigned or retired. In a survey sent to 2575 employees by the Committee on the Judiciary, 56% said they would not report another employee's misconduct for fear of retaliation—the Federal Blue Wall of Silence. This exaggerated sense of brotherhood is common in all LEO cultures.

The Office of the Inspector General of the Department of Justice examined cases of sexual harassment and sexual misconduct reported by the FBI, ATF, DEA, and USMS from October 1, 2008 to September 30, 2012 and found 621 sexual misconduct and sexual harassment allegations for the four federal law enforcement agencies (see Table 1.1). The offense types for the cases reported are presented in Table 1.2. Law enforcement sexual misconduct has its roots in the historical development of moral/sin policing in democratic systems of formal social control—criminal justice system.

**Table 1.1** Sexual harassment and sexual misconduct by federal law enforcement agencies (2008–2012)

|      | Employees | Offenses | Rate by Population |
|------|-----------|----------|--------------------|
| ATF  | 4716      | 51       | 10.8               |
| DEA  | 11,053    | 136      | 12.3               |
| FBI  | 33,344    | 343      | 9.7                |
| USMS | 5602      | 91       | 16.2               |

*Source* DOJ (2015: 88)

**Table 1.2** Alleged sexual harassment and sexual misconduct by offense type

| Offense | ATF | DEA | FBI | USMS | Total |
|---|---|---|---|---|---|
| Inappropriate relationship (supervisor/sub-ordinate and colleagues) | 10 | 18 | 77 | 15 | 120 |
| Sexting | 14 | 23 | 36 | 4 | 86 |
| Sexual harassment | 3 | 28 | 50 | 4 | 85 |
| Misuse of govt. property to facilitate sexual activity (office/vehicle) | 4 | 8 | 56 | 6 | 74 |
| Inappropriate sexual comments and/or gestures | 9 | 1 | 29 | 22 | 61 |
| Improper association with a criminal element | 3 | 13 | 9 | 8 | 33 |
| Solicitation of prostitutes (overseas) | 0 | 19 | 6 | 8 | 26 |
| Solicitation of prostitutes (domestic) | 1 | 2 | 15 | 1 | 19 |
| Supervisor failure to report sexual misconduct | 2 | 2 | 8 | 4 | 16 |
| Alleged sexual assault | 0 | 3 | 10 | 3 | 16 |
| Alleged sexual abuse (minor) | 1 | 3 | 11 | 1 | 16 |
| Improper association with confidential source | 1 | 7 | 6 | 0 | 14 |
| Child pornography | 1 | 2 | 7 | 1 | 11 |
| Retaliation for reporting sexual harassment/misconduct | 0 | 1 | 9 | 0 | 10 |
| Obstruction of an official inv. | 0 | 3 | 5 | 1 | 9 |
| Alleged sexual abuse (inmate) | 0 | 0 | 0 | 8 | 8 |
| Indecent exposure | 0 | 0 | 3 | 3 | 6 |
| Videotaping undressed women without consent | 0 | 1 | 3 | 0 | 4 |
| Assault | 0 | 2 | 0 | 0 | 2 |
| Solicitation of sex (multiple partners) | 1 | 0 | 1 | 0 | 2 |
| Inappropriate relationships (foreign nationals | 0 | 0 | 1 | 0 | 3 |
| Misuse of position (Strip club) | 0 | 0 | 1 | 0 | 1 |
| Unprofessional conduct—off-duty strip club | 1 | 0 | 0 | 0 | 1 |
| Grand total | 51 | 136 | 343 | 91 | 621 |

*Source* DOJ (2015: 89)

# Mala Prohibita Policing—Moral/Sin Policing

LEOs enforce laws that are *mala en se* acts (wrong in themselves such as murder, rape, theft) and *mala prohibita* acts (wrong because they are forbidden). Mala prohibita crimes are forbidden by statute, not because there is anything inherently wrong with them. Policing *mala prohibita* acts leads to public law enforcement officers becoming involved in Moral or Sin police work. Public police work as moral/sin policing evolved in England from a need to control the lives of the dangerous classes—the poor and the disorderly working class. Moral policing was a means for the "elite" to constrain the activities of the dangerous/marginalized classes in 1600s England because "Crime, illegitimacy, idleness, irreligion, poaching, dancing, drinking, the playing of games and so forth were believed to be linked" (Rawlings 2002). Laws were passed to control these "moral" transgressions and assure social harmony—crime prevention through moral regulation. At first, justice's of the peace and other parish officials enforced laws on drinking, prostitution, swearing, Sabbath-breaking, and "lewd and disorderly conduct." In the eighteenth century, the watch system was created to assume the duties of moral policing (Critchley 1967). Following the watch system reforms, *policework* inched toward an occupation of public order policing.

The Metropolitan Police Act of 1829 created the occupation of public paid policing but many, particularly the poor and working class, thought the new police as public order police would enforce a moral code that would destroy or disrupt their recreations and lifestyles (Rawlings 2002). The working classes and the poor had reason to worry because the proactive policing model of the time is what is known as "quality of life" policing today, that is, arrests for petty offenses in the streets (drunkenness, gaming, and other social order offenses), and other acts that are not inherently evil. This new occupation was transported to the United States where moral policing became the norm and the dangerous classes were defined by race and ethnicity through the actions of the politically elite (Barker, forthcoming).

*Policework* once developed in the United States became heavily involved in moral policing by enforcing a multitude of *mala prohibita* laws viewed as "victimless crimes" because they only harm the offender, like drug use, and other vice activities. *Mala prohibita* policing involves law enforcement officers in the moral policing of the marginalized classes—those without power and status, creating opportunities for police sexual misconduct on carefully selected targets—low-risk targets with credibility problems (Barker 2011). Sex workers—male, female, and transgender—represent a special population of victims for police sexual misconduct in police agencies worldwide.

## Sex Workers—An At-Risk Population Targeted for PSM

The sexual exploitation of sex workers by police officers occurs throughout the world. Law enforcement officers with the *inclination* for forbidden sex have seized on the *opportunities* for *low-risk* targets for sexual abuse. Numerous studies find that the inherent and widespread discretion associated with the moral policing of sex workers increased the opportunities for police sexual abuse worldwide (Williamson et al. 2007). Williamson and her colleagues reported sex workers throughout the world are subject to police sexual misconduct that includes harassment, inappropriate touching, rape, and sexual extortion. Marginalized women such as prostitutes are vulnerable targets because the complaints from these "un-rape able" women are automatically dismissed. They cite studies in Europe and Asia, Great Britain, and the United States in support of their findings.

Decker and her colleagues reviewed over 800 studies and reports for their comprehensive study of human rights violations against sex workers—male, female, and transgender—globally (Decker et al. 2015). State reaction to sex work varies from full decriminalization—New Zealand and New South Wales, Australia to capital punishment in Sharia law countries such as Iran. In some countries—Switzerland, Turkey, Hungary—sex work is legalized but regulated through mandatory, registration, health examinations, testing, and criminal prosecution in some specific regions—in public or near churches and schools. However, according to Decker et al. (2015), the dominant state response worldwide is criminalization of sex work by criminal and administrative punitive law. These punitive laws directly criminalize the selling of sex or criminalize purchasing sex or earning money through sex work—pimps and brothels. Many countries, such as the USA, fully criminalize almost all aspects of sex work, such as selling sex, buying sex, earning money from someone's sex work, and running a brothel. In the USA, certain areas of Nevada allow brothels under heavily regulated restrictions.

Decker et al. (2015) concluded from their global studies that regardless of state reaction to sex work, sex workers were denied equal access to police protection and there was an climate of impunity toward violence, including murder of sex workers. Violence against sex workers was treated as moral punishment, after all sex workers cannot be raped. Throughout the world, the primary action against sex workers is street-level policing by uniformed police officers—the largest category of sexual abuse aggressors. Male, female, and transgender sex workers in all countries that criminalize all or some parts of selling sex report police gang rape, forced sex, and sexual extortion at the stop, arrest, or detention settings. Whenever police officers have the power of arrest and the sexual act occurs under the threat of harm, this constitutes implicit or direct police sexual violence (Decker et al. 2015: 189). Police officers extort fines and information from sex workers under the threat of arrest, physical violence, and gang rape. The overwhelming numbers of these forced sex or extorted actions are not reported, increasing the real or perceived low risk of PSM.

Globally, the typical reason for not reporting police sexual misconduct is fear and mistrust of the police. Sex work is illegal in Serbia, but a qualitative semi-structured interview study of 31 female and transvestite sex workers in Belgrade and Pancevo, Serbia, documented free sex to police officers to avoid arrest, detainment, or fine (Rhodes et al. 2008). Twenty-five of the FSWs were street workers and 15 of them were Roma's—a discriminated group. All the FSWs were subjected to violence, especially the transvestites and Roma's as a form of moral punishment. A study of 1680 female sex workers—FSWs—in a semi-rural area in the Andhra Pradesh state in southern India found that 372 of the women had sex with a police officer to avoid trouble (Erausquin et al. 2015). Although sex work is not illegal in India, soliciting for sex in public is illegal, making the street worker "occupation" vulnerable to arrest. The sex worker's venue is always important because some venues are more visible than others. They concluded their study by saying "FSW's interactions with police are characterized by police power over sex workers in a variety of ways including police discretion in when and under what charges to arrest a sex worker" (p. 1114). A study of female sex workers in two Mexican-US border towns found that 46% of the 496 FSWs had police or military as clients in the past six months (Connors et al. 2016). In Tijuana—sex work was legal with work permit. In the other city—Ciudad Juarez—sex work was illegal and underground. Regardless of the legality, the police sexually harassed sex workers in both cities.

Sex work is not legal in Russia and is subject to administrative fines and not imprisonment. In what the authors say is the first quantitative study of police coercion experienced by Russian sex workers, the study found that police coercion for free sex in lieu of paying a fine when arrested by sex workers and their pimps was widespread (Odinokova et al. 2012). Eight hundred and ninety-six (896) sex workers in two Russian cities—St. Petersburg and Orenburg—were interviewed. St. Petersburg is a major tourist city with a population of over 5 million people. The city has a large sex industry with about 10,000 FSW workers operating on the street—67%, 21% in brothels, 5% in railway stations, and almost 5% in hotels. Orenburg, an industrial city of approximately 600,000 gas and oil workers and their families, has a different sex worker industry with 76.63% of the FSWs operating on the street and the rest working in the city's three hotels. Thirty-eight percent of the total FSW's in both cities reported police sexual coercion in the past year. The street FSWs reported the highest incidence of police sexual coercion, a not unexpected finding due to its visibility.

The studies discussed above demonstrate a major thesis of this book. *Policework* is a morally dangerous occupation for police workers and represents one of many abuse-prone occupations. This is true no matter what country we examine or its system of government. Police sexual misconduct is a rational choice action whenever and wherever a police worker with a sexual inclination is presented with the opportunity under a real or perceived low-risk situation.

## Sex Workers in the United States

A study of 35 sex workers in Baltimore, Maryland, found that several subjects had been forced or pressured to have sex by police officers. One African-American victim said, "I've had sex with cops that arrested me. After I've given them a blowjob. They put on a condom, so you aren't touching anything…You've got some of them that they use their authority to get what they want" (Decker et al. 2013). Another African-American victim described what happens if you are caught with something illegal.

> If they [the cops] catch you with a stem [crack pipe] on you or some drugs on you or something or they catch you doing something wrong or illegal sometimes they'll let you do something for them. Mostly it's a blowjob because it's really quick… There's no money, no tip, no nothing, but you're just staying free. (Decker et al. 2013)

The study found that the women did not report the police sexual predators because they came from communities where no one trusted the police—a common finding in minority communities where police misconduct including sexual misconduct is a tradition.

Williamson and her colleagues found that when marginalized women, including sex worker in the United States, are victims of crimes such as assaults, robberies, and failure to pay their complaints are dismissed by police officers annoyed by their calls for help. These women are at the bottom of the list of those "to serve and protect." The Williamson study placed these law enforcement officers in a category of Nonresponsive Officers who felt they [the victim] got what they deserved.

> First of all, when the police came [called for help after assault]:
>
> Asked me, "Well, how did you get in this situation?" And I said, "Well, I ain't gonna lie about it. I'm a prostitute. I work the streets, because I have a crack habit." And they said, "Well I guess you got what you deserve." (Williamson et al. 2007: 24)

Another example of a Nonresponsive Officer came when a Detroit prostitute was picked up and taken to the perpetrator's house. At knifepoint, she was tied to a bed and then sodomized with various objects. She described her contact with the police:

> At the time there was a lot of women getting raped…It's hard to get the police to do anything when you're a prostitute. They'll tell you, you deserved it. That's the mentality they have.…Once I called the police

because this guy had threatened to kill me if I told anybody what he did to me. I was hysterical…They said I got what I deserved, cause I was out there like that… They didn't ask for a description. They didn't take any reports or nothing, nothing. And after that, I stopped [calling]. (Williamson et al. 2007: 25)

The study identified a type of police officer who not only coerces sex workers into sexual situations, but also is physically and verbally abusive to them—Police Officers as Perpetrators (Williamson et al. 2007: 27). The Police Officers as Perpetrators overtly demonstrated their disdain for sex workers and other "disreputable" persons—the dangerous classes not worthy of police protection.

The Williamson study found other evidence of police sexual misconduct. Fifteen percent of the female sex workers reported being forced to have sex with an officer, 45.5% had paid sex with a police officer, and 18 had sex for free. The most common form of police sexual misconduct was sexual shakedowns. Fifty-six percent of the women had sex with the officer, and he let them go without charges (Williamson et al. 2007).

\* \* \*

The global and the US studies presented demonstrate that wherever sex work is criminalized, FSWs suffer from punitive moral policing with few legal remedies. Police officers throughout the world think they have special privileges when it comes to sex workers. Whom are the FSWs going to complain to?

On occasion, police agencies treat the murders of sex workers as examples of "misdemeanor murders"—a police term describing murders of disreputable individuals such as career criminals, police fighters, "whores," and other douche bags and scum (personal experience as a former cop and police academy instructor). Sex worker assaults are treated as "Misdemeanor assaults." Their murders and assaults are viewed as an occupational hazard for marginalized women working in a disreputable line of work (personal police work experience and interviews with numerous officers). Police agencies are criticized for being lax in the investigations of murders, including serial murders, and kidnappings of black women and children (Schechter 2003).

## Constantly Changing Target Pool

Moral policing in the United States has become a confusing part of police work in a continually changing society. US police work is in a constant state of flux as new acts are defined as crimes—*mala prohibita*—and agencies to deal with these new illegal behaviors are created, merged, and disbanded. Historically, the United States has created, merged, and disbanded law enforcement agencies in reaction to the efforts of moral entrepreneurs, powerful interest groups, moral panics, and perceived and real threats, for example, prohibition, the war on drugs, terrorism, illegal immigration, and sexting. This chaos creates law enforcement fragmentation, organizational confusion, and expanded opportunities for misconduct.

The victim selection pool—targets—for law enforcement officer sexual misconduct has gotten more extensive with the creation of an alphabet soup of federal, state, local, and special district law enforcement agencies (ABC, ATF, BART, DEA, DIA, DART, FBI, ICE, IRS, ISDP, MARTA, TSA, USMP, USSS, ad infinitum) involved in US police work.

## Police Sexual Misconduct Victims—Pool of Low-Risk Vulnerable Targets Worldwide

The everyday activities of law enforcement workers present *sexually inclined* LEOs with the *opportunities* to come into contact with sexually vulnerable persons—male and female—of all ages. Many of these vulnerable persons have credibility issues making them "perfect victims"—*low risk*—for illicit sexual advances and coercion. Victims with criminal records do not report officer misconduct because they do not want to draw attention to themselves (Lersch 1998). Police departments with poor relationships with their communities have lower rates of citizen complaints, increasing the likelihood of police sexual misconduct— safe targets for sex predators (Lersch and Mieczkowski 2000). Paradoxically, police departments with dysfunctional relationships with their citizens or specific areas of their community have lower rates of complaints, increasing the likelihood of police sexual misconduct. Whom do you call when the police are the problem?

On-duty police sexual aggressors in low political power communities choose their victims, male and female, from a pool of vulnerable victims that include: children and minors; individuals involved in sex work or the commercial sex industry; immigrants and undocumented persons; individuals under the influence of drugs or alcohol; individuals with limited English proficiency; people with mental illness or developmental challenges; individuals with physical disabilities; crime victims seeking help; those who have committed crimes and are on probation or have outstanding warrants; vulnerable victims seeking help—domestic violence victims, runaways, and inmates in custodial settings. Recent examples of this diverse pool of targets follow.

A 2015 report from Radio-Canada revealed several allegations of sexual abuse of indigenous (Aboriginal) women—marginalized low-risk population—by Quebec provincial police officers (Shingler, November 16, 2016). One retired Quebec police officer pleaded guilty and another committed suicide after being charged (MacKinnon, October 27, 2018). The current influx of illegal aliens has exponentially increased the pool of venerable targets for US law enforcement sexual aggressors. Male and female illegal aliens are terrified of being deported, they are not familiar with American laws, and most cannot speak English. The mere threat of legal consequences is a coercive weapon. However, as we have stressed policing as a worldwide occupation provides publicly paid law enforcement officials with similar or the same pool of vulnerable victims. What follows are illustrative not exhaustive examples of police sexual misconduct worldwide. *Illustrative Examples*—I.E.s—is a term used in lieu of case study because of the nature of our topic—hidden deviance—and the reliance on secondary data sources. The secondary data sources provide limited sources of information and missing data sources that are common in case study research (Yin 2003).

A Philippines police officer was accused of raping a 15-year-old girl in exchange for releasing her on drug charges (Anonymous, November 1, 2018). The officer said that the practice of "palit-puri"—exchanging sex for dropping charges—was a common practice among the police.

According to a "whistle blower," custodial sex between prison staff and inmates is commonplace in Australia (Graham, July 27, 2018). A London newspaper reported that it found 156 police sexual misconduct complaints being investigated by the police in England, Scotland, and Wales (Hamilton, October 22, 2016). The newspaper reported that 400 complaints had been made in the previous five years. The complaints included rape, sex on duty, sex with victims, and groping, harassing, and making inappropriate sexual advances to their colleagues. A 2007 New Zealand Commission of Inquiry—Bazley Report—found systematic sexual abuse and violence against women going back three decades in some New Zealand police agencies (Lewis, April 3, 2007). The Commission made 60 recommendations for reform.

## What Is the Actual Extent of Police Sexual Abuse?

The answer to this question is unknown and unknowable. There are no official US statistics on police sexual misconduct, or for that matter police crime or misconduct in general. However, one police abuse watch group the National Police Misconduct Reporting Project run by a private citizen and now the Cato Institute reported in 2010 that police sexual misconduct was the second most reported form of police misconduct. Finding reliable information is difficult. Police sexual abuse is discovered and becomes public in a limited number of ways. First, working police officers reveal the sexual misconduct of a fellow officer. This is an unlikely event, but it does happen. Second, formal complaints of sexual abuse to the police are recorded and examined. This is also an unlikely event because many victims are reluctant to report their victimization (see Box 1.1). Furthermore, police departments are loath to admit police misbehavior. They discourage reports and engage in cover-up acts. Criminal charges and civil lawsuits are filed thereby, forcing an investigation. Lastly, the most likely event leading to the exposure of law enforcement sexual misconduct is the act/s become a scandal and a media feeding frenzy occurs. The s.... hits the fan. This happened in 2014.

---

**Box 1.1   Why Police Sexual Abuse Is Not Reported**

The readily available pool of "perfect victims" is filled with low-risk targets with credibility problems or they are members of the "dangerous classes." This is not a politically correct world, and disparaging labels apply. The victims or potential victims are not treated or addressed as African-Americans, sex workers, or undocumented persons they are known as blacks, N_____, sluts, whores, illegal aliens, wetbacks, and other derogatory terms. Marginalized victims are justifiably scared of their sexual predators and fear the consequences of reporting them. The police sexual abuse incidents are not reported for a variety of reasons: trauma, embarrassment or ashamed, victim fears retaliation, previous bad experiences with police or criminal justice system.

---

*   *   *

The 2014 arrest, trial, and conviction of a white racist Oklahoma City Police Officer for the rape and sexual abuse of 13 black women became a social media sensation. Following his arrest, the *Associated Press* examined the only available, but severely flawed, "official source" of information on police sexual misconduct at the state and local levels. The *AP* report examined officers who had lost their state certifications for on-duty sexual misconduct.

The journalists obtained official records of 41 states with police decertification processes for prohibited behavior. The behaviors prohibited by the 41 states varied. The only standard definition of prohibited behavior among the states was the conviction of a felony involving moral turpitude. The journalists found 1000 police officers were decertified in the six-year period 2009 through 2014 for sexual misconduct offenses. Five hundred and fifty (550) officers lost their licenses for sexual assault, including rape, sodomy, sexual shakedowns, or groping pat-downs. Over four hundred licenses were revoked for other sexual offense such as child pornography and other patterns of sexual misconduct. One hundred and fifty-four officers lost their certification for forced and "consensual" sex in detention facilities.

The victims of these police sexual predators fit into the pattern of vulnerable victims—young, poor, addicts, criminal past, and other marginalized persons with creditability issues. New York journalists conducted a second study.

*Buffalo News* staff journalists reported a second print media national study of police sexual misconduct in 2015. They examined news reports and court records to develop a database of "credible" cases from a 10-year period state-by-state and county-by-county. All but 5 of the 700 officers were men who averaged 38 years in age with an average of nine years of service. The police sex predators chose their victims from motorists, crime victims, prisoners, informants, students, and young people—160 offenses against young people. Police officers pulled over drivers to "fish" for dates and extorted sex through threats of arrest and resorted to rapes with reluctant victims. The victims fit the vulnerability profile of the earlier *AP* report—police officers preying on possible accusers with credibility problems. Again, victims are selected from among those least likely to complain.

Complicating the search for reliable PSM data is the spatial and secret environment in which the acts take place. Many police-citizen encounters occur late at night in most cases with no witnesses and no audio or visual recordings. These conditions make police sexual misconduct a low-risk behavior.

## Police (LEO) Sexual Misconduct as a Low-Risk Behavior

The socialization process through occupational experiences well-known in police work creates an occupational culture that condones, facilitates, or ignores acts of nonviolent police misconduct and on occasion overlooks or by silence supports nonviolent police sexual misconduct (Barker 1977, 1978, 2011). Oftentimes, sexual predators labeled "skirt chasers," "stick daddy's," and "pretty boys" are well known in the agency. The peer group does not define the officers as deviant, especially when their acts appear to involve "consensual" sex or involve marginalized groups such as sex workers, drug addicts, or criminals. The police peer group sees these sex acts as "fringe benefits of the job" (see Stamper 2005: 121–128). Stamper (2005), a former police chief in several departments, estimated that at least 5% of the officers in any police department are "on the prowl for women." As long as police sexual predators choose victims from the low-risk pool, he or she may remain safe and protected. Even when caught, police offenders are often allowed to move on without consequences—Gypsy Cops—further exacerbating the police sexual misconduct problem.

## Gypsy Cops or Passing the Trash

The dark side of police sexual misconduct is hidden from public view by the well-known practice of "impression management" or "normalization of deviance" (see Lemert 1967) techniques engaged in by law enforcement agencies. These techniques hide a recidivist population of police sexual offenders who move from agency to agency (Rabe-Hemp and Braithwaite 2013). Law enforcement agencies and other sexual abuse-prone occupations are loath to admit their problems. Therefore, they attribute acts of deviance to a few "rotten apples," a seemingly perfect explanation for their "bizarre" behavior. It is common practice among police agencies to allow these "rotten apples" to resign instead of prosecution thus keeping the acts secret and allowing the perpetrator to move onto another agency and continue their deviant activities (Goldman 2003; Goldman and Piro 1987, 2001; Rabe-Hemp and Braithwaite 2013). These deviant traveling officers are known as "Gypsy Cops" and are a real problem in police work and responsible for a significant number of police misconduct incidents. A constant finding in criminological research is that past criminal behavior is a good predictor of future criminal behavior. The cops rules of loyalty and brotherhood perpetuate "the officer shuffle," leading to a small number of recidivist sexual offenders who engage in police sexual misconduct and other forms of police misconduct in different police departments (Shockley-Eckles 2011; Rabe-Hemp and Braithwaite 2013). Deterrence/rational choice theory tells us that an increase in the certainty, severity, and celerity of punishment increases the real or perceived risk of prohibited behavior and discourages it occurrence (Beccaria 1963; Gibbs 1975; Pogarsky and Piquero 2004). The presence of Gypsy Cops in police organization by the same logic increases the likelihood of police sexual misconduct in their new department. We continually address this issue.

## Scholarly Research on Police (LEO) Sexual Misconduct

In spite of the problems of identifying police sexual misconduct in a secret and powerful occupation, there have been empirical investigations into this dark side of policing. An exhaustive review of the academic literature reveals a slowly developing body of research beginning in the late 1970s. The early discussions of police sexual abuse were mostly non-theoretical narrow descriptive approaches limited to adult female victims. These studies for the most part ignored minors, children, transgender, lesbians, and gays as victims, and federal law enforcement officers as sexual predators. The research studies steadily evolved from the "consensual sex assumptions" to the recognition of police sexual violence consisting of police sexual aggressors who deliberately chose victims from groups of vulnerable persons. Then, sexual abuse by corrections officers was introduced into the discussion along with the phenomenon of sexually related police homicides. Slowly, the academic community recognized that there are male and female victims and LEO sexual abuse occurs on and off duty with and without violence. Deviant sexual acts involving gay and lesbian sexual contacts were uncovered along with police sexual abuse in law enforcement agencies at all levels of government. A body of twenty-first-century scholarly research applying sociological/criminological theories to police misconduct in general is developing that applies to police sexual misconduct. The empirical studies provided the bedrock for the development of the PSM Causal Equation Model and the proposed typology. The academic police sexual misconduct is presented in historical order.

## Barker 1978

Barker's (1978) study expanded his research on police occupational deviance and identified five patterns of police misconduct other than police corruption—police perjury, police brutality, sleeping on duty, drinking on duty, and sex on duty. The research was based on his "retrospective participant observation" of "on the job" years as a working police officer. Retrospective participant observation literally translated as "experience recollected in academia" of observations "made on the job." The researcher is first a total participant in the activity and then becomes an academic (in Barker's case a Ph.D. Sociologist). The researcher develops a research interest in the former work experiences and retrospectively examines these experiences (Blumer 1982). Such research has a long history in sociology—Becker's study of dance musicians (Becker 1963), Polsky's study of poolroom hustlers, and Holdaway's research on the British police (Holdaway 1979). More recent examples, and there are many, include John Irwin's writing on his prison experiences and James Quinn describing his life as an outlaw biker. Barker supplemented his "retrospective participant observation" with formal and informal interviews with current and former police officers and surveys administered to officers in a 50-person police department.

Barker conducted his research from a rational choice perspective of the intersection of inclination, opportunity, and peer group support for certain patterns of deviant conduct, including sex on duty. Barker's survey revealed 32% of those surveyed believed officers in their department had sex on duty. The respondents gave sex on duty the second lowest perceived deviance or "wrong" scale, reflecting a "high" level of reinforcement and encouragement from the peer group [Akers' social learning theory would identify this phenomenon as differential reinforcement]. Those surveyed identified numerous opportunities for on-duty sex: intoxicated females, promiscuous females seeking to avoid the inconvenience of a ticket or arrest, women who operate on the fringe or outside the law—sex workers, barmaids—who have something to gain from "good relations" with the police, and police groupies who love the "boys in blue." He did recognize that "rogue" cops forced some women into sexual relations on less than willing terms. For the most part, the women discussed were willing participants in the sex on-duty encounters. The sex on-duty acts were considered a police perk just like accepting free meals and discounts. None of these interviewed knew of a police officer in their department being disciplined for either act.

# Sapp 1986

Sapp's (1986) article is the first scholarly article directly investigating the range of possible police sexual misconduct behaviors. He opined that the police occupation is a sexually abusive-prone occupation and provides more opportunities for sexual misconduct than any other occupation. Sapp's research was an attempt to "provide a preliminary categorization of police sexual misconduct behaviors as a heuristic device to further research in this area" (Sapp 1986: 3). The research was based on interviews with 47 police officers and supervisors in several large metropolitan municipal in five states. Sapp recognized the possibility of female police officers sexually harassing male citizens and same-sex sexual harassment but limited his discussion to male officers and female targets. Sapp cautioned that some of the activities might not be overtly sexual but they are sexually motivated or sexual harassment, i.e., aggressive pressure or intimidation of a sexual nature. Sapp identified seven categories of police sexually motivated or sexual harassment categories (see Box 1.2):

---

**Box 1.2   Sapp's Seven Categories of Police Sexually Motivated or Sexual Harassment Behaviors**

**1. Non-sexual contacts that are sexually motivated**
The female may not recognize behaviors in this category as sexual; for example, the officer makes an invalid traffic stop or runs a license plate check to obtain information or start a conversation. If the female provides no encouragement or the officer makes no follow-up calls or stops, there is little likelihood of a sexual harassment complaint. Sapp points out that some officers are well known by their peers as "likely to check out the ladies."

**2. Voyeuristic Contacts**
A minority of officers spend varying amounts of their on-duty time seeking out opportunities to view unsuspecting women partially clad or nude. One of Sapp's subjects described his time as a "rookie" and working with a veteran training officer. Sapp identified police voyeurs who spend time sneaking up on parked cars in "lover's lanes" hoping to catch

---

couples engaged in sexual activity. Sapp is the first to recognize that some patterns of LEO sexual misconduct do not require victim contact.

### 3. Contacts with Crime Victims
As Sapp points out, crime victims are particularly susceptible to sexual harassment [sexual intimidation] by police officers. The victims are emotionally upset and turn to the police for support and assistance, and the officer takes advantage of them. Unnecessary callbacks to crime victims, according to Sapp, are one of the most common forms of police sexual misconduct.

### 4. Contacts with Offenders
As Sapp opines "Police officers" have relatively frequent opportunities for sexual harassment and sexual contact with offenders. Offenders are not only aware of the authority of the officer but are also in a position where their complaints may be disregarded or played down. Sexually harassing offenders through unnecessary body searches, frisks, and pat-downs are examples of sexual misconduct. Sex with offenders in police lockups and jails is included in this category. Sapp describes detention officers seeking "out opportunities to observe females in various degrees of undress" and making sexual demands to inmates.

### 5. Contacts with Juvenile Offenders
Sapp's study reveals runaways, truants, and delinquents are targets of police sexual abuse because of the disparity of their position in contacts with police and their credibility problems. He discussed the firing of a school liaison officer because of his sexual involvement with female students.

### 6. Sexual Shakedowns
Sapp considered sexual shakedowns "Demanding sexual service from prostitutes, homosexuals, or other citizens involved in illegal or illicit activities" as the most severe form of sexual harassment. They involve an unwilling citizen yielding "solely on the basis of the police authority to arrest and prosecute."

### 7. Citizen-Initiated Sexual Contact
Every working police officer or former police officer is familiar with female citizens who initiate sexual contact with police officers. Sapp opines that "police groupies" attracted sexually to the uniform, weapons, or powers of the police officer are a common feature of police work. There are lonely and mentally disturbed women seeking attention and affection from a police officer.

\*   \*   \*

# Kraska and Kappeler 1995

Kraska and Kappeler (1995) examined police sexual abuse from a feminist perspective and were among the first researchers to call attention to the violent nature of some acts of police sexual misconduct. They correctly pointed out that a view of police sexual misconduct that assumes the "consensual" nature of the sex act masks the coercive/violent nature of many encounters. Some acts, they argue, are coercive assaults and rapes. They opined that police sexual violence (PSV) was a form of occupational sexual harassment and defined as *those situations in which a female citizen experiences a sexually degrading, humiliating, violating, damaging or threatening act committed by a police officer through the use of force or police authority* (Kraska and Kappeler 1995: 93. Italics in original).

Kraska and Kappeler (1995) developed a *Continuum of Police Sexual Violence* based on the behavior's "obtrusiveness." The broad categories in the continuum subsumed various types of police sexual misconduct. **Unobtrusive** behavior includes voyeurism, viewing sexually explicit photographs or videos of crime victims and other invasions of privacy—*contact with victim not necessary*. **Obtrusive** sexual behavior was unnecessary, illegal, or punitive pat-down searches, strip searches, body cavity searches, police services or leniency for sexual advantage, deception to gain sexual favors from citizens and some instances of sexual harassment. **Criminal** behavior was specific forms of sexual harassment, sexual assault, and rape.

Their data consisted of media accounts from one national newspaper over an 18-month period and all published Federal District Courts cases between 1978 and 1983 where someone claiming some form of sexual abuse sued the police—mass media and court records as data. They found 124 cases of PSV—33 from the news survey and 91 from the legal database. Eighty (64.5%) of the cases came from municipal agencies; twenty-six (21%) came from sheriff's departments; and ten cases (8%) came from state and federal agencies. The remaining cases came from multiple jurisdictions. These jurisdictional findings support the conclusion that police sexual misconduct is an occupational police deviance phenomenon that occurs in all types of police agencies at all levels of government. Thirty percent (37 cases) involved rape or sexual assaults by a police officer. Twenty (16%) of all the cases involved administrative or supervisory police officers and 15 cases involved two or more police officers. These last findings challenge the "rogue" officer being responsible for police sexual misconduct (Kraska and Kappeler 1995: 96). Their research emphasizes violence involved in police-citizen sexual encounters and points out that state and federal law enforcement officers are involved in police sexual violence. Their seminal approach is important to the development of PSM research and the most widely quoted. However, it is too narrow for the twenty-first century where all police sexual encounter are not male–female in nature, and numerous examples of police sexual misconduct do not involve violence and range from consensual sex and no police victim contact to sexually motivated murder.

## Haarr 1997

The purpose of Haarr's (1997) study was to examine the link between organizational commitment and police occupational deviance. Specifically, she discussed four types of police occupational deviance identified by Punch (1985). The four types were (1) work avoidance and manipulation—such things as overlooking a crime to avoid extra work and overtime, sleeping on duty and staying out of sight; (2) employee deviance against the organization—pilfering or stealing, sabotage, absenteeism, and neglect; (3) employee deviance for the organization—bending the rules and regulations and violating policies, procedures, and the law to get the job done; and (4) informal rewards—perks, discounts, services, and presents. Her research was conducted in a 285-person unnamed police department and consisted of field observations and interviews with a sample (57 officers) selected from the patrol division.

Police sexual misconduct is subsumed under the broad category employee of deviance against the organization. She gave the example of a group of five to seven patrols officers regularly visiting strip bars and arranging for sex on duty. One female officer said she acted as a "lookout" for the male officers while they engaged in sex in the police car. I know of numerous male officers who acted as lookouts during sex on-duty incidents, but this is the only example of a female officer acting as a lookout I am aware of. Haarr observed officers propositioning waitresses, convenience store clerks, and women on the streets. Most of the sexual misconduct encounters were considered consensual on-duty acts; however, she was told the story of five officers accused of gang-raping a female at an off-duty party. An interesting finding from the study is officers who engaged in misconduct, such as sleeping on-duty or consensual sex sought out partners with other officers who had a reputation for similar behavior. A sensible decision by officers engaged in police misconduct of any type.

## Eschholz and Vaughn 2001

Eschholz and Vaughn (2001) posit that criminal justice personnel, including police and corrections officers, use the same "rape myths" used by convicted rapists to justify police sexual violence (PSV). PSV is defined as unobtrusive viewing (police and corrections workers), sexual harassment (police and corrections workers), kidnapping, rape, and murder (*police sexual homicide*). They describe unobtrusive viewing PSV in jails and prisons such as strip and body searches of prisoners and opine that sexual harassment such as sexualized touching, sodomy, and rape is systematic within all the criminal justice subcultures (Eschholz and Vaughn 2001: 390). This is the third reference to correction workers sexual misconduct being included in a police sexual misconduct definition. *Police sexual homicides* are included in the definition of PSV for the first time when they discuss a Monroe, North Carolina police officer, Josh Griffin, found guilty of the kidnapping and murder of a woman who rebuffed his sexual advances.

The "Rape Myths" used by police and corrections workers to neutralize sexual violence against women are:

1. The victim "asked for it" by their behavior and dress (i.e., "blaming the victim"). The victim's reluctance and resistance to sexual

overtures to sexual overtures is a normal part of sexual foreplay (i.e., no means yes).

2. Sex is a commodity that victims trade for favors (i.e., she/he owes me).

3. The victim suffered no injury, so no crime occurred (i.e., "denial of injury"). Eschholz and Vaughn (p. 397) says that some corrections officers view prisoners in their custody as sexual objects or commodities that entitles the officer to engage in sexual groping. Since there is no injury involved, there is no crime, and no one got hurt. Police officers used the same neutralization technique.

4. The victim is not raped because they did not physically resist sexual overtones, i.e., no one can be raped against their will.

5. After consensual sex, the victim regretted his/her consensual behavior and cried rape.

6. The victim is objectified by virtue of their sexual availability, promiscuous, and/or tainted image as an offender for example, "sluts/whores cannot be raped."

7. Only men are capable of committing sexual violence (i.e., women cannot rape). Eschholz and Vaughn cite the case of a male inmate who claimed a female correctional counselor subjected him to repeated sexual abuse—female sexual aggressor. She unsuccessfully invoked three "rape myths" in her defense—(1-no means yes, 2-he owes me, and 3-women cannot rape).

## Walker and Irlbeck 2002 and 2003 Update

Walker and Irlbeck's (2002, 2003) research opined that driving while female (DWF) was as significant a problem as driving while black (DWB). They provided a list of media reports of police sexual abuse running the gamut from harassment to murder. The case of *police sexual related murder* is the case of Cara Knott killed in 1986 by a California Highway Patrol Officer after a traffic stop. This was the second instance of police sexually related murders cited in police sexual misconduct research.

# Findings

**First,** there is a pattern of police officers using their traffic enforcement powers to abuse women. They maintained the "driving while female" problem was as large as the "driving while black" problem. They mentioned that in certain areas of the United States, police officers stop motorists based on their Hispanic/Latino ethnicity—driving while brown. The authors suggest these behaviors are the result of "rogue" officers violating the law and departmental policy.

**Second,** a significant part of the PSM problem is the failure of police departments to investigate allegations that come to their attention. They conclude that in some cases supervisors disregarded citizen complaints filed by female victims. Once again, they lay the blame on "rogue" officers who continue their predatory behavior because of the department that looks the other way—rotten apple impression management technique—and provides a real or perceived safe setting through differential reinforcement.

**Third,** abuses continue because police departments continue to tolerate them by failure to act on complaints and do not adopt appropriate policies and training and fail to properly supervise their officers. This once again creates a real or perceived safe setting for PSM—differential reinforcement.

Walker and Irlbeck suggest several remedies to the problems of driving while female (DWF) and driving while black/brown (DWB).

**Step One: Data Collection**—Departments need to begin gathering data to determine if there is a DWF problem in their agency.

**Step Two: Official Policies and Training**—All police agencies should have formal policies prohibiting "driving while female." The policies should define DWF as "the use of law enforcement powers to stop females where there is no suspected criminal activity or traffic law violation." The policy should be a part of pre-service and in-service training programs.

**Step Three: Better Supervision**—On the street, the supervision of police officers should be improved. This would increase the real risk.

Officers should be aware that sexual abuse is a serious violation and not tolerated.

**Step Four: An Open and Accessible Citizen Complaint System Should be Developed**—The developed complaints system should be open and readily available to the public. Police accountability is necessary for a free society.

**Step Five: Hire More Female Officers**—The five remedies they suggest would apply as remedies to many police misconduct problems and make the police occupation more accountable to the public and more transparent. We address many of these issues throughout the book.

## 2003 Update

Their 2003 Update on "Driving While Female" made a number of important contributions to the study of police sexual misconduct: (1) It revealed the pattern of police officer sexual exploitation of teenage girls and (2) the problem of same-sex police sexual misconduct was exposed along with the problem of sexual abuse in police-/community-sponsored programs. Walker and Irlbeck presented six "cases," taken from newspaper reports describing police sexual encounters with police-sponsored Police Explorers Programs. Five of the "cases" involved molested male victims, including the notorious "case" of LAPD Deputy Chief David Kalish who was suspended after being accused of sexually molesting a young male Explorer in the 1970s; (3) the "Update" introduced the use of case studies from newspapers as a data source. They said, "This report is based on a survey of police abuse cases reported in the news media. Cases are identified through conventional and academic electronic index web sources." The authors concluded that the findings from both their 2002 and 2003 reports "are police officers are using their law enforcement authority to take advantage of vulnerable people." Forty percent of the incidents cited involved teenage boys and girls, 30% involved traffic enforcement-related cases, and nine cases involved prostitutes. Of particular interest to the study of PSM are the recommendations they made to provide better oversight of Police Explorer Programs (see Box 1.3).

---

**Box 1.3   Recommendations for Better Oversight of Explorer Programs**

- Police chiefs need to give special attention to departmental-sponsored Explorer programs.
- Police chiefs need to screen with special care officers assigned to Explorer program. [This would identify the inclination for PSM.]
- Police chiefs should personally interview officers assigned to Explorer programs, emphasize the gravity of any inappropriate sexual acts, and indicate that any misconduct will result in significant discipline. [A core finding of deterrence theory—increase risk.]
- Police chiefs should consider assigning a male and a female officer as a co-leader of the Explorer program [guardian in routine activities theory].
- The leaders of local Explorer offices should discuss the problem of sexual misconduct with law enforcement officers and ask what steps the department is taking to guard against the inappropriate activity.

---

\*   \*   \*

# Texeira 2002

Mary Texeira, like several others—Barker, Kappeler, Maher, and Stinson—writing and conducting research on police sexual misconduct is a former police officer-turned academic. The African-American woman was a deputy sheriff from 1968 to 1986. Her research began with her "retrospective participant observation" of the "on the job" years as a working police officer and the sexual harassment she suffered from being an African-American woman in a predominately white police organization (Texeira 2002). She began her research by interviewing African-American women she knew from "on the job" experiences and then used the snowball technique to increase her sample size. She ended up with a sample size of 50 active and 15 retired African-American female police officers. Her interview results revealed seven (7) patterns of sexual harassment experienced by her subjects.

**Assault (Actual or Attempted Rape or Sexual Assault)**
There were six incidents reported of male officers grabbing the women's crotches, fondling their breasts, and rubbing their bodies against them.

**Favors (Unwanted Pressure for Sexual Favors)**
Twenty-one incidents involved a type of quid pro quo arrangement in which the women were asked to perform sex acts in return for favorable assignments. One woman was forced to have sex on a regular basis with her training officer to avoid being reassigned back to the jail.

**Touch (Unwanted Deliberate Touching), Leaning Over, Cornering, or Pinching.**
Twenty-one subjects reported inappropriate touching. The women reported men in the police agency had the attitude that women officers were property, to be touched and spoken to sexually whenever they wanted.

**Gestures (Unwanted Sexually Suggestive Look or Gestures)**
Fifteen incidents occurred where male peers or supervisors grabbed their crotches to manually stimulate sexual intercourse or masturbation.

**Calls (Unwanted Letters, Phone Calls, or Materials of a Sexual Nature)**
Seventeen incidents of this nature were reported.

**Dates (Unwanted Pressure for Dates)**
This was the most common pattern reported—27 incidents.

**Jokes (Unwanted Sexual Teasing, Jokes, Remarks, or Questions)**
Sexual innuendos and joking were relentless, especially around the station. Ten incidents were reported, but Texeira thought it was underreported because it happened so frequently—differential reinforcement.

## Collins 2004

Collins (2004) research examined sexual harassment complaints against Florida police officers from 1993 to 1997 as reported to the Florida Criminal Justice Standards and Training Commission—the

Commission. The Commission is responsible for certifying and decertifying police officers in Florida. Florida requires that police officers must possess "good moral character." "Officers lack good moral character if they commit any one of a specified list of criminal offenses or other acts, including "sexual harassment" involving physical contact or misuse of official position" (Florida Administration Code 1997e as cited in Collins 2004: 514). Collins used the commonly accepted definition of sexual harassment "three related but conceptually different dimensions: sexual coercion, unwanted sexual attention, and gender harassment" (Collins 2004: 522). Reported cases included four cases of dual-certified officers who committed sexual harassment while employed as corrections officers. One victim was a *correction's* officer. Two cases involved same-sex sexual harassment. Two complaints involved female police officers sexually harassing male officers—female sexual aggressor. Gender harassment was the most frequent complaint by women—25 cases. Twenty cases of unwanted sexual attention were reported to the Commission along with eight cases of sexual coercion.

## Maher 2003

Maher, a former police officer turned academic, drew attention to what Barker (2011) later described as *policework*, being a "morally dangerous occupation" due to the numerous opportunities for deviance, including sexual misconduct, unsupervised atmosphere of police-citizen contacts, and the isolated nature of those encounters (Maher 2003). His research examined two aspects of police sexual misconduct: (1) police officer's perception of the extent of sexual misconduct and (2) what factors influence an officer's decision to engage in or refrain from engaging in sexual misconduct—self-control (see Chappell and Piquero 2004 for an examination of 1 and 2 applying social learning theory—discussed later). Maher used Sapp's taxonomy of police sexual misconduct plus one added category "Officer-initiated sexual contacts" in his research (Maher 2003: 360).

Maher used a "snowball" sample of 40 working police officers from 14 police agencies in the St. Louis, Missouri area. He administered a survey and conducted personal interviews. The officers were asked to recall instances of police sexual misconduct during the past year and in their career. He found three categories accounted for the majority of the incidents—non-sexual contacts, voyeuristic behavior, and officer-initiated contacts. The Sapp categories of contacts with juveniles and sexual shakedowns were reported as very low. The remaining categories—citizen-initiated contacts, contacts with crime victims and contacts with offenders—revealed a moderate to low level of occurrence—differential reinforcement. Although the officers reported police sexual misconduct was common, the subjects perceived that those incidents involving violence were rare. The officers struggled when asked to define police sexual misconduct and reported their department did not have a policy on police sexual misconduct and suggested the behaviors probably came under the common policy issue of the vague "Conduct unbecoming of an officer." The author reported his "most surprising" finding was the availability of police sexual misconduct opportunities. He concluded that most sexual misconduct acts occur at night when officers are less busy, few people around, and supervisor oversight is the lowest—low risk. The male subjects reported that an estimated 36% of the officers engaged in some form of police sexual misconduct. A later study with female subjects reported that 46% of the male officers engaged in some form of police sexual misconduct.

## Maher 2007

In an address to the Miscarriages of Justice Conference: Current Perspectives held at the University of Central Missouri on February 20, 2007, Maher expressed the view that one does not have to be arrested to suffer a miscarriage of justice. A person becomes a miscarriage of justice victim when they become a victim of some type of deviant police behavior; in this case, he was talking about was police sexual misconduct (Maher 2007). Reacting to what *he sees as the trend to define police sexual misconduct in the narrow sense as Police Sexual Violence he developed a definition of police sexual misconduct that contains violent and non-violent "varieties" of Police Sexual Misconduct* [emphasis supplied]:

Any behavior by a police officer whereby an officer takes advantage of his or her unique position in law enforcement to misuse their authority or power to commit a sexually violent act or to initiate or respond to some sexually motivated cue for the purpose of personal sexual gratification.

The definition includes violent and nonviolent varieties of police sexual misconduct, including "consensual" sex relationships that violate the common acceptable behavior for law enforcement officers—on-duty sexual misbehavior. His police experience and the studies he reviewed led him to conclude that police sexual misconduct is common in police work and ranges from serious behaviors like rape, sexual assault, and sex with juveniles to less serious crimes that included inappropriate touching of suspects or rubbing against someone in a pat-down search. Officers make illegal stops to fish for victims. Consensual sex on duty was not illegal, but it was unacceptable behavior for a working police officer. Maher believed that data from media sources or court cases only exposed the "tip of the iceberg" of police sexual misconduct, so he decided to survey three samples of working police officers—police officers, police chiefs, and female police officers.

## Maher 2008

This research addresses the extent and nature of police sexual misconduct as perceived by a sample—20—of male police chiefs from the St. Louis metropolitan area (Maher 2008). Eight of the chiefs were from large departments, more than 50 officers; seven were from median-sized ages; and five from small agencies, less than 25 officers. They had an average of 33.5 years as police officers and 7.5 years as chief with their departments, clearly an experienced group of police officers and chiefs. Each of the chiefs was interviewed—semi-structured and informal. They were asked 13 questions about their perceptions of the nature, extent, and causes of police sexual misconduct.

The majority of the chief's divided police sexual misconduct into serious and non-serious incidents—differential reinforcement by the chief executive officers. Serious offenses included acts such as rape, sexual assaults, sexual shakedowns, and sex with juveniles. Non-serious offenses were the non-criminal offenses of flirting, making unwarranted traffic stops to check out attractive drivers, or sex on duty. They did agree that non-serious offenses are a problem for the department and could be subject to discipline.

The chiefs agreed that police sexual misconduct was common, but they did not believe it was widespread or engaged in by most officers in their department. This conclusion appears contradictory or they may have thought police sexual misconduct was common in other police departments but not theirs. As expected, they believed serious offenses were far less common than non-serious sexual misconduct. The chiefs believed police sexual misconduct had declined over the years because of police professionalism, improved hiring practices, and advanced education about sexual harassment and technological innovations such as video cameras in patrol cars, audio recorders worn by officer, and vehicle tracking devices.

The chiefs noted several factors contributing to sexual abuse: **lack of knowledge about police sexual misconduct**—the chiefs were in general agreement that their officers received little training on the subject. This is probably because none of the departments had written policies on police sexual misconduct; **police complaint systems**—most chiefs reported sexual misconduct complaints were received and investigated internally. However, many chiefs would not accept complaints not filed in person and writing. Most of the chiefs recognized the opportunity structure in police work contributes to sexual misconduct. Lastly, they recognized that the **police occupational culture** affects the likelihood of reporting a fellow officer for acts of police sexual misconduct—differential reinforcement. One police chief remarked that police officers have a "'good-ole-boy network' and if you are one of the good old boys, then you don't have to 'sweat the little things'."

## Maher 2010

Maher points to the recent interest in police sexual misconduct as a result of concerns over "sexual exploitation among many service professionals—e.g., psychologists, therapists, teachers, and clergy."

He opines that sexual abuse in these service professions and police work results from social and cultural aspects of the organization—occupational deviance in sex abuse work settings where *inclination, opportunity, and real or perceived low risk* are common. This research is his third to use a snowball sample of police officers in the St. Louis, Missouri metropolitan area. He interviewed twenty female officers to explore the female perspective on the nature and frequency of police sexual abuse (Maher 2010).

His findings are similar to findings from the earlier studies. The female officers believe the less serious police sexual misconduct patterns are common in police work and their departments. However, the serious patterns—rape, sexual assault, sexual shakedowns, and sex with juveniles—are rare occurrences. The female officers felt that sexual harassment was a significant problem in police work and in their department—75% reported their fellow male officers or supervisors had sexually harassed them. Only two of these victims reported the sexual harassment because they wanted to avoid trouble or did not want to call attention to themselves—differential reinforcement. They also suggested the police culture exerts pressure not to report misconduct by fellow officers—differential reinforcement. The female officers believed changes in police sexual misconduct would have to come with a change in the male-dominated police culture. He recommended a common deterrent solution to PSM—a zero-tolerance approach and policies that make clear that PSM is a high-risk behavior.

## Shockley-Eckles 2011

This research and the research that follows examined Gypsy Cops and the phenomenon known as "officer shuffle" that allows "disreputable" officers to remain in law enforcement positions. The research is an ethnographic case study of officers in the St. Louis Metropolitan Police Department. A brief discussion is provided here, and a more expansive discussion was provided earlier.

The study's purpose was to describe "the effects on, and perceptions of officers serving alongside the gypsy cops," and relied on a combination of semi-structured interviews and 50 hours of participant observation in the form of ride-a-longs with police officers, unobtrusive observation, and informal interviews. Shockley-Eckles found that the "officer shuffle" even for sexual offenders was quite common and known by the research subjects. However, the research subjects objected to the "officer shuffle" because they knew it damaged the reputation of their department and they were concerned about discredited officers providing sufficient back up when needed. Reputable officers were concerned about working side-by-side with Gypsy Cops.

Shockley-Eckles recommended: (a) the adoption of decertification policies in all 50 states, (b) standardization of decertification criteria across jurisdictions, (c) mandatory reporting of employment histories of those decertified, and (d) the creation and maintenance of a national database of revocation with accessibility granted to all employing agencies nationwide (Shockley-Eckles 2011: 304).

## Rabe-Hemp and Braithwaite 2013

Their research sought to identify the existence of repeat police sexual violence offenders in the US Midwest region who "shuffle" from agency to agency continuing their sexual depravations. The researchers identified sexual problem-prone officers and the agency's reaction to them. They use the definition of police sexual violence-PSV—proposed by Kraska and Kappeler (1995) as those sexual acts experienced by a **female** [italics supplied] that are "sexually degrading, humiliating, damaging, or threatening act committed by a police officer through the use of force, fear or intimidation, or police authority."

The researchers conducted a content analysis of newspaper accounts of police sexual violence offenses from 1996 to 2006 in the Midwest region. The keyword search of the newspapers in the LexisNexis database was "police," "sexual," "police violence," "sexual violence," and "sexual harassment." They were seeking officers found guilty of PSV and those who had been accused of PSV in the past. The finding supported the existence of problem-prone PSV offenders. A small group of repeat offenders was responsible for the majority of sexual misconduct reported in the newspapers. Repeat or problem-prone officers sexually abused almost three-fourths of the victims. The police sexual misconduct problem-prone officers averaged four victims over an average of 3 years. Fourteen percent of these repeat offenders were allowed to resign and resume police employment in another police agency—*Gypsy Cops or officer shuffle*. They likened this approach to the well-known "pass the buck" phenomenon when dealing with sexually abusive priests. Many of those officers accused of sexual misconduct in one department left with favorable recommendations for employment and committed sexual misconduct in their new agencies. Among the recommendations the authors suggested was increasing the power and presence of Peace Officer Standards and Training (POST) boards.

## Cotter et al. 2014

Cotter and her colleagues conducted a systematic research study from a women's perspective and added significantly to the understanding of police sexual misconduct (Cotter et al. 2014). Their sample of 318 women was enrolled in a drug court program. The women were vulnerable targets for police sexual misconduct: 70% African-American, low education (48% high school or GED), low employment (42% had worked in the last 12 months), 39% were homeless, and 70% had been arrested 4 or more times in their lifetime. Fifty-five percent of the sample had been sexually abused as a child. All of the women were drug users, some multiple drug users, and 25% reported having traded sex for favors with an on-duty police officer to avoid an arrest or charge for a crime. A disturbing finding was that some police sexual victims were as young as 15. There was a violent component to many encounters. Thirty-one percent of the sample characterized the encounter with the police officer as rape. Most of the women reported multiple sexual encounters with the same officers. Another disturbing finding was 24% reported that another police officer was present during the sexual encounter, giving evidence to the peer group support for police sexual misconduct.

# Stinson et al. 2014

The researchers concluded that police work fits into what Barker (2011) posited earlier, "*policework* is a morally dangerous occupation" where law enforcement officers acting alone without direct supervision interact with a vulnerable pool of victims that are subject to their power and coercive authority.

Stinson et al. (2014) identified and described the arrests of 548 sworn non-federal officers arrested for sex-related crimes. The arrests were found in a quantitative analysis of Google Alerts and court records from 2005 to 2007. Their findings revealed serious forms of sex-related crimes with victims typically younger than 18 years of age—236 victims under 18 with the modal age of 14–15 years of age. Almost all of the arrested officers were male, and most of the cases came from officers working in patrol. The most serious charges were forcible rape ($n = 117$) followed by forcible fondling ($n = 107$), statutory rape ($n = 59$), forcible sodomy ($n = 54$), and child pornography ($n = 39$). The most disturbing findings are the youth of the victims, and the finding that the "most egregious forms of police sexual violence are *not* isolated events," 118 cases of rape occurred over the course of three years.

# Barker 2015

Barker's (2015) analysis of federal and non-federal police sexual misconduct incidents obtained from Google News Alerts from 2009 to 2015 identified 759 cases of on- and off-duty sexual abuses. There was no attempt at statistical analysis in what was a qualitative analysis to develop categories or types of police sexual misconduct based on this study and previous empirical studies. The 2015 findings revealed 26 incidents where police officers had coerced sex with three different victims. Eight of this deviant group was classified as *Serial Rapists*, including an openly gay deputy sheriff who sexually assaulted 20 illegal immigrants. *Sexual Extortion*—sexual shakedowns—was the most frequent form of on-duty sexual misconduct—110 cases. Seventy-three incidents involved police officers sexually assaulting victims who came or called the police for help—*Betrayal of Trust*. Forty-five cases of supposedly *consensual on-duty sex* were documented. This category included sex in the patrol cars, offices, or other official buildings, including sex with a police groupie in a patrol car during the funeral for a fallen officer. Thirty-nine cases were reported of sexual misconduct between inmates and custodial staff in detention facilities—lockups, jails, or prisons—*Custodial Sexual Misconduct*. There were 36 reports of *Sexual Harassment/Discrimination*, including one case where a female chief of police was accused of sexually harassing her male subordinates. There were 88 reported incidents of on-duty sexual contact between a police worker and minors under the age of eighteen—*Police Child Molesters*. Three police child sexual predators had histories of sexual assaults with multiple victims. One 22-year police veteran was accused of 39 sex acts with an unknown number of minor male victims. He was found guilty of 13 counts of child molestation. Twelve police officers, including a high-level Immigration and Custom Enforcement official, viewed, transmitted, or possessed child pornography—*Child Pornography*. The last category points out that direct contact with a victim is not a necessary condition of police sexual misconduct. Forty-five incidents of sexual misconduct were reported between police officers and minors in police/community-sponsored programs such as Police Explorer, School Resource Officers, and DARE officers—*Sexual Exploitation in Joint School Police and Community Programs*.

Barker's study identified numerous examples of off-duty illegal sexual conduct by law enforcement officers: statutory rape, pornography/obscenity offenses, and online solicitation of children, child molestation—male and female—and incest. There were a surprising number of pedophiles and child molesters carrying a badge. For the most part, these off-duty incidents are not discussed in the patterns presented, except when they are used to make a specific point.

## Lopez et al. 2017

The study grew out of a commissioned analysis of PSM in "Central City" a metropolitan municipal city (Lopez et al. 2017). They compared their central city results to media coverage—Google search—of police sexual misconduct in Atlanta, Boston, Detroit, Houston, Portland, San Antonio, and San Diego from 2000 to 2009. Their study only included non-federal officers and excluded workplace sexual misconduct. The researchers identified 42 PSM events—a surprising but unexplained low number. The events were listed in an Appendix. I could not determine the nature of many events but of the ones I could identify were: 9 sexual assaults, 5 child sexual abuse, 4 rapes, and 3 official misconduct charges. They concluded that police sexual misconduct occurred on a continuum from less serious acts—voyeurism, sexual harassment in the form of callbacks to crime victims, suspects, or witnesses—to serious criminal offenses such as sexual assaults, rape, sexual shakedowns, and child molestation.

## Jones 2018

Barker's 2015 research raised the ugly menace of *police child molesters,* and the production, viewing, possession, and distribution of *child pornography.* However, Professor Samuel Jones—Associate Dean and Professor of Law at the John Marshall Law Chicago—goes further and makes a controversial claim "police involved sex trafficking, and related police-involved sex offenses against children, represent a continuous and constitutive threat to child safety" in the United States (Jones 2018: 1012). The data for his study of US police-involved child trafficking comes from qualitative studies, investigative and journalistic reports from law enforcement executives, human rights advocates, and survivor testimonials.

In support of his argument, he cites ten cases from 2016 to 2018 where law enforcement officers "have allegedly attempted to; or reportedly engaged in" some form of child sex trafficking. Jones also cites thirty cases where US law enforcement officers at all levels of government have allegedly possessed, produced [actual violent child molestation], or marketed child pornography in the same two-year time period. Lastly, he provides a list of sixty US LEOs—not including the previous forty cases—where US LEOs from all levels of government have "reportedly been arrested, charged, or convicted for, conduct linked to child sexual abuse, since 2016" (Jones 2018: 1046). The listed cases are disturbing and demonstrate a pattern of police sexual misconduct. His article should stimulate discussion of further research.

The crux of his argument is that the "heoroification" of law enforcement has had the unintended consequences of contributing to the inability to identify, quantify, and deter police officers from sexually exploiting children. This has created an adjudicating system that ignores police sexual violence. The victims of police sexual misconduct, according to Jones, struggle against the "hero cop narrative" when they report their victimization—no one believes them or is skeptical of their complaints. This supports the claim by other researchers that this phenomenon creates a *real or perceived low-risk* setting (Barker 2015). Jones posits that the typical child sex trafficking comes from a vulnerable pool—*opportunity*—of runaways, child victims of sexual or physical abuse, child drug user, homeless child, or immigrant children coming alone.

Jones is critical of the Blue Wall of Silence-BWOS-common in the police culture. He is right in pointing out that the BWOS has a chilling effect on victims reporting LEO sexual abuse. No one will accept his or her uncorroborated complaints. The powerless victims rightly fear other officers may harm them or not protect them from retaliation. They also fear harsh interrogations without any outside support. The BWOS increases the likelihood that other officers will commit PSM when they view it as LEO job perk—differential reinforcement plus low risk. The Blue Wall of Silence insures that PSM remains secret deviance and further damages the police-community relations in the minority and marginalized neighborhoods. Lastly, Jones recognizes that the BWOS allows offenders to receive light or no punishment and move on to other agencies to continue their deviant sexual abuse—Gypsy Cops. This particular research is sure to spawn discussion—pro and con. However, his research supports the rational choice interaction of inclination—motivated actor—opportunity, and real or perceived low risk to produce certain types of police sexual misconduct.

# Empirical Typology of Police Sexual Misconduct

At this time, there is no inclusive taxonomy or typology of police sexual misconduct. However, the literature review and previous studies make clear that the broad array of police sexual misconduct acts is more complex than originally thought. The acts lie on a continuum of seriousness from consensual sex to murder. Some PSM acts arise from the officers arrest power and some do not. There is violence in many PSM acts while other acts do not require contact with a victim. Many PSM victims cannot give consent, while others may give consent but the act is still illegal.

At this time, the proposed remedies are a hodgepodge of competing suggestions. Will the professionalization of the police and improved administrative rule-making end or lessen police sexual misconduct? What if police agencies improve the screening of applicants or only hire college graduates? What would be the effect on PSM? Surely, if the police agencies train their officers better and pay them more, we can have an impact on PSM or some forms of PSM? How do we resolve this conundrum? The first step is to separate and classify the varied PSM behaviors. For example, the typology shows that the different PSM types have varied target pools. A rational approach would be to limit access to the potential victims. A common element in the different patterns was the real or perceived risk of such behavior. Increasing the risk and certainty of punishment should deter the sexually inclined police sexual offender—a necessary condition for all types.

The proposed empirical typology is based on real-life experiences not on created ideal types of police sexual misconduct (Box 1.4). The typology is grounded in the previous research studies, and the author's personal experiences plus forty years of structured and semi-structured interviews with police officers at all levels of government. The typology of recurring patterns of behavior is the necessary first step toward the understanding, explanation, and elimination of police sexual misconduct.

## Box 1.4    Empirical Typology of Police Sexual Misconduct

**Type 1: Sex-Related Criminal Homicides**—The Rarest Pattern

**2 Categories**

1. **Police serial sexual murderers—personality disorders**
   **ACTS**—Sadistic murders committed by disturbed individuals.
   **AGGRESSORS**—Male police officers. No evidence of female involvement.
   **VICTIMS**—Males, females, transgender, and same sex.
   **PEER GROUP SUPPORT**—No peer group support. However, the peer group often is aware of prior "bizarre" Sexual behavior.
   **RISK**—A high-risk behavior once the murders become known; however, many have long histories because of the police agencies failure to take action on known sexual misconduct act.
   **FREQUENCY OF OCCURRENCE IN POLICE AGENCIES**—Rare and episodic. Examples have been identified worldwide.
   **PREVENTIVE ACTION**—Proper background checks and psychological testing would eliminate these "rotten apples."

2. **Rape or sexual assault plus murder—no personality disorder**
   **ACTS**—Impulsive or murders that are the end result of a police sexual assaults. The sexual aggressor murders his victim by accident or design to conceal his crime, or stop resistance. Generally, no personality problems indicated.
   **AGGRESSORS**—Male, no female police aggressors, found in the literature.
   **VICTIMS**—Male, female, transgender, and same sex.
   **PEER GROUP SUPPORT**—Little peer group support when the act results in murder; however, there is often low to moderate peer group support for the underlying police sexual misconduct.
   **RISK**—A high-risk behavior if a murder results from a police sexual assault.
   **FREQUENCY OF OCCURRENCE IN POLICE AGENCIES**—Rare and episodic.
   **PREVENTIVE ACTION**—Proper background checks, psychological testing, internal discipline and certification systems.

**Type 2: Serial Rapists and Sexual Predators**

**2 Categories**

1. **Serial Rapists**
   **ACTS**—The police officers in this category are "rotten apples" even in rogue police departments. Impulsive and violent rapes could have resulted in murder and in some instances may have.

AGGRESSORS—At this time, only males are known to be involved.

VICTIMS—Females.

PEER GROUP SUPPORT—Varies with type of agency. In corrupt police agencies where all patterns of police misconduct and crime are present the peer group will give direct or implicit support for these "rotten Apples" (Barker 2011).

RISK—Varies by type of agency.

FREQUENCY OF OCCURRENCE IN POLICE AGENCIES—Rare and episodic, except in corrupt agencies.

PREVENTIVE ACTION—The type of agency and its history will determine the best course of action, varying from the identification of "rotten apples" to "rotten barrels."

2. **Sexual Predators**

ACT\S—Repetitive sexual assaults with coercion, including the threat of violent acts. However, there is always the possibility of violent action. Further research may reveal little difference between category one—serial rapists and sexual predators. For now, we maintain that there is a difference.

AGGRESSORS—At this time, the evidence suggests that the police aggressors are male.

VICTIMS—Marginalized females and same sex.

PEER GROUP SUPPORT—Varies. More research is needed along the lines of that conducted by Klocker and his colleagues.

RISK—Varies by agency.

FREQUENCY OF OCCURRENCE IN POLICE AGENCIES—There are no official or scientifically accurate estimates of this type of police sexual misconduct. However, the estimates by knowledgeable experts range from 5 to 25% of the officers in any police are sexual predators.

PREVENTIVE ACTION—Proper background checks, internal discipline, and certification systems.

**Type 3: Sexual Extortion aka Sexual Shakedowns**

ACTS—During routine proactive activities, sexually inclined police officers enter into a quid pro quo sexual relationship.

AGGRESSORS—Police aggressors are male, female, and same sex.

VICTIMS—Male, female, transgender, and same sex.

PEER GROUP SUPPORT—Moderate to high support depending on police agency.

RISK—Low to moderate risk behavior depending on the agency.

FREQUENCY OF OCCURRENCE IN POLICE AGENCIES—This type is probably the second most common type of police sexual misconduct in police agencies worldwide.

PREVENTIVE ACTION—Improved administrative rule-making and early warning systems to identify potential sexual offenders.

### Type 4: Betrayal of Trust

**ACTS**—Reactive police strategy sexual misconduct. Generally does not involve quid pro quo interactions. The police take advantage of vulnerable persons, perverting the motto—To Serve and Protect.

**AGGRESSORS**—Police aggressors are male, female, or same sex.

**VICTIMS**—Male, female, or same sex.

**PEER GROUP SUPPORT**—Low to moderate, depending on the peer group's social definition of consent. The exposure of these acts creates scandals; therefore, many peer groups condemn open behavior.

**RISK**—Low to moderate varies by setting, and the age and disability of the victim.

**FREQUENCY OF OCCURRENCE IN POLICE AGENCIES**—These acts appear episodically in American and UK agencies. More research is needed in other police agencies worldwide.

**PREVENTION**—Administrative rule-making and internal audit and discipline systems. Gypsy cops and "disturbed" individuals have been identified. This calls into question the vetting process.

### Type 5: Consensual On-Duty Sex

**ACTS**—The most numerous act of police sexual misconduct. Consensual on-duty (CS) sex is present, and has always been, in all police agencies worldwide. Nevertheless, CS is unethical, often coerced, and criminal in some circumstances and settings.

**AGGRESSORS**—Male, female, and same sex.

**VICTIMS**—Male, female, same sex, and transgender.

**PEER GROUP SUPPORT**—High peer group support often looked on as a perk of the *policework* occupation—one of many sexual abuse-prone occupations.

**RISK**—Low risk.

**FREQUENCY OF OCCURRENCE IN POLICE AGENCIES**—Occurs in all police agencies, depending on the agency's culture.

**PREVENTION**—Administrative rule-making and a zero-tolerance stance by the administration.

### Type 6: Custodial Sexual Misconduct

**ACTS**—Custodial sexual misconduct is the exemplar of the PSM Causal Model—custody/detention workers with the *inclination* for sexual misconduct have a captive pool of vulnerable targets—*opportunity*—with credibility problems, and the environment is a *low or no risk* setting. Some of the most egregious examples of PSM occur in jails and prisons. Furthermore, the available evidence suggests that all the types except serial sexual killers and PSM in joint police and community-sponsored programs.

AGGRESSORS—Male, female, and same sex.
VICTIMS—Males, females, same sex, and transgender.
PEER GROUP SUPPORT—Varies by type.
RISK—Low to no risk.
FREQUENCY OF OCCURRENCE—Widespread depending on the setting and level of government.
PREVENTION—Administrative rule-making, vetting of workers, and zero tolerance for violations.

### Type 7: Harassment/Discrimination in the Police Workplace

ACTS—Sexual harassment/discrimination can be one or any combination of the following acts: gender discrimination, unwanted sexual attention, and sexual coercion.
AGGRESSORS—Male, female, and same sex.
VICTIMS—Male, female, gay, or lesbian.
PEER GROUP SUPPORT—Medium to high depending on the agencies culture.
RISK—Low to moderate.
FREQUENCY OF OCCURRENCE IN POLICE AGENCIES—Widespread.
PREVENTION—Administrative rule-making.
MALE AND FEMALE VICTIM CONTACT—Police sexual misconduct police sexual misconduct high peer group support. Generally, a low-risk behavior.

### Type 8: Child Molestation

ACTS—Sexual relations with child under 18 years of age. Consent not possible.
AGGRESSORS—"Rotten apples" can be male, female, or same sex.
VICTIMS—Male and female.
PEER GROUP SUPPORT—None, however in some departments there is a tendency to not publicly identify the child molesters which create a perceived safe setting.
RISK—High risk.
FREQUENCY OF OCCURRENCE IN POLICE AGENCIES—Rare. However, a surprising number of child molesters on and off duty were found in Barker's study. More research is needed.
PREVENTION—Improved vetting and a zero-tolerance policy by police agency.

### Type 9: Child Pornography

ACTS—The viewing, possessing, producing, or possessing of child pornography.

AGGRESSORS—Male "Rotten Apple" police officers.
VICTIMS—Male and female children.
PEER GROUP SUPPORT—No agency peer group support but small groups of like-minded officers are possible.
RISK—High risk.
FREQUENCY OF OCCURRENCE IN POLICE AGENCIES—Occurs world-wide. This is the most organized type of police sexual misconduct.
PREVENTION—Zero tolerance.

**Type 10: Sexual Exploitation in Joint School Police and Community-Sponsored Programs**
ACTS—Sexual abuse in the school setting.
AGGRESSORS—Male, female, and same-sex police officers.
VICTIMS—Male, female, and same sex. Most not legally able to give consent.
PEER GROUP SUPPORT—The support depends on the agency. It appears that in some agencies, the sexual acts are considered a perk of the assignment. More research is needed.
RISK—Appears to be a low-risk behavior.
FREQUENCY OF OCCURRENCE IN POLICE AGENCIES—The evidence suggests that this PSM type is widespread in US police agencies with police/school and community-sponsored programs.
PREVENTION—Zero-tolerance and internal auditing.

\* \* \*

Typologies are important in understanding the similarities and differences between and among the identified PSM types. It should be clear from the PSM typology that police sexual misconduct begins with a sexually motivated offender—inclination. The opportunities for each type of PSM will vary by such things as officer's assignment and the social characteristics of the neighborhood or community. LEO sexual misconduct is most common in those officers who have direct face-to-face contact with citizens such as uniformed officers and detectives/special agents at all levels of government. Most PSM studies concentrate on local municipal patrol officers and fail to see it as a problem in federal agencies and custodial settings. Some PSM acts are internal to the agency—harassment/discrimination, and only involve agency members, while other types are external to the agency and involving the public as victims—betrayal of trust. Some types are personal crimes requiring victim to officer interaction, others are not. The real or perceived risks of the sexual misconduct types vary—from less serious rule violations to sexually motivated murders. We have known for some time that the police peer group differentially supports or condemns various types of police misconduct, including PSM.

Each PSM types will be the subject of separate chapters. The understanding of what types of PSM exist in any police setting is important in learning the environment in which the behavior occurs in order to provide appropriate remedial action. For example, the setting, officers involved, and victims are different in sexual shakedowns, custodial sexual misconduct, and harassment/discrimination in the workplace. The sex misconduct problem in an agency can vary on a continuum from individual, group, or agency involvement—rogue police department (Barker 2011). We examine each type according to inclination, opportunity, and risk dimensions using a PSM Causal Model.

## The Police Sexual Misconduct Causal Equation Model

A Police Sexual Misconduct Causal Equation Model is used to explain each of the types of police sexual misconduct. The model has three dimensions/elements—inclination, opportunity, and real or perceived risk. Each dimension is a necessary but not sufficient factor and is supported in whole or in part by deterrence, social control, and social learning theories. The types require a sexually motivated police actor. The opportunities for police sexual misconduct are readily available to all members of the *policework* occupation, but only a small number engage in this deviant behavior. Empirical studies and retrospective participant observations demonstrate that the police peer group defines the risk for certain types of deviant behaviors, including PSM. The model is based on the previous scholarly research on PSM, "on the job" police experiences, forty-plus years of research on police misconduct, and formal and informal interviews with "on the job" and retired law enforcement officers since the 1960s.

# Inclination

Rational choice theory is based on the decision-making process of the individual offender (Anonymous 2014). The rational choice model we follow in explaining police sexual misconduct assumes that police sexual predators—except police sexual serial killer—are rational sexually motivated offenders with the inclination in favorable settings. He or she makes their decision in their own self-interest based on their evaluation of the cost—risks and benefits—sexual pleasure—when presented with the opportunity under a real or perceived low-risk situation. Several rational choice theories assuming a motivated offender apply to police sexual misconduct.

# Routine Activities Theory

The occupational routine activities of a police sexual predator provide the settings for PSM. The settings create the hunting grounds for sex victims. The routine activities theory of crime introduced by Cohen and Felson (1979) had three components that converged together to produce crime: (1) a motivated offender who has the inclination and the ability to commit the act. In our causal model that is a sexually inclined police sexual predator, (2) a suitable target—the pool of vulnerable victims, and (3) an ineffective or absent guardian (see Tewksbury et al. 2008 for a routine activities theory analysis of sexual residency laws). Barker and Roebuck (1973) used an expanded version of the last component—an ineffective or absent guardian—years before the publication of the routine activities theory. Their control mechanisms included the police agencies discipline system, or lack thereof, and the police peer group support for police corruption that creates a real or perceived low-risk environment. The police peer group as a "risk factor" considered before a police officer engages in police misconduct—police corruption—or reports a fellow officer has been a consistent finding in police misconduct studies since Barker and Roebuck (1973) introduced it as a dimension in corruption. Barker (1978) introduced peer group support as a dimension in police misconduct other than corruption including police sexual misconduct. Klockers et al. (2000) study of police misconduct in 30 US police agencies—sample size of 3235 officer—concluded:

> The more serious the officers considered a behavior to be, he more likely they were to believe that more serious discipline was appropriate, and the more willing they were to report a colleague for engaging in that behavior. (2000: 1)

Their study did not include federal officers or state officers, and officers from the West, Northwest, or Midwest. Furthermore, the scenarios only covered police corruption and still do; however, the offer of sex or coerced sex could easily be substituted for monetary gain in many of the scenarios. For example Case 2: Free meals, discounts on Best— *Type 5-Consensual on-duty sex;* Case 4: Holiday gifts from merchants— *Consensual on-duty sex;* Case 8: Cover-up of Police DUI accident—*Type 3-Sexual Extortion;* Case 3: Bribes from speeding Motorist; and Case 9: Drinks to ignore Late Bar Closing—*Type 3-Sexual Extortion.*

According to Ivkovic and Haberfeld (2015), the original police integrity scenarios have been revised to include five scenarios describing police corruption, four describing use of excessive force and two describing false reports and failure to execute a search warrant. These scenarios, still absent police sexual misconduct, have been administered to police officers in 23 countries on four continents—North America, Europe, Africa, and Asia. The same revisions to include sexual misconduct still apply. The proposed Empirical Typology of Police Sexual Misconduct should stimulate the corruption research conducted by the late Carl Klockers and his colleagues to include similar more expansive police misconduct US or worldwide PSM research.

Barker (1978) used the rational choice concept—motivated actor, opportunity, and real or perceived risk—to analyze police sexual misconduct as a type of police occupational deviance. The rational choice calculus of the inclined actor is not infallible. Sometimes, the police sexual offender miscalculates in his or her risk assessment and the event leads to exposure and adverse consequences—loss of job or arrest and prosecution—or in worst-case scenario the victim's murder (see Beauregard and Leclerc [2007] study of a routine activities analysis of serial sex offenders miscalculations in a Canadian sample).

The Beauregard and Leclerc (2007) study found that sexual assault victims were more likely to be killed if the attacker had a gun—a disturbing finding for police sexual misconduct victims who resist or threaten to expose the officer. Police sexual misconduct research and the identification of sexually inclined police officers that are repeat sexual predators raise the specter of "rotten apples" again.

## "Rotten Apples" Revisited

A study of 60 Norwegian police officers—"rotten apples"—prosecuted for misconduct and crime from 2005 to 2010 found that 4 officers were convicted and sentenced to more than 2 years in prison—(1) theft of money, weapons, and passports to help criminals; (2) theft of confiscated drugs from police station for personal use; (3) paid by prison inmate to arrange frequent trips; and (4) sexual harassment, sexual abuse, and rape of several intoxicated women (Gottschalk 2010: 175).

The study of Norwegian police officers charged with criminal offenses, including sexual misconduct, is presented for several reasons. The study of police "rotten apples" in Norwegian police forces demonstrates the nature of police occupational deviance in what is considered a misconduct-free police organization (Gottschalk 2010). The study from the "rotten apple" perspective confirms the utility of studying individual rational choice deviance in what are generally considered to be deviance-free police agencies. As Barker (2011) pointed out, it is time to revisit this widely considered impression management technique. There are a number of individual officers or small groups of officers who commit deviant acts in an otherwise deviant-free police organization. Barker (2011) posited that "true" "rotten apples" are misconduct-prone individuals who because of lax or nonexistent background checks slip through the screening process and succumbed to the temptations inherent in the *policework* occupation. There are deviant individuals who continue their deviant practices in an environment of ample opportunity.

The true "rotten apples" came to the job with the inclination for misconduct, including PSM. Gypsy Cops are an example of known deviant "rotten apples" that enter police agencies without proper vetting. The police officer that killed twelve-year-old Tamir Rice is another example of a "rotten apple." The Cleveland, Ohio, police department should not have hired this officer (Doherty 2018). The Cleveland PD did not examine the personnel records from his previous agency. If they had they would have discovered that he resigned right before he was fired—a common tactic for handling "rotten apples," resignation before termination. Four previous police agencies rejected him because of his background. The hiring of "rotten apples" who are known sex offenders happens. In 2004, an Oregon police officer was fired for sexual misconduct with a ten-year-old girl (Doherty 2018). Part of his sentence agreement was that he would not seek police employment again. Three months later, he was hired by a small rural agency as their police chief. While he was at this department, he was investigated for another alleged child molestation charge before being convicted of burglary and criminal conspiracy. The "rotten apple" or "seriously flawed individual theory" explains some but not all police sexual misconduct.

Barker (2011) suggested this in a *Continuum of Officers in Corrupt Departments* ranging from **White Knights**—a rare category who engage in no forms of corruption—to **Rogue Officers** ("**rotten apples**"—a rare category of officers who have few bounds on their acts of corruption). The continuum suggests that any police officer has the potential to succumb to the temptations always present in the morally dangerous occupation on an occasional basis. The same continuum applies to police sexual misconduct. Proper vetting processes, increased supervision, and reactive and proactive—sure and swift punishment—deterrence practices and a national system of decertified officers will have an effect on this continuum of possible misconduct-prone officers who are impulsive or lack self-control.

## Self-Control Theory

There are without doubt individuals who are impulsive or lack self-control that are misconduct-prone when presented with the opportunity (Pogarsky and Piquero 2004). Self-control theory suggests that the Commission of police misconduct is the expression of a police officer's natural expression to pursue pleasure and avoid pain—rational choice (Donner et al. 2016). Self-control theory or variations of self-control theory are useful to predict police misconduct, the likelihood of future misconduct and reduce some or all types of police misconduct.

According to Donner et al. (2016), two self-control theories have implications for police misconduct. The first self-control theory proposed by Gottfredson and Hirschi (1990) is a general theory of crime that does not require any specific motivation. The potential criminal expresses his or her natural predisposition-inclination—to pursue pleasure and avoid pain. Those individuals with low self-control have difficulty calculating the long-term costs for such rational action. Thus, those with low self-control act impulsively and are more likely to engage in criminal or deviant behavior when the opportunity presents itself.

Hirschi (2004) revised the theory to include factors that establish a social bond—internal value system—that the actor uses to calculate the potential costs of the behavior. The social bond factors include attachments to family, commitment to social norms and institutions such as the police agency. The higher one's stake in conformity, the less likely one is to engage in deviant or criminal behavior. Social control is self-control because the internal value system guides one's behavior. Donner and his colleagues were the first to use the revised self-control theory to examine police occupational deviance.

Their self-control study of police supervisors assumed that the desire to preserve social bonds would impact on the willingness to engage in police occupational deviance (Donner et al. 2016: 844). Data was collected from a sample—101—of first-line police supervisors attending a National Police Research Forum funded by the National Institute of Justice. Survey data measured the past behavior on ten self-reported acts of police occupational deviance and the inclination to engage in such behavior in the future. The past behavior acts were minor acts not including serious occupational deviance such as corruption, drinking on duty, sexual misconduct, sleeping on duty or perjury in court—the authors pointed this out as a limitation of the study. The use of "minor" acts of misconduct is typical in police integrity studies especially those who use the scenarios developed by Klockers and his colleagues (Hickman et al. 2015). The acts used in this study were: fix a ticket, conduct an unauthorized record check, fail to arrest or ticket a friend or relative, display your badge to avoid a ticket, sleep while on duty, speed when no emergency exists, fail to report an excessive force incident, illegally stop and frisk a suspect, illegally search a suspect, and falsify an arrest report. Following the self-reports were questions regarding the likelihood of engaging in these acts in the future.

The police supervisors top three reported acts were: (1) speeding when no emergency exists (82.20%); (2) displaying one's badge to avoid a traffic ticket (51.5%); and (3) sleeping while on duty (49.5%). The bottom three self-reported acts were: (1) falsify an arrest report (1%); (2) illegally stop and frisk a suspect (4%); and (3) illegally search a suspect and failure to report an excessive force incident tied at one percent (1%). The measures for the most likely to engage in the behavior in the future were: (1) sleeping on duty (64%); (2) displaying one's badge to avoid a traffic ticket (52.3%); and (3) failure to arrest or ticket a friend or relative (25.2%). The least likely behaviors to occur were: (1) falsify an arrest report (1%); (2) failure to report an excessive force incident (1.8%); and (3) illegal stop and frisk a suspect.

The results suggest that self-control is a predictor of self-reported police misconduct among this sample of police supervisors. Police supervisors who have higher self-control levels are less likely to engage in the minor types of occupational deviance noted in the study. These findings have implication for pre-employment—background checks—and post-employment—training—strategies.

The authors opine that in order to reduce misconduct, the identification of low self-control police officers must pursue certain strategies: (1) pre-hiring detection and (2) post-hiring detection (Donner et al. 2016: 853). Low self-control applicants should not be hired. Stringent hiring practices—psychological exams and interviews—should be adopted by all agencies. Thorough background checks must look for applicants with a history of problematic behaviors—arrests and poor work histories. As we shall see, these obvious disqualifiers are not used by some agencies. Post-employment strategies should include ethics training—rookie school and in-service, and reactive and proactive measures to identify problem officers in need of remediation or termination.

Self-control theory "assumes that human actions are based on 'rational choices;' that is, they are informed by the probable consequences of that action" (Akers 1991: 654). The majority of police officers abide by the rules because of moral and characters issues buttressed by the fear of agency and social sanctions when they encounter a PSM opportunity—self-control and lack of inclination. However, there are other factors at play in the police work setting that influence PSM. Nevertheless, the sexually motivated actor—*inclination*—is a necessary condition for the occurrence of police sexual misconduct. However, there are other necessary elements. One of those necessary elements is the opportunity structure of the law enforcement occupation.

## Opportunity

The opportunity theories of crime and delinquency such as routine activities theory and self-control focus on the physical and social environment characteristics that facilitate deviant acts (Hollis et al. 2013). Routine activities refer to that activity that makes up the actor's daily routine and posits that crime is based on opportunity (Cohen and Felson 1979). For our purposes, the daily activity of working law enforcement officers creates opportunities for sexual misconduct and other patterns of police misconduct. As stated earlier, Barker and Roebuck (1973) were the first researchers to focus on the police work opportunity structure and its connection to police crime and misconduct. Barker and Roebuck focused on the motivated police officer—*inclination*—and the opportunities for opportunistic or systematic corruption—*opportunities*—that came together to produce corrupt acts, depending on the social, definition, and support from the police peer group. They proposed that efforts directed at any of the elements—inclination, opportunity, and peer group support—can and has affected the nature and extent of police corruption over time in some police agencies. Barker (1978) extended this assumption to other forms of police misconduct, including police sexual misconduct.

The routine activities theory as first proposed consisted of three necessary elements for predatory crime—crimes that harm the victim or takes property from the victim—to occur. Those three elements are a motivated offender, an available, vulnerable victim and the absence of a capable guardian. The first two elements—a motivated offender and an available, vulnerable victim—are essential to the study of police sexual misconduct. We discussed a motivated offender—inclination—earlier. Our inquiry is now how the routine activities of law enforcement officers, and in some cases the routine activities of potential victims, affect the PSM Causal Model.

PSM is occupational deviance where the routine activities and consequently the opportunities to engage in this predatory behavior vary by the law enforcement agency's jurisdiction, location, and the victim's characteristics. The PSM opportunities vary by the officer's assignment—task environment—in the agency—patrol, traffic, custody/detention, and detective for most municipal, county, and state officers. This calls for a structural analysis of the routine activities of any individual police officer (Ede et al. 2002). For example, patrol officers are most likely to engage in field stops and proactive sexual shakedowns. Detectives are more likely to engage in *Betrayal of Trust* sexual misconduct with victims or witnesses. Police officers in administrative positions are more likely to be accused of sexual harassment than general service officers. The structural setting for *Custodial Sex* is obvious. Further complicating the discussion is that the opportunities for PSM in many LEO agencies are "hot spots" of opportunity that vary by demography (Ede et al. 2002). PSM like crime is not randomly distributed—criminology of place. The *criminology of place* was first proposed by Sherman and his colleagues in the application of the Routine Activities Theory to Hot Spots of Predatory Crime in Minneapolis (Sherman et al. 1989).

The criminology of place suggests that PSM opportunities are different situational and structural moments depending on the delivery of police services. Police sexual offenders make contact with victims in places. The places vary by the law enforcement agency. In the United

States, essential police services—patrol, traffic control, investigation, and custodial/detention—are the primary responsibility of 15,328 general-purpose law enforcement agencies—municipal, county, and regional police departments; most sheriffs offices; and primary state and highway patrol agencies (US Department of Justice, August, 2018). These general-purpose law enforcement agencies employ an estimated 701,000 full-time sworn officers in agencies ranging from one person to 30,000 plus. Over half of these agencies employ 10 or fewer officers. There are also special purpose/special district agencies—tribal, park, school, airport, subway, hospital, housing authority, and governmental—law enforcement agencies. Two hundred fifty federal law enforcement agencies employ approximately 120,000 officers with arrest and firearm authority (Reaves 2012). The four largest federal agencies are two in the Department of Homeland Security—Customs and Border Control, Immigration and Customs Enforcement—and two in the Department of Justice—FBI and Secret Service. Police sexual misconduct of some type/s occurs in all these agencies.

The majority of predatory police sexual incidents, but not all, occur in general-purpose agencies with the most opportunities. Our fragmented system of municipal policing is organized into decentralized beats/districts and precincts. According to the social ecology theory of police misconduct, police beats/districts with high crime rates and evidence of social disorganization increase the opportunity for sexual opportunities as prostitutes, drug sellers, and users loiter in public places (Klinger 1997). These potential PSM victims create their own victimization by citizens and the police by their routine risk behaviors (Kane 2002).

The nature of police work worldwide is that street-level officers make a clear distinction between the "rough and respectable" members of their work environment (Chan 1997). Ethnic and racial profiling, immigration status and sexual orientation are a part of this distinction of making, targeting, and selecting PSM victims. Sexually motivated police officers in these "hot spot" environments know where to look for sexual victims. They know the locations of bars, taverns, crack, and drug houses in their beats where there are opportunities for trading sex for leniency with intoxicated drivers. Kane (2002) hypothesized that the primary factors for police misconduct, including PSM, across police territorial settings, such as beats/divisions were the opportunities determined by social ecology.

Experienced police officers know that areas with evidence of social disorganization have more opportunities for police misconduct ranging from abuse of power, corruption for profit, to police sexual misconduct. Police misconduct opportunities vary by defined neighborhoods in any city no matter how large or small. I knew this from my on the job police experiences before I ever took a sociology course.

Police officers make the rational choice guided by their internal value system not to engage in these available deviant patterns of behavior when the opportunity presents itself. Inclination plus the opportunity are necessary but not sufficient elements in the PSM Causal Equation Model. There is one more necessary condition in our causal model.

## Real or Perceived Risk

The last dimension—*real or perceived risk*—is for sexually inclined police officers a necessary and sufficient condition for PSM, when agency's culture and peer group define one or more types of PSM as low-risk actions. Only an estimated three to 5% of law enforcement officers in any agency, except a rogue police department, reach this stage in the causal equation (see Stamper 2005; Kane and White 2009; Barker 2011).

The social learning theorists and other rational behavior advocates consider the support—tacit or implied—and the risk of informal and formal punishment as an example of *differential reinforcement* (Akers et al. 1979). Accordingly, the more officers in any particular police agency that engage in or define a forbidden sex act as "good" or at least acceptable, the more likely it is to occur when the opportunity presents itself.

Chappell and Piquero (2004) recognize that the police occupation provides numerous opportunities and justifications for various patterns and forms of behavior occupational deviance. They choose three of Barker's (1977) outlined deviant patterns—accepting free gifts and meals from the public, opportunistic thefts, and excessive use of force—to test the efficacy of Akers' social learning theory and the differential reinforcement formula on police misconduct. They examined "how officer attitudes and perceptions of peer attitudes and ideas about the likelihood of punishment influence officially documented citizen complaints." They examined three hypotheses: (1) officers who associate with deviant peers are more likely to have citizen complaints; (2) officers who consider misconduct to be less serious will have a higher likelihood of citizen complaints; and (3) officers who anticipate less punishment for misconduct are more likely to have citizen complaints.

According to social learning theory, the same learning processes produce conforming and nonconforming behavior. Support or disapproval for behavior is acquired through *differential association* with those whom you associate most frequently. For the police that group of persons is the occupational peer group—the primary group provides the definitions, models, and support for accepted or prohibited behavior (Barker 1977, 1978, 2011). The police peer group defines what is deviant or "approved"—*differential reinforcement* according to the social learning theory.

Their study surveyed a random sample—504—of the 3810 members of the 23 Philadelphia patrol districts in January 2000 after roll call. The number of citizen's complaints each officer had received measured the dependent variable. Each subject was presented with five scenarios showing the three deviant patterns and asked to rate the seriousness of each misconduct behavior and the reaction to each type if the officer was discovered. The study found that accepting gifts were the norm, but the officers considered stealing and excessive force to be more serious offenses. The subject believed that the acceptance of gifts would result in verbal or written reprimands. However, if they were caught using excessive force, they would be suspended without pay, and if they were caught stealing, they would be dismissed. This supports the differential reinforcement formula of the social learning theory. On the matter of citizen complaints, the results showed that attitudes toward gifts and thefts were not significantly related to citizen complaints. However, those subjects who felt that excessive force was not serious were more likely to have citizens' complaints that is engaged in misconduct—also supported by social learning theory.

Chappell and Piquero (2004) concluded that a law enforcement officer chooses to engage in or not engage in a range of opportunities for sexual misconduct present in his or her police work social environment, that choice is affected by the real or perceived risk of discovery and punishment—differential reinforcement.

\* \* \*

The **PSM Causal Equation Model** has empirical and theoretical support. However, the overwhelming conclusion from all the studies of police sexual misconduct is that minorities of police officers engage in any type of PSM, notwithstanding the opportunity or low risk. The NYPD Mollen Commission found that even in a department with systematic opportunities for corruption and misconduct, and where most officers tolerate the misconduct and profit-motivated corruption, most officers do not engage in this deviant behavior (Kane and White 2009). Kane and White (2009) examined the personal and career histories of 1543 NYPD officers who were separated for cause—misconduct—during 1975–1996. The forms of misconduct included: police crime, police corruption, and abuse of authority. Five hundred and eighty-one (581) officers were terminated for police crime and serious misconduct—profit-motivated corruption, perjury, criminal abuse of authority, or other criminal offenses. Administrative misconduct—serious violations of department rules—costs 430 officers their positions. Four hundred and twenty officers (420) failed or refused to take a drug test. Even though this is a large number, it only represented 2% of the approximately 78,000 officers employed during the study's time period. Several pre-employment risk factors such as prior arrest and documented employment problems were found to be predictors of police misconduct. This points out the importance of the vetting process as a preventive strategy in police misconduct. The authors opine that this finding is consistent to control theories that suggest that prior deviance predicts future deviance through low self-control (Kane and White 2009: 763). However, this study only represents the most severe sanction—dismissal—that can be imposed for police misconduct in the NYPD. It is not an accurate measure of NYPD police misconduct and makes no mention of police sexual misconduct. Police sexual misconduct is not explicitly mentioned in any of the nine categories in the "classification scheme of police misconduct" (Kane and White 2009: 745). This does not discount the role that self-control plays in the PSM Causal Model.

Self-control is an essential element in the PSM Causal Model that assumes the presence of a sexually inclined individual as a necessary but not sufficient factor, a rational sexually motivated law enforcement officer—opportunity and real or perceived risk are the other factors. Studies have shown that police officers who receive their first misconduct complaint early in their careers tend to persist in misconduct (Kane and White 2009; Harris 2010; Harris and Worden 2014).

## Conclusion

The review of the existing literature and empirical study of police sexual misconduct leads to several conclusions. *Policework* is a morally dangerous occupation that presents its workers with a myriad of opportunities for misconduct and crime, including police sexual conduct. The review revealed ten (10) patterns of police sexual misconduct—**Empirical Typology of Police Sexual Misconduct**. The occurrence and prevalence of any of the ten types of police sexual misconduct vary with the presence or absence of inclination to offend, opportunity to offend, and the real or perceived risk of offending. The typology does not rank the types in seriousness other than the obvious first three types: (1) Sex-Related Criminal Homicides; (2) Serial Rapists and Sexual Predators; and (3) Sexual Extortion that involve physical violence—threat of violence in sexual extortion—and an unwilling victim. There is a need for empirical studies similar to those conducted by Ivkovic and Haberfeld to address police sexual misconduct. The typology should stimulate this research. However, there is empirical and theoretical support for a testable **PSM Causal Equation** Model.

### PCM CASUAL EQUATION

**Inclination + Opportunity + Real or Preceived Low Risk = PSM**

The *inclination* to commit police sexual misconduct plus the *opportunity* to target a pool of victims with credibility problems that occur under *real or perceived low-risk* situations leads to police sexual misconduct. The strength, presence, or absence of the dimensions of this causal equation can increase or decrease the likelihood of police sexual misconduct and has the potential to be a factor in other patterns of police misconduct. The rest of the book will examine each of the proposed types and provide Illustrative Examples of each.

# References

Akers, R. A. (1991). Self-control as a general theory of crime. *Journal of Qualitative Criminology, 7*(2), 201–211.

Akers, R. T., Krohn, M. D., Lanza-Kaduce, L., & Radosevich, S. (1979). Social learning and deviant behavior: A specific test of a general theory. *American Sociological Review, 44*(4), 636–655.

Anonymous. (2014). Rational choice theory: Deviance and social control. *EBSCO Research Starters.*

Anonymous. (2018, November 1). Unending police misconduct. *Philippine Daily Inquirer.*

Barker, T. (1977). Peer group support for police occupational deviance. *Criminology, 15*(3), 353–366.

Barker, T. (1978). An empirical study of police deviance other than corruption. *Journal of Police Science and Administration, 6,* 264–272.

Barker, T. (2011). *Police ethics crisis in law enforcement.* Springfield, IL: Charles C. Thomas.

Barker, T. (2015, March). *Sleazy blue line: Police sexual misconduct.* Paper presented to the Annual Meeting of the Academy of Criminal Justice Sciences.

Barker, T., Hunter, R. D., & Rush, J. P. (1994). *Police systems and practices: An introduction.* Englewood Cliffs, NJ: Prentice Hall.

Barker, T., & Roebuck, J. (1973). *An empirical typology of police corruption.* Springfield, IL: Charles C. Thomas.

Beauregard, E., & Leclerc, B. (2007). An application of the rational choice approach to the offending process of sex offenders: A closer look a the decision-making. *Sex Abuse, 19,* 115–133.

Beccaria, C. (1963). *On crimes and punishments.* Indianapolis, IN: Bobbs Merrill (Original work published in 1764).

Becker, H. S. (1963). *Outsiders.* New York: Free Press.

Blumer, M. (1982). When is disguise justified? Alternatives to covert participant observation. *Qualitative Sociology, 54*(4), 252–264.

Bryant, C. (1974). *Deviant behavior: Occupational and organizational bases.* Chicago: Rand McNally.

Calhoun, A. J., & Coleman, H. D. (2002). Female inmates' perspectives on sexual abuse by correctional personnel: An exploratory study. *Women and Criminal Justice, 13*(2–3), 101–124.

Chaminda, J. (2019, May 18). Scale of police sexual abuse claims revealed. *The Guardian.*

Chan, J. B. L. (1997). *Changing police culture: Policing in a multicultural society.* Cambridge, UK: Cambridge University Press.

Chappell, A. T., & Piquero, A. R. (2004). Applying social learning theory to police misconduct. *Deviant Behavior, 25,* 89–108.

Cohen, L. E., & Felson, M. (1979). Social change and crime rate trends. *American Sociological Review, 44,* 588–608.

Collins, S. C. (2004). Sexual harassment and police discipline: Who's policing the police? *Policing: An International Journal of Police Strategies & Management, 27*(4), 512–538.

Committee on the Judiciary-House of Representatives. (2015, April 15). *Analyzing misconduct in federal law enforcement.* Washington, DC: GPO.

Conners, E. E., Silverman, J. G., Ulibarri, M., Magis-Rodriguez, C., Strathdee, S. A., Staines-Oruzco, H., et al. (2016). Structural determinants of client perpetrated violence among female sex workers in two Mexico-U.S. border cities. *Aids Behavior, 20,* 215–224.

Cotter, L. B., O'Leary, C. C., Nickel, K. B., Reingle, J. M., & Isom, D. (2014). Breaking The Blue Wall of silence: Risk factors for experiencing police sexual misconduct among female offenders. *American Journal of Public Health, 104*(2), 338–344.

Critchley, T. A. (1967). *A history of police in England and Wales—900–1966.* London: Constable and Company.

Decker, M. R., Crago, A.-L., Chu, S. K. H., Sherman, S. G., Seshu, M. S., Buthezi, K., et al. (2015). Human rights violations against sex workers: Borders and effect on HIV. *The Lancet.*

Decker, M. R., Pearson, E., Illangasekare, S. L., & Sherman, S. G. (2013). Violence against women in sex work and HIV risk implications differ qualitatively by perpetrator. *BMC Public Health.*

Doherty, O. (2018). A reform to police departments hiring preventing the tragedy of police misconduct. *Case Western Law Review, 68*(4).

DOJ. (2015, March). *The handling of sexual harassment and misconduct allegations by the department's law enforcement components.* GPO: Office of the Inspector General, Department of Justice.

Donner, C. M., Fridell, L. A., & Jennings, W. G. (2016). The relationship between self-control and police misconduct: A multi-agency study of first-line police supervisors. *Criminal Justice and Behavior.*

Ede, A., Homel, R., & Prenzler, T. (2002). Reducing complaints against police and preventing police misconduct. *Australian and New Zealand Journal of Criminology, 35*(1), 27–42.

Erausquin, J. T., Reed, E., & Blankenship, K. M. (2015). Change over time in police interactions and HIV behavior among female sex workers in Andhra Pradesh, India. *AIDS Behavior, 19*, 1108–1115.

Eschholtz, S., & Vaughn, M. S. (2001). Police sexual violence and rape myths: Civil Liability under Section 1983. *Journal of Criminal Justice, 29*(5), 389–405.

Fosdick, R. A. (1915). *European police systems.* Montclair, NJ: Patterson Smith.

Gibbs, J. P. (1975). *Crime, punishment, and deterrence.* Amsterdam: Elsevier.

Gottfredson, M. R., & Hirschi, T. (1990). *A general theory of crime.* Stanford, CA: Stanford University Press.

Gottschalk, P. (2010). Police misconduct behavior: An empirical study of court cases. *Policing, 5*(2), 172–179.

Goldman, R. I. (2003). State revocation of law enforcement officers' licenses and federal criminal prosecution: An opportunity for cooperative federalism. *Saint Louis University Public Law Review, 22*, 121–150.

Goldman, R. L., & Puro, S. (1987). Decertification of police: An alternative to Traditional remedies for police misconduct. *Hastings Constitutional Law Quarterly, 15*, 45–79.

Goldman, R. L., & Ruro, S. (2001). Revocation of police officer certification: A viable remedy for police violence? *Saint Louis University Law Journal, 45*, 541–580.

Graham, B. (2018, July 27). Sexual encounters between prison staff and inmates is 'commonplace' says whistleblower. *News.com.au.*

Haarr, R. N. (1997). They're making a bad name for the department. *Policing: An International Journal of Police Science and Management, 20*(4), 786–812.

Hamilton, F. (2016, October 22). Hundreds of police sex pests uncovered: Predatory officers face tough new punishments. *The Times.*

Harris, C. J. (2010). Problem officers? An analysis of problem behavior problems from a large cohort. *Police Quarterly, 12,* 192–213.

Harris, C. J., & Worden, R. E. (2014). The Effects of Sanctions on Police Misconduct. *Crime and Delinquency, 60*(8), 1258–1288.

Hickman, M. J., Piquero, A. R., Powell, Z. A., & Greene, J. (2015). Expanding the measurement of police integrity. *An International Journal of Police Strategies and Management, 39*(2), 246–267.

Hirschi, T. (2004). Self-control and crime. In R. Baumeister & K. Vohs (Eds.), *Handbook of self-regulation: Research, theory, and applications* (pp. 537–552). New York: Guilford Press.

Holdaway, S. (1979). *The British police.* London: Edward Arnold.

Hollis, M., Felson, M., & Welsh, B. C. (2013). The capable guardian in routine activities theory: A theoretical and conceptual reappraisal. *Crime Prevention and Community Safety, 15*(1), 65–79.

Ivkovic, S. K., & Haberfeld, M. F. (2015). Chapter 12: A comparative perspective on police integrity. In S. K. Ivkovic & M. F. Haberfeld (Eds.), *Measuring police integrity throughout the world.* New York: Springer.

Johnson, M. S. (2003). *Street justice: A history of police violence in New York City.* Boston: Beacon Press.

Jones, S. V. (2018). Police, heroes, and child trafficking: Who cries when her attacker wears blue. *Nevada Law Journal, 18,* 1007–1118.

Kane, R. J. (2002). The social ecology of police misconduct. *Criminology, 40*(4), 867–896.

Kane, R. J., & White, M. D. (2009). Bad cops: A study of career-ending misconduct among New York City police officers. *Criminology, 6*(4), 737–769.

Klinger, D. (1997). Negotiating order in police work: An ecological theory of police response to deviance. *Criminology, 35,* 277–306.

Klockers, C. B., Ivkovich, S. K., & Haberfeld, M. R. (2000, May). *The measurement of police integrity* (Research in Brief). Washington, DC: National Institute of Justice.

Lewis, P. (2007, April 3). NZ inquiry finds 30 years of sexual misconduct in parts of police force. *ABC.*

Lopez, M. K., Forde, D. R., & Miller, M. J. (2017). Media coverage of police sexual misconduct in seven cities. *American Journal of Criminal Justice, 42,* 833–844.

Kraska, P. B., & Kappeler, V. E. (1995). To serve and pursue: Exploiting police sexual violence against women. *Justice Quarterly, 12*(1), 86–111.

Lemert, E. M. (1967). *Human deviance, social problems and social control.* Englewood Cliff, NJ: Prentice-Hall.

Lersch, K. M. (1998). Police misconduct and malpractice: A critical of citizen's complaints. *Policing, 23,* 80–94.

Lersch, K. M., & Mieczkowski, T. (2000). An examination of the convergence and divergence of internal and external allegations of misconduct filed against police officers. *Police Practice and Research, 3,* 135–147.

MacKinnon, C. (2018, October 23). Police officer charged following Val-d'Or investigation pleads guilty. *CBC.*

Maher, T. M. (2003). Police sexual misconduct: Officer's perceptions of its extent and causality. *Criminal Justice Review, 28,* 355–377.

Maher, T. M. (2007). *Cops on the make: Police officers using their job powers, and authority to pursue their personal interests.* Presented at Miscarriage of Justice Conference: Current Perspectives, University of Missouri at St Louis.

Maher, T. M. (2008). Police chief's views on police sexual misconduct. *Police Practices and Research, 9,* 239–250.

Maher, T. M. (2010). Police sexual misconduct: Female police officer's views regarding its nature and extent. *Women and Criminal Justice, 20*(3), 263–282.

Manning, P. K. (2009). Bad cops. *Criminology & Public Policy, 8*(4), 787–794.

Odinokova, V., Rusakova, M., Uranda, L. A., & Silverman, J. G. (2012). Police sexual coercion and its association with risky sex work and substance abuse behaviors among female sex workers in St. Petersburg and Orenburg, Russia. *International Journal of Drug Policy, 25,* 96–104.

Pogarsky, G., & Piquero, A. R. (2004). Studying the reach of deterrence: Can deterrence theory help explain police misconduct. *Journal of Criminal Justice, 32,* 371–386.

Porter, L. E., & Prenzler, T. (2016). The code of silence and ethical perceptions: Exploring police officer unwillingness to report misconduct. *Policing an International Journal of Police Strategies & Management, 39*(2), 370–386.

Punch, M. (1985). *Conduct unbecoming: The social construction of police deviance and control.* London: Tavistock.

Rabe-Hemp, C. E., & Braithwaite, J. (2013). An exploration of recidivism and the officer shuffle in police sexual violence (PSV). *Police Quarterly. XX*(X), 1–21.

Rawlings, P. (2002). *Policing: A short history.* Portland, OR: William Publishing.

Reaves, A. (2012, June). *Federal law enforcement officers, 2008.* Washington, DC: U.S. Department of Justice, Bureau of Justice Statistics.

Reiss, A. J. (1971). *The police and the public*. New Haven, CT: Yale University Press.

Rhodes, T., Simic, M., Baros, S., Platt, L., Zikic, B., & Brooks, G. (2008). Police violence and sexual risk among female and transvestite sex workers in Serbia. *British Medical Journal, 337*(7669), 560–563.

Sapp, A. (1986). Sexual misconduct and sexual harassment by police officers. In T. Barker & D. L. Carter (Eds.), *Police deviance*. Cincinnati, OH: Pilgrimage Press.

Schechter, H. (2003). *The serial killer files*. New York: Ballantine Books.

Sherman, L., Gartin, P. R., & Buerger, M. E. (1989). Hot spots of predatory crime: routine activities and the criminology of place. *Criminology, 27*(1), 27–55.

Shingler, B. (2016, November 16). No charges in Val-d'Or abuse scandal will breed further mistrust, indigenous leaders say. *CBC*.

Shockley-Eckles, M. L. (2011). Police culture and the perpetuation of the officer Shuffle: The paradox of life behind "The Blue Wall". *Humanity & Society, 35*, 290–309.

Stamper, N. (2005). *Breaking rank: A top cop's expose of the dark side of American policing*. New York: Nation Books.

Stinson, P. M., Liederbach, J., Brewer, S. L., & Matina, B. E. (2014). Police sexual misconduct: A national scale study of arrested officers. *Criminal Justice Review, 21*.

Tewksbury, R., Mustaine, E. E., & Stengel, K. M. (2008). Examining rates of sexual offenses from a routine activities perspective. *Victims and Offenders, 3*, 75–85.

Texeira, M. T. (2002). "Who protects and serves me?" A case study of sexual harassment of African American women in one U.S. law enforcement agency. *Gender and Society, 16*(4), 524–543.

Vaughn, M. S. (1999). Police sexual violence: Civil liability under state tort law. *Crime and Delinquency, 45*(3), 334–357.

Waddington, P. A. J. (1999). *Policing citizens*. London and New York: Routledge.

Waegel, W. B. (1984). How police justify the use of deadly force. *Social Problems, 32*(2), 144–155.

Walker, S., & Irlbeck, D. (2002). *Driving while female: A national problem in police Misconduct*. Omaha: Department of Criminal Justice, The University of Nebraska at Omaha.

Walker, S., & Irlbeck, D. (2003). *Police sexual abuse of teenage girls: A 2003 update on driving while female*. Omaha: Police Professionalism Initiative, Department of Criminal Justice, University of Nebraska at Omaha.

Williamson, C., Baker, L., Jenkins, M., & Cluse-Tolar, T. (2007). Police-prostitute interactions: Sometimes discretion, sometimes misconduct. *Journal of Progressive Human Services, 18*(2), 15–37.

Yin, R. K. (2003). *Applications of case study research* (2nd ed.). Sage: Thousand Oaks, CA.

# Part I
## Police Sex Related Criminal Homicides

## Introduction

Homicide—the killing of a human being by a human being—includes justifiable (self-defense and by law), excusable (accidents), and criminal (manslaughter and murder) killings. Murder is the killing of a human being by another human being with "malice aforethought" or evil intent. Criminal homicides by law enforcement officers are extremely rare and a matter of speculation and sensational reporting. Every police-citizen homicide, especially unarmed minorities, elicits 24/7 social media attention as cries of murder fill the news. There are valid reasons to be skeptical of what police spokespersons say following a police homicide. Police spokespersons obfuscate the discussion to protect the agency from criticism and scandal (see Davis 2017; Prator 2018). The police agency repudiates the victim with information on past crimes or indiscretions, even mental status. These same techniques are used to discredit those who file PSM complaints.

Government officials and police spokespersons circle the wagons and fabricate a narrative they often know is false. The most egregious example occurred with the killing of Laquan McDonald in Chicago in 2014. A Chicago police officer shot the 17-year-old McDonald sixteen times as he walked away and posed no threat to anyone. The police video was concealed from public view for over a year and created a scandal when released. Three Chicago PD (CPD) officers were indicted for lying about the events and were eventually acquitted (Puskar and Li, January 17, 2019). The judge declared that the state had failed to meet its burden. The police shooter was indicted and convicted at trial on October 5, 2018, for first-degree murder. He was sentenced to seven years in prison. The shooting and the obfuscations coming from elected officials, the police department, and the police union contributed to weeks of protests, the firing of the police superintendent, and a scathing Department of Justice report. Complicating the strained police-community relations following the police-citizen shootings is the lack of reliable information on police violence.

There are no nationwide official statistics on police violence, or police homicides—accidental, justified, or criminal. However, there are limited of mass media outlets that shed some light on general police violence against civilians. Although rare, police criminal homicide violence, including manslaughters and murders, occurs. Included within this category are police criminal homicides by police sexual predators. Veteran police officers know sexual predators join police agencies for the opportunity to commit sexually abusive acts—personal work experience and forty years of interactions and conversations with on-duty and retired police officers. Retired Seattle Police Chief Norm Stamper, a progressive reform chief devoted an entire chapter to "Sexual Predators in Uniform" in his memoir (Stamper 2005). Stamper estimates that five percent of the officers in any department are "on the prowl for women." Police sexual predators view sex as "fringe benefits of the job." Numerous former and working police officers have expressed the same sentiment to me. However, there are ways to prevent the entry of potential police sexual predators.

Identifying likely problem officers in the vetting process must be the number one priority in any law enforcement agency. Marilynn Johnson (2003) published a definitive work on the history of police violence in New York City from its founding in 1845 to the end of the twentieth century. Many of those problem officers had a known tendency toward violence and other forms of police misconduct including police sexual abuse—improper vetting. Obviously, once hired those with identified misconduct tendencies should be terminated and/or prosecuted when their aberrant known behavior-second dimension. The following Illustrative Example shows the outcome of not properly vetting and dealing with a known problem officer who became a police murderer.

Michael Griffith, a former Sergeant with the Harris County, Texas Sheriff's Department, was executed on June 6, 2007, for Capital Murder. In January 1993, Griffith was fired following his plea-bargained conviction for misdemeanor domestic violence. The events leading to his arrest and conviction warranted felony charges and prison time. He held his girlfriend hostage in her apartment for twelve hours repeatedly threatening to kill her. The victim escaped and he was arrested. The sheriff's department knew or should have known that he had the potential for future violence against women.

Griffith had a history of violence against women during his ten years with the sheriff's department. His first wife testified that Griffith beat her during their marriage and once held a gun to her head. He broke her ribs when confronted with an affair he was having. She left him when he injured their daughter during a fight. His second wife recounted the violence during their three-year marriage. He beat her four months into the marriage and threatened to kill her for wearing a tight dress. Following the divorce of his second wife, Griffith dated a co-worker who he choked and threatened her with a gun. He was finally fired, but that did not prevent the escalation of his violent behavior.

On October 10, 1994, the former deputy robbed, sexually assaulted, and murdered a Houston woman in a flower shop. Griffith a frequent customer bought roses for his domestic violence victims at the shop. He stabbed the victim 11 times with a butcher knife. Four days later, he robbed a woman at a savings and loan company, and shot her in the back of the head. The bullet only grazed her skull and she survived. On October 28, 1994, Griffith robbed a bridal salon and sexually assaulted the salesperson. He was arrested, charged, and convicted of murder.

The penalty stage after his murder conviction revealed how violent and dangerous Griffith was (*Griffith v. State* 1998). According to the appeals court, the state proved Griffith had violent reputation and a volatile temper. Griffith was known by his police peers to be angry, physically and verbally abusive. He was extremely possessive and controlling toward two ex-wives and two ex-girlfriends and violent with his children.

A state's witness, a psychologist from the FBI's Behavioral Science Unit, testified that Griffith was a sexual predator "who will continue to look for similar outlets for sexual gratification, and if isolated from females, he will look for a similar victim within the available population, which could include weaker males." His evil career could have been stopped if the Harris County Sheriff's Department would have taken appropriate action—arrest and prosecution for his domestic violence. He was known to have the *inclination* for violent sexual behavior when presented with the opportunities. The department's failure to deal with his violent inclinations increased the likelihood of more violent behavior. There are other police murderers.

## Police Criminal Homicides

Police homicides, in the past, have been divided into three broad categories: *professional killings*—officer kills a citizen within legal parameters; *vigilante killings*—the officer kills a citizen for a noble cause-a community service homicide—the ends justify the means; and *civil rights oppressors*—police homicides resulting from the police acting as oppressors of marginalized citizens (Hirschfield and Simon 2010; Barker, forthcoming). There are at least two other categories of police homicides that receive little study or social attention. There are *"bad" violent individuals*, such as Michael Griffith, who would commit horrendous crimes, even murder, no matter what line of work they are in. They are "bad to the bone" criminals in blue who lie, steal, and murder (Barker, forthcoming). A second category is *police sexually related criminal homicides*—the focus of the next two chapters.

# References

Barker, T. (Forthcoming). *Police homicides: Accidents to murder.* Lexington Books.

Davis, A. D. (ed.). (2017). *Policing the Black man.* New York: Pantheon Books.

*Griffith v. State*, 983 S.W. 2nd 282 (Tex. Cr. App. 1998).

Hirschfield, P. J., & Simon, D. (2010). Legitimizing police violence: Newspaper narratives of deadly force. *Theoretical Criminology*, 14(2): 155–182.

Johnson, M. (2003). *Street justice: A history of police violence in New York City.* Boston: Beacon Press.

Prator, L. P. (2018). *Excessive use of force: One women's struggle against police brutality and misconduct.* Lantham, MD: Rowman & Littlefield.

Puskar, S. & Li, D. K. (2019, January 17). 3 Chicago officers acquitted of covering up for colleague who shot Laquan McDonald. *NBCnews.com.*

Stamper, N. (2005). *Breaking rank: A top cop's expose of the dark side of American policing.* New York: Nation Books.

# 2

# Police Sex-Related Criminal Homicides: Sexually Motivated Police Serial Killers

Sexual homicides involve sexual activity before, during or after the homicide. In spite of the sensationalized media attention they receive, sexual homicides are rare. On occasion, sexual homicides are a hybrid offense between sexual assault and murder. The perpetrator did not have the intention of killing his victim (Stefanska et al. 2017).

**Police Sex-Related Criminal Homicides** is the first of the ten types of PSM we discuss. There are two categories in this type—serial murderers and rape plus murder. Serial sexual murderers intend to kill their victims. Serial sexual murders are driven by personality disorders. Sexual serial murderers are psychopaths or sociopaths, who show no remorse, lack empathy, and see others as objects for their sexual pleasure. Torture is there "turn on" (Ressler and Shachtman 1992). An unknown number of these disturbed individual's are law enforcement officers.

FBI profiler John Douglas found that serial killers are drawn to police work because of the power, and the authorization to hurt "bad people for the common good" (Douglas and Olshaker 1995). Kenneth Bianchi, one of the serial killers known as the Hillside Stranglers was turned down for several police positions after successful vetting processes before working as a security guard, a not uncommon work

© The Author(s) 2020
T. Barker, *Aggressors in Blue*,
https://doi.org/10.1007/978-3-030-28441-1_2

substitute for rejected police applicants. However, deranged individuals have become law enforcement agencies. Other sexually motivated serial killers began their reign of terror as law enforcement officers and continued after leaving police work. They no longer carry a badge but they use their law enforcement experience and training to facilitate their deprivations.

Should these disturbed individuals ever been given a badge? Where there known, or knowable reasons for rejecting the sexual aggressors. What were the known or knowable characteristics of the police sexual predators? We can discuss what we know now that they have been unmasked.

Our discussion begins with the worst-case scenario of law enforcement serial killing history in American history—Gerald Schaefer. That may change. DNA analysis has recently revealed that the notorious Golden State Serial Killer and Rapists of the 1970s and 1980s—50 rapes and at least 12 murders—were a police officer. Further information may eclipse Gerald Schaefer's reign of terror and murder (McNamara 2018). There is also an unfolding story of a US Custom and Border Patrol Agent supervisor who has been charged with the serial killing of four women and attempted murder on a fifth (Horton, September 17, 2018). These two cases remind us that unidentified police serial sexual murderers may be present in today's police agencies.

## Does the Devil Exist?
## Yes He Does—Gerard J. Schaefer Jr.

At the top of any list of sexually motivated serial killer cops is Gerard John Schaefer Jr. The grim reaper could be seen in his eyes a former lover remarked (Mason 2008). A psychiatrist opined, "Schaefer is an anti-social personality, which is manifested by sexual deviation and erotic sadism." He killed his victims in pairs and sometimes threes because "Doing doubles is far more difficult than doing singles, but on the other hand it also puts one in a position to have twice as much fun" (Mason 2008).

Schaefer's reign of terror was an act of whore cleansing—a noble cause often used as a rationalization for serial murder. Schaefer claimed that he killed his victims to stop them from being whores or to release them from the life of being a whore. Any girl out on the street, especially hitchhikers, was a whore in his twisted logic—*psychologically disturbed inclination*. He went into a puritanical rage at the sight of a woman exposing her naked self, even if it were not for his viewing. That they were whores justified their sadistic deaths to this sexual psychopath who grew up Catholic, attended parochial school and attempted at one time to become a priest. His interest in the priesthood was dashed when he was told he was not religious enough. He quickly renounced Catholicism. That he became a law enforcement officer is regrettable. There were good reasons to reject him.

Schaefer's early life was not as idyllic as one would expect for a "devout Catholic boy." He frequently fought with his verbally abusive alcoholic father, especially when the senior Schaefer called his mother a whore. At twelve, the budding psychosexual murderer wore women's underwear and discovered autoerotic asphyxiation while slipping into the woods and hanging himself from a tree while masturbating.

During this same time period, the father was going on business trips. Gerard suspected his father-committed adultery with whores on these trips. These suspicions increased his hatred for whores who violated Catholic values and the sanctity of the Sacrament of Marriage and caused problems in his family.

Classmates described Gerard, a loner in high school, as weird. However, the tall, smiling blonde teenager did attract a girlfriend. They went together for almost two years before breaking up, because of his bizarre sex games. The young Schaefer was only able to have sex if he pretended to play-rape her and tear off her clothes while talking dirty to her. After the split, the odd teenager returned to the woods for self-gratification with women's panties and a hangman's noose.

According to his next girlfriend, lover, and biographer, Sondra London, the teenager added voyeurism to his perverted sexual behaviors (Schaefer 1989). London recounts the young Schafer watching a neighbor girl undress at night. He railed on in a fit of rage saying that the girl, Leigh Hainline, was flaunting her naked charms at him through the window. He vowed to put a stop to her behavior. He made good on the threat years later. In 1969, Leigh Hainline disappeared and was never seen again.

A background check would have discovered the red flags and disqualified his police application, but it was never done (Green 2018). One red flag was hard to miss, but it was. Gerard pretended to be a transvestite to avoid the draft during the Vietnam War. He writes that the Society of Friends came to campus and described ways to avoid the draft, a common practice during this unpopular war (Schaefer 1989). The Society of Friends suggested 1-Y deferment for personality disorders. After being drafted, Schaefer reported to the Army induction center wearing panties, garter belt, and nylons and asked "is it gonna be OK to be in the Army if I'm queer?" As expected, he was granted a 1-Y deferment.

In August 1970, the confused young man got married and received a B.S. degree in geography from Florida Atlantic University. Within a month after his graduation and marriage, the small town Wilton Manor Police Department hired him without a background check or psychological tests. He completed basic academy training, fulfilled his six-month probationary period and hit the streets as a sworn, and trained certified police officer. There is speculation that the disappearance of a young blonde female driver during his rookie year was his first victim. FBI profilers Ressler and Shachtman (1992) report that he was disciplined for stopping cars driven by young women and then running their licenses for computer checks to learn more about them—a *common technique to identify sexual targets*. Two years into the job, the rookie officer received a commendation for a drug arrest, but his commendable arrest was soon marred by a confrontation with the chief of police. The chief was set to fire him, but Schaefer begged him out of it.

The disgruntled Schaefer applied for a position with the Broward County Sheriff's Office, without notifying his chief. Schaefer failed Broward County mandatory psychological exam and was disqualified—*proper vetting*. This information was not shared with any other law enforcement agency. At the time, Florida did not have a certification and decertification system. Two months later, he interviewed with the Martin County Sheriff's Department, using a forged letter of recommendation from the Wilton Manor Chief of Police. He was fired immediately when the Wilton Manor chief learned he interviewed with the Martin County SO, but he was hired by the sheriff's office.

The Martin County 27-year-old sheriff was a first-time sheriff and only in office for about two months. He was desperate for personnel. Gerald John Schaefer was now a *Gypsy Cop*, moving from department to department under suspicious circumstances. The sheriff's first hiring mistake was colossal and would put him, his department and Martin County, Florida on the front page of newspapers around the world.

Twenty-eight days into his new position, Schaefer's law enforcement career came to an inglorious end on July 21, 1972, when he picked up two teenage girls. Nancy Ellen Trotter, age 19 and Pamela Sue Wells, age 18, had hitchhiked from Michigan to Florida for some fun in the sun. Inclination and opportunity come together under a perceived low-risk setting. Deputy Schaefer, in uniform and driving a police vehicle, picked them up and lectured them on the dangers of hitchhiking. He gave them a ride to the halfway house where they stayed and arranged to meet the next day for a guided tour of the area. Later they testified they trusted him; after all, he was a cop.

Instead of a tour Schaefer abducted them, took them to remote woods on deserted Hutchinson Island—*safe space*. He bound and gagged them, put a noose around their necks and tied them to trees while threatening to kill them or sell them into prostitution. For some reason, he left the girls handcuffed, gagged, with nooses around their necks tied to a tree, leaving them at risk of hanging if they slipped. He told the horrified girls he would be back shortly. Ressler and Shachtman (1992: 142) opine that he left the scene to answer roll call because he returned to the scene two hours later in uniform, but they were gone. One of the girls managed to escape her noose and run to a nearby road where a passing motorist stopped and picked up the urine-soaked survivor and drove to a police station. When Schaefer returned, he found the girls missing.

Schaefer called Sheriff Crowder and confessed he had done something foolish. He said he played a joke on two girls who were hitchhiking, and he pretended to kidnap and threaten them to scare them out of this risky behavior. Sheriff Crowder ordered him to the station where he was stripped of his badge, fired, and arrested for false imprisonment and aggravated assault.

Schaefer was in jail from July 1972 until September 1972 and then released on his own recognizance. The killing spree began. While out on bond, young girls started disappearing. The investigation revealed Schaefer abducted and slaughtered Susan Place, 17, and Georgia Jessup, 16 during that time period. Place's mother last saw the girls leaving with a man named Gerry Shepherd. Suspicious of Shepherd she wrote down the car's license plate number. Later, their mutilated remains were found on Hutchinson Island. Almost a year later, the police finally got around to trace the number, by that time other young girls were butchered and Schaefer was charged with other murders. Following the disappearance of Jessup and Place, two young girls Mary Briscolina age 14, and Elsie Farmer, age 14, disappeared. They were last seen hitchhiking in the Fort Lauderdale area. A piece of Elsie's jewelry would be found in Schaefer's trophy stash and he would "sort of confess" to killing these young girls.

Schaeffer returned to court on the first kidnap victims in December 1972 and pleaded guilty to picking up Trotter and Wells, taking them to the remote Hutchinson Island. He was sentenced to six months to a year in jail and three years probation after all the charges, except for one count of assault, were dropped. His former status as a cop was taken into consideration in dropping the charges and his light sentencing. The sentencing judge remarked:

> It is beyond this court's imagination to conceive how you were such a foolish and astronomic jackass as you were in this case. (Mason 2008)

The day before Schaefer was to report to jail to begin serving his six-month sentence Collette Goodenough, age 19 and Barbara Wilcox age 18 disappeared while hitchhiking from Sioux City, Iowa to Florida. The available evidence confirms the belief that Schaefer was operating under a delusional false *sense of low risk*. Some of their personal items were found in Schaefer's trophy stash, but their remains were not found until four years later, well after Schaefer had been convicted of the murders of Susan Place and Georgia Jessup. In April 1973, the decomposing, butchered remains of Place and Jessup were found in shallow graves on Hutchinson Island. The location of their remains was in the same general area where Trotter and Wells were held. The similarities of the abduction to the earlier false imprisonment and aggravated assault cases and the evidence that victims Place and Jessup had been tied to a tree led to a search warrant for Schafer's apartment and his mother's house.

Nothing incriminating was found in Schaefer's apartment but the search of his mother's house produced a mother's lode of evidence, leading to his prosecution for the murders of Place and Jessup, and implicated him in a number of unsolved disappearances. The police found detailed writings from the killer's perspective describing the torture, rape, and murder of women referred to as whores and sluts. Also found was his stash of victim's trophies—personal belongings such as jewelry, driver's licenses, passports, diaries, and teeth from at least eight young women and girls who had gone missing in recent years. It was learned that Schaefer had given Susan Place's purse to his wife. Jewelry and two gold-capped teeth belonging to Leigh Hainline were found in his stash of victims' trophies. Her body was found in 1978, but Schaefer died without being charged with her murder.

After a circus of motions to declare him insane failed, Schaefer's trial for the murders of Susan Place and Georgia Jessup began in a packed courtroom on September 17, 1973. A six-member jury with one alternate decided the case. The death penalty was not an option because the murders occurred during a period when the US Supreme Court declared the death penalty unconstitutional. The amount of evidence against him was shocking, scary, brutal, and immense. Prosecutors brought in actual tree limbs that held the victims, with the noose markings on them. Large roots from the scene were dug up and brought to court to show how the victims had to balance themselves to keep from being hung before being filleted by the defendant. Several jurors appeared shaken and pale. Susan Place's mother took the stand and identified Schaefer as the man who was last seen with her daughter. The medical examiner came to the stand and described the decomposition and mutilation of the young girls. He showed the detailed cuts on the bones and told them where their body parts had been separated with a large knife.

Nancy Trotter and Pamela Wells testified about their encounter with Deputy Schaefer and their narrow escape. Their testimony ended with a video presentation enactment of what they had endured, including them reenacting being bound and gagged hanging by nooses from trees. The jury was given a copy of one of Schaefer's writings found during the searches. The manuscript titled "How to Go Un-Apprehended in the Perpetration of an Execution-Style Murder" went into gory detail after gory detail explaining how to choose and murder women, even up to selecting victims in pairs. A weak defense followed and the jury began its deliberation on September 27, 1973. The jury returned a verdict of guilty after several hours of deliberation. On October 4, 1973, the former deputy sheriff was sentenced to life in prison. Twenty appeals were turned down by a variety of courts.

While in prison Schaefer, who had taken several creative writing courses in college, developed what he called a new writing genre called "killer fiction" described as "where the writer takes violence as an artistic medium and instead of glorifying it, makes the reader see it as the cruel and horrid act as it is in reality. I don't represent violence as good or bad, merely as it is" (Mason 2008). Among his gory stories was a collection of five brief homicidal scenarios titled "Whores—What to *DO* About Them." The sadistic and bloodcurdling tales describes five whores who were shot, stabbed, hung, and eviscerated with a razor-sharp skinning knife by a serial killer. Schaeffer bragged that he killed at least 80 women; he wrote, "I killed women in all ways from shooting, strangling, stabbing, beheading, to odd ways such as drowning, smothering, and crucifixion. One I whipped to death with a strap, another I beat to jelly with a baseball bat while she was hanging by her wrists." All described in his killer fiction writings.

Schaefer was linked to murders of an unknown number of other girls and women. He was never charged for these other murders. On December 3, 1990, an inmate burst into Schaefer's cell and slit his throat and stabbed him in both eyes, claiming he was a "rat" and troublemaker.

\* \* \*

Gerald Schaefer was a seriously disturbed individual who was a law enforcement officer because of poor vetting and the lack of attention to his bizarre behavior patterns—*inclination*. This Gypsy Cop selected his known victims, except Leigh Hainline, from pairs of young teenage girls hitchhiking—*opportunity*. He began his targeting, selection, and murder while an active law enforcement officer and continued his sexually moti-vated murders after he was fired—*delusional sense of low risk*.

What makes Schaefer's so disturbing is that the murders could and should have been prevented. We know more about Schaefer because of the volume of nonfiction and true crime books written about him and his disturbed behavior. Unfortunately, that is not true for former police officer David Middleton.

David Middleton began his disturbed sexually motivated killings while a police officer and continued killing after being fired. There is evidence that his murder streak, like Schaefer's, could have ended long before it was.

## David Middleton the Cable Guy Killer Aka the Prince of Darkness

"That dude's evil man—I can feel it." Interviewing Reno, Nevada Homicide Detective. (Kaye 2008: 109)

The following narrative is from two sources (Kaye 2008 and *Middleton v. State of Nevada* 114 Nev. Adv. Op. 120—No. 31499, November 25, 1998).

Former police officer David Middleton was first identified as a sexual predator while a working police officer, and then continued his sexual depravations after leaving police work. He was convicted of two murders and sentenced to death. However, he is suspected of several other murders.

## Victim Number 1—Katherine Powell

Katherine Powell, the first known Nevada victim was forty-five years old, a third-grade school teacher, divorced and lived alone in Reno, Nevada. She did not report to her teaching position on Monday, February 6, 1995 and was reported missing by school workers who went to her home and could not get an answer to repeated knocks. The police responded and entered the residence but found nothing suspicious. Five days later on Saturday, February 11, Reno Police received a report that a homeless "dumpster diver" found a body in a dumpster. The police found a yellow plastic bag covering a sleeping bag that contained a naked bound female body—Katherine Powell. She had been sexually assaulted, tortured, and brutally murdered.

A neighborhood canvass revealed that David Middleton, a black "cable guy" technician, in a TCI Cable red truck was seen in front of Powell's home on Saturday February 4, 1995. On Sunday February 5, a male disguising his voice to appear female called a Reno store and ordered a $1900 piece of stereo equipment using Powell's credit card. A woman, who turned out to be Middleton's longtime live-in girlfriend, picked up the stereo equipment. She drove a red truck with TCI Cable on the side and Colorado plates to the store.

During the investigation, detectives discovered the yellow plastic bags covering the sleeping bag were sold at two local hardware stores. One store sold a box of the 33-gallon bags three days before Powell's body was discovered. The description of the purchaser fit David Middleton.

Middleton was interviewed and admitted he made a service call to the Powell house on January 28, 1995 and did own a red truck. He denied knowing anything about the stereo or Powell's credit card. He said he knew nothing about the yellow garbage bags. One of the detectives noticed what looked like keys for a lock that would fit on a storage unit on his key ring, so he asked Middleton if he had a rented storage unit. Middleton said no and walked out of the interview.

On March 5, 1995, an anonymous caller-never identified—informed the detectives that Middleton and his live-in girlfriend had a storage unit and gave its location. The next day the police executed a search warrant on the storage unit and found a "treasure load" of incriminating evidence, including a box of yellow 33-gallon plastic bags with one missing, and the stereo equipment purchased with Powell's credit card. Powell's house and car keys and her camera, computer, and other personal items were also found.

Inside the storage unit, a refrigerator lay on its back on the floor. Fibers found in the refrigerator matched those found on Powell's body.

The refrigerator was modified and served as the "torture chamber" for Powell. According to court transcripts, Powell was stored in the refrigerator and Middleton would come by and torture her while engaging in vaginal and anal sex. When finished, he would place her back in the refrigerator and come back again until she died. The investigation revealed Powell lived for two days until the air coming in from two holes drilled in the bottom was exhausted and she suffocated. A foam ball with teeth marks on it was found in the storage unit. This was stuffed in the victim's mouths to muffle their screams while he engaged in his depraved sex acts. A stun gun and rope similar to that used to tie Powell's body was also found.

As the search continued, more ominous pieces of evidence were discovered, including orange-handled tension clips containing hair and fiber, black canvas belts with Velcro, black wire ties, handcuffs, condoms, and partial rolls of duct tape. The detectives discovered a second makeshift "torture and storage" container—a large speaker box with a space behind the speaker about 14 inches deep, 30 inches wide, and 36 inches high. The speaker box could hold a small woman or child, raising the distinct possibility of one or more victims. Hair and fibers found in the speaker box confirmed their suspicion. A nearly empty industrialized jug of Clorox bleach found inside the storage unit and the obvious smell of Clorox used to clean up the unit led to the suspicion that someone with police experience who knew that bleach will obliterate DNA was involved.

The detectives discovered that David Middleton was a convicted sex offender and former police officer. His original charges on November 19, 1989 were kidnapping and sexual assault, and he was convicted of the charges of false imprisonment and aggravated battery in June of 1990—*light treatment because of police status?* He was sentenced to two concurrent five-year prison terms and released in 1993 after serving a little more than two years. His records revealed Middleton was a Boston PD police cadet for two years before resigning. He then became a police officer with the Miami, Florida PD for eight years before resigning. His resignation date revealed he was a cop when he was arrested for the original charges of kidnapping and sexual assault. The Reno detectives speculated that the bad outcome of the first known kidnapping and rape led him to kill future victims.

The investigators found other possible sexual murder victims. Ex Miami cop David Middleton was listed as a suspect in the disappearance of a Montrose, Colorado 18-year-old girl before moving to Reno. The Reno detectives went to Colorado and discovered incriminating evidence but there was no body or indication of murder. They returned to Reno with the firm belief that Middleton was indeed a serial killer. The Reno detectives flew to Florida to see what they could learn about his eight-year tenure as a Miami-Dade police officer.

What they found solidified their suspicion that David Middleton was a seriously disturbed sexually motivated serial killer and police sexual predator. The Miami prosecutor said he was "a bad cop who was twisted enough to use his badge and uniform to hunt down women and sexually abuse them" (Kaye 2008: 159). She said that when he was arrested he had tapes of him having sadomasochistic sex with women, believed to be prostitutes. The women in the tapes were in handcuffs and obviously in pain. The former prosecutor regretted that a bureaucratic mistake prevented her from introducing the tape as evidence that would surely lead to a rape conviction and a long prison sentence. She also admitted that she wanted to file federal charges but her supervisor stopped her. Officers who worked with Middleton at Miami-Dade described him as obsessed with sex and bragging about having tapes of him having sex with women. His peer group knew of his bizarre sexual habits, but none reported him. All seven of the cops interviewed stated that Middleton had sexually deviant tendencies long before he moved to Reno.

## Victim Number 2—Thelma Davila

Two months after Powell's body was found, the body of a second and prior victim who left the hair and fibers in the speaker box in the storage unit was found. On April 9, 1995, a man walking his dog found a skull and human remains and notified the Washoe County Sheriff's Office. Earlier in 1994, the remnants of a sleeping bag had been found with bone fragments strewn nearby.

A dental bridge in the skull was identified as belonging to Thelma Davila, a forty-two-year-old woman who lived with her sister in a one-bedroom apartment in Sparks. She was reported missing on August 10, 1994. A blanket, a black lacy top and other personal items belonging to Davila were found in Middleton's storage unit. Hairs found on duct tape in the storage unit were consistent to Davila's. Knots found in the ropes on Powell and Davila's bodies and remains were the same.

She and Middleton met at a Latin dance club in downtown Reno and had been seen in each other's company numerous times by friends. Middleton had installed the TV cable in the sisters' apartment—*opportunistic victim selection same as first known victim.*

David Middleton went on trial in 1997 and was convicted of two counts of first-degree murder, and two counts of first-degree kidnapping. He was sentenced to death. The ex-cop serial murderer is on Nevada's death row and is a "person of interest" in several unsolved murders of women in Colorado, Florida, and Nevada.

*    *    *

Police sexual serial murderers occur in police forces worldwide-occupational deviance consistent with the **PSM Causal Equation** nexus of *inclination, opportunity and real or perceived risk.* A disturbed gay British law enforcement with same-sex victims who began his murders as a working police officer, as did David Middleton—and continued his murders after leaving police work. A second police serial murderer was a Russian police officer discovered a DNA match committed long after his crimes.

## Dennis Nilsen—British Police Serial Killer—Aka Britain's Jeffrey Dahmer

Dennis Nilsen was hired as a police officer, even though he was seriously psychologically disturbed—*not properly vetted.* His behavior became more disturbed and noticeable while he was in police work and then evolved into repetitive sexual homicides after he resigned from the London Metropolitan Police. There is evidence to suggest that his contacts with potential victims as a police officer, and his prior police training and acquired knowledge facilitated his reign of terror.

The former English "Bobby," killed 12–15 young men from December 1979 to February 1983. The key to his predatory behavior was in his past. Becoming a killing machine is not an overnight event; it is a long slow process with a lot of clues along the way, according to FBI profilers (Ressler and Shachtman 1992). A withdrawn and lonely child, Nilsen struggled with the knowledge he was homosexual. After an 11-year tour of duty with the British Army, where he engaged in sexual fantasies and masturbation, the conflicted young man joined the London Metropolitan Police Force and was posted to a seedy and diverse section of London. While a police officer he acted on his homosexual tendencies and frequented gay pubs engaging in casual sexual liaisons—*there is evidence to suggest that his bizarre behavior was known to his police colleagues* (Ressler and Shachtman 1992). He resigned from the police force after a year's service and became a security guard and then a British civil servant.

According to Ressler and Shachtman (1992), Nilsen's increasing male sexual encounters disturbed him and increased his loneliness, leading to more bizarre behavior and sexual fantasies that turned to sadism and necrophilia—*psychologically disturbed inclination*. His first known murder victim, a young man he met in a gay pub, was invited to his house for drinks. In a deranged desire to keep the man from leaving, Nilsen strangled his victim to unconsciousness then drowned him in a bucket of water. He washed his victim's body, placed it in his bed, spending the night sleeping with the corpse. He placed the corpse under the floorboards for seven months before burning the decaying remains in his back garden. Thus began, one of the most macabre tales of sexual perversion in English history.

Nilsen selected victims from a *vulnerable target pool* of gay, homeless, orphans, drunks, and males prostitutes. Homeless, unemployed, and male prostitute victims are not likely to be reported missing, cops know that. Nilsen knew that—*opportunity and low risk*. The disturbed serial killer strangled and drowned his next 11 or 14 victims, slept with their corpses, dismembered their bodies, boiled their heads before flushing their remains down the toilet or burning them (Ressler and Shachtman 1992).

Body parts and putrefying human flesh were discovered in the attempt to free the clogged drains, bringing the authorities into the investigation. Nilsen readily confessed when confronted; he was proud of what he had done. Thousands of bone fragments were found in his backyard-burning pit. Several plastic bags, containing human remains, dismembered heads and larger body parts were found in his apartment. At trial, he was charged with six murders; pleaded not guilty even after giving a lengthy confession. The shocked and sickened jury was unable to reach a unanimous verdict, with some jurors opting for diminished responsibility due to mental illness. However, the judge agreed to accept a majority verdict and Nilsen was convicted on all six counts. Currently serving a life sentence in a British maximum-security prison, he is on the list of prisoners never to be released.

## Mikhail Popkov—"The Werewolf"—Most Prolific Police Serial Killer in Russian History 1994–2000

During the years 1994–2010, Mikhail Popkov a Russian police officer known as the "Werewolf" killed and mutilated 82 women. The nickname "Werewolf" came after one of his victims was beheaded, and her heart cut out. Popkov assumed the women were prostitutes, a few were, but the majority were not—one was a medical student and another his daughter's teacher. As stated earlier, killing prostitutes or whores is a commonly stated motivation for serial sexual killers operating on a perceived moral crusade—*disturbed inclination.* He slaughtered his victims with axes, knives, and screwdrivers. His police identity facilitated his killing spree. He committed his heinous act in uniform and while driving a police car "to fool his victims," he confessed—*opportunistic victim selection.* The following narrative comes from two sources (Barbash, January 12, 2017; Wikipedia 2019).

Popkov confessed to murdering 82 women between 1992 and 2010. The murders followed the same planned method of operation (MO), making full use of his police identity. When the desire became strong—*inclination,* Popkov went on the hunt. He knew where to find vulnerable victims during his routine patrol activities—*opportunity.* Popkov parked his police car outside nightclubs, restaurants, and other public places where drinking was common and waited for unaccompanied women to emerge. He would call them over to his car and offer help in getting home or suggest that they have some fun with him. Those that agreed fit his "loose women" definition. They had to die.

His justification for murder blames the victims, "The victims were those who, unaccompanied by men, at night, without a certain purpose were on the streets behaving carelessly, who were not afraid to enter into conversation with me, for the sake of entertainment, ready to drink alcohol and have sexual intercourse with me." He had a "desire to teach and punish" these loose women. After the trap was sprung, Popkov drove to the woods, raped his victims and killed them with hand-held weapons, some of which he took from the police evidence locker.

His murders continued after he retired, even though he was rendered impotent by a venereal disease caught from one of his victims in 2000. The number of victims brought on extreme efforts to identify the possible police serial killer. In 2012, 3500 current and former Russian police officers in the region where the murders took place were forced to provide DNA samples. The DNA analysis linked Popkov to 22 murders. Popkov lamented the use of DNA analysis in his downfall stating, "I could not anticipate the examination of DNA. I was born in another century. Now there are such modern technologies, but not earlier…" The Werewolf confessed to 22 murders and sentenced to life in prison. In January 2017, according to the Russian Investigative Committee [Federal Investigation Agency, FBI equivalent], Popkov confessed to 60 more sexual murders and began taking the police to graves of women reported as missing. The stimulus for his new confessions was to prevent his transfer to a tough penal colony to serve out his life sentence. The Russian police believe his final total is 82.

## Conclusion

The brief Illustrative Examples—I.E.—demonstrate that sexual homicides, in fact all sexual crimes, are pattern forms of deviant behavior with characteristics common to the offender, victims, and the selection of victims. It is possible to identify possible repetitive police sex offenders prior to employment with proper vetting. It is also possible to take proper action when problem officers are identified to deter their future acts in any law enforcement setting. Real evidence is always present at a sexual encounter. Modern technology—DNA analysis and technical assist, such as body and dash cameras—have made sex crimes easier to solve. The use of DNA in the Russian example and the recent identification of the Golden State Killer and Rapist make this point clear.

# References

Barbash, F. (2017, January 12). "Werewolf" of Siberia ranked among worst serial killers ever after confessing to 81 victims, says Russian media. *The Washington Post*.

Douglas, J. E., & Olshaker, M. (1995). *Mindhunter: Inside the FBI's elite serial crime unit*. New York: Scribner.

Green, R. (2018). *Killer cop: The deviant deputy who kidnapped, raped and killed*. Lexington, KY: Ryan Green.

Horton, A. (2018, September 17). A woman's daring escape from a Border Patrol agent helped reveal a 'serial killer', police say. *The Washington Post*.

Kaye, J. (2008). *Beware of the cable guy: From cop to serial killer*. Palm Springs, CA: Polimedia Books.

Mason, Y. (2008). *Silent scream*. Dressing Your Book.

McNamara, M. (2018). I'll be gone in the dark. New York: Harper Collins.

Ressler, R. H., & Shachtman, T. (1992). *Whoever fights monsters: My twenty years tracking serial killers for the FBI*. New York: St. Martin's Paperback.

Schaefer, G. J. as told to Sondra London. (1989). *Killer fiction*. Los Angeles: Feral House.

Stefanska, E. B., Higgs, T., Carter, A. J., & Beech, A. R. (2017). When is a murder a serial murder? Understanding the sexual element in the classification of serial killings. *Journal of Criminal Justice, 50*, 53–61.

Wikipedia. (2019). Mikhail Popkov. Accessed June 3, 2019.

# 3

# Sex-Related Criminal Homicides: Rape Plus Murder

## Introduction

The following three murderers are not included in Chapter 2 because the homicides do not result from some personality defect, as is the case for serial killers. The sex-related murders described occur when the victim is killed to eliminate a witness, reduce the chances of the sexual aggressor being identified, or the victim resists the sexual aggression. They are situational or instrumental murders (James and Prouix 2016; Stefanska et al. 2017). The murderers are best described as a "rape plus murder" killer who kills to avoid detection (Healey et al. 2014). The murder was not a source of sexual stimulation as in the case of serial murderers. Killing is an integral source of sexual stimulation for serial sexual killers. However, sexual abuse by an armed police sexual aggressor always involves the possibility of murder as an outcome (Higgs et al. 2015). These murders are rare and not supported by the police peer group.

The sexual aggressor's status as a law enforcement officer with ties to respectability exacerbates the likelihood of murder. We expect a certain way of behavior—a way of life—from those who carry a badge.

© The Author(s) 2020
T. Barker, *Aggressors in Blue*,
https://doi.org/10.1007/978-3-030-28441-1_3

They have a lot to lose by exposure as a sexual predator—a stake in conformity. Furthermore, the person who becomes a law enforcement officer is forever defined as a former or ex-law enforcement officer. Their behavior will always be judged by the expected behavior for law enforcement officers. Rightly or wrongly, law enforcement officers on or off duty retired or former will still be accepted, rejected, or judged by the pattern of behavior deemed appropriate for the *policework* occupation. Because of this Master Status, a rape-murder that follows a sexual assault by police officers or former police officers receives extensive media attention whenever or wherever they occur. What follows are illustrative examples of police rape plus murderers.

## California Highway Patrolman—George M. Gwaltney—1982

The first California Highway Patrol Officer charged with an on-duty murder was George M. Gwaltney. He is also the first California police officer to be tried federally for the violation of a person's civil rights under the color of law. Outwardly, he was an unlikely candidate for these sordid firsts. Gwaltney, a ten year highly respected California Highway Patrolman, was at one time the agency's Officer of the Year. Well known in the community for his good deeds and helpfulness, the jovial "officer friendly" had a secret. On duty, alone and unsupervised, he was a sexual predator stopping women and young girls to bargain leniency for sex. Give it up or get a ticket or go to jail—a Sexual Shakedown to be described later. His first known murder victim was hunted and stopped on a deserted road.

On January 11, 1982, an attractive 23-year-old aspiring actress, Robin Bishop, was driving alone from Los Angeles to her home in Las Vegas (*U.S. v. George M. Gwaltney* 1986; The FBI Files 2008). It was slightly past 8:30 p.m. on a pitch-dark evening. Unknown to Bishop, Gwaltney spotted her coming out of a fast-food establishment and noticed her Nevada license plate. The *inclination* to commit a sexual offense plus the *opportunity* intersects with a *perceived low-risk* setting. However, the rational decision would turn out to be flawed.

Gwaltney guessed the route she would take. He began hunting for her. In the high desert area northeast of Barstow, California, he saw her car and made his move.

Gwaltney stopped Bishop in a desolate area on Interstate 15 some 30 miles northeast of Barstow. As described in the court testimony, he encountered an agitated young woman with a problem. Robin Bishop had a terrible driving record. One more speeding ticket would cause her to lose her driver's license. She is now a vulnerable victim with credibility problem, adding to the low risk of a sexual attack. According to the theory of her murder, Robin argued with him to no avail. "The speed limit is what it is for a reason," he sternly countered according to The FBI Files (2008). Gwaltney in his twisted logic had hit the "jackpot."—A vulnerable victim he could bargain with—sex or a citation or arrest. "Maybe, we can work this out," he allegedly said.

Gwaltney took the young victim out of her car, handcuffed her, and put her in the back seat of his police vehicle. He drove to an isolated frontage road just off the interstate and parked and started taking off his uniform. The investigation revealed that Gwaltney used this same frontage road for other sexual liaisons with other victims—*his safe place*. Secluded from the interstate by brush and darkness, the officer took the handcuffs off the 23-year-old sexually assaulted her. Again, the theory of the case describes what happened next (*U.S. v. George M. Gwaltney* 1986). The sexual violation over the distraught victim sat on the ground putting her boots on. At that very moment, a San Bernardino County Deputy Sheriff drove by on the interstate and flashed his spotlight on the California Highway Patrol car. It was a signal of recognition from a fellow law enforcement officer. This unplanned event disrupted the seemingly rational choice actions of Gwaltney. The theory of the murder is that Miss Bishop probably sensed help would come and said something to the effect of "see they saw you, and now you are going to pay for what you've done to me." The rattled rapist, fearing job loss and possibly prison, walked up behind the distraught victim and shot her in the back of the head with his .357 caliber service revolver. Gwaltney, voice quivering and short of breath, called in and reported a body, possibly a suicide at the location.

Speculation is that he had intended to let the young girl go, but the passing deputy sheriff caused him to "lose his cool" and murder, Robin Bishop—*sexual assault plus murder*. Finding himself in a desperate situation, the veteran officer continued his attempt to conceal the crime. Moving the body and turning it over to locate the bullet, he disturbed the crime scene. The veteran law enforcement officer knew a ballistic examination would reveal the bullet was fired from his service revolver. He could not find the bullet. The bullet did not exit Robin's head; instead, it lodged in her jaw. His House of Cards would soon implode.

The detectives called to the scene discovered troubling details. Miss Bishop's car was found about 200 feet from the location of her body. The car was in gear with the keys in the ignition and no evidence of any malfunctions that would cause her to stop where she did. There were visible handcuff marks on her wrist. The autopsy revealed the recovered bullet came from a .357 caliber weapon, a common police weapon and the required weapon for the California Highway Patrol. These facts suggested that a police officer or someone pretending to be a police officer was the murderer. Robin Bishop trusted whoever got her to stop. Still, the focus was not on Gwaltney; after all, he found the body and no one believed he would murder someone. His peer group knew he would hit on a pretty girl like Robin, but kill her absolutely not. Not George M. Gwaltney whose brother was also a CHP officer.

The next move was clear to the investigators. To eliminate officers working the night of the murder, the officers were ordered to turn in their service weapons for ballistic examination. They all did except one—Gwaltney. Investigators and a California Highway Patrol Captain went to his house to retrieve his service revolver. He didn't have it; he told them. Incredibly, he explained, it had been stolen in an unreported burglary sometime after his shift ended. According to the trial documents and documentary, the stunned officers now considered Gwaltney a suspect. With his consent, a search was conducted of his home and surrounding area. The stripped-down frame of his service weapon was found in his truck with the barrel missing. Gwaltney made no attempt to explain the missing barrel or how the stolen stripped-down weapon was in his truck. Later, he would claim that someone was trying to frame him.

Investigators canvassed gun shops in the area asking if Gwaltney had attempted to buy a new barrel for the weapon. Why else would he keep the frame? None of the gun shops reported an order for a new barrel. Then three women came forward saying that Gwaltney had stopped them and made sexual advances toward them. Gwaltney was fired, arrested, and based on the overwhelming circumstantial evidence arrested for Robin Bishop's murder.

George M. Gwaltney was tried twice by the state of California, and both trials ended in hung juries: 8-4 for acquittal the first time and 7-5 for acquittal the second time (*U.S. v. George M. Gwaltney* 1986; The FBI Files 2008). A third trial by the state was ruled out, and the charges were dismissed. He was home free, at least that is what he thought. In the early 1980s, there were not many police-involved shootings drawing the media's attention. There were no 24-hour 7-day TV news shows repeating the same stories as they filled in the time. However, one agency noticed the murder and the two state hung juries. The Los Angeles FBI office monitored the case from the beginning, primarily because it was an alleged murder committed by an on-duty police officer, a clear civil rights violation if true. Federal authorities decided to try the "clearly" guilty police officer for a civil rights violation on the theory that he had murdered Robin Bishop on duty and in uniform, thereby depriving her of her civil rights under cover of law. Under the federal microscope, it was not long before the series of lies told in his first trials started falling apart.

His alibi for the time of the murder was shown to be off by at least 30 minutes, giving him ample time to commit the murder and establish an alibi. Semen found on the victim was determined to come from a person who had a reversed vasectomy. Gwaltney had a vasectomy and then had it reversed. A forensic serologist testified that rare anti-sperm antibodies found in the sperm of men who have vasectomies reversed were found on Bishop's clothing and on the back seat of Gwaltney's patrol car. The FBI lab made a match on one of the tools in his garage and the marks on the gun frame, showing the tool had been used to remove the barrel.

When investigating crimes, it is always smart law enforcement tactics to knock on the same doors more than once (personal experience).

FBI agents re-interviewed the gun shop owners. The agents reminded the gun shop owner that it was a felony to lie to a federal agent conducting an investigation. One admitted he lied at both state trials. Gwaltney had asked him to order a new gun barrel for his service weapon. The FBI agents pulled all of Gwaltney's citations for the last year of his employment and interviewed all the females who received tickets. No rape victims were found, but dozens of women revealed that he had solicited sex from them in return for no ticket, thus demonstrating a pattern of sexual coercion during traffic stops. The trial in Federal District Court in Los Angeles lasted six-weeks, and the jury was out for one and a half days. George M. Gwaltney was found guilty of the murder of Robin Bishop, thereby depriving her of her civil rights under cover of law. He was sentenced to 90 years in prison and died twelve years later of a heart attack. At his sentencing, the unruffled Gwaltney said, "I have been thinking of what I should say for the last 40-some odd days. I will stand by my plea of innocence. I killed nobody" (Anonymous, June 28, 1994). Four years later, another California Highway Patrolman would murder another young woman during a sexual encounter.

## California Highway Patrolman—Craig Peyer—1986

The arrest of a veteran California Highway Patrol Officer for murder created a shockwave in the San Diego area. The neighbors and friends of Craig Peyer, the 13-year veteran of the California Highway Patrol (CHP) and Vietnam veteran, were stunned by his arrest for the murder of Cara Knott, a 20-year-old college student.

The investigation, testimony, and court documents painted a much different picture of Peyer and his murder of twenty-year-old Cara Knott (Leaf, December 27, 2014; Wikipedia, May 7, 2019). He was a known sex offender by his peer group who refused to report him. The events as alleged by the court documents and newspaper accounts describe the intersection of *inclination, opportunity* and a *perceived low-risk* setting leading to a sexual assault plus murder Type 1-Police Sexual Homicide.

The events also describe the results of a seemingly flawed rational choice decision.

The young women were driving home from her fiancé's house in Escondido to her parent's home in El Cajon on a foggy night December 27, 1986. Her fiancé had the flu, and she acted as an angel of mercy to see about him. The attractive University of San Diego honors student never completed the 33–35 mile trip down Interstate 15, because Craig Peyer, the husband, father, son, and neighbor revered by his friends, was also a calloused sexual predator with a badge who often trolled for female drivers on the lonely road Cara traveled—*inclination*. He often stopped his prey and ordered them to pull off the road in deserted dark spaces—*opportunity and perceived low risk*. He would then detain them for long periods of time engaging in personal "flirting" conversations.

Court testimonies indicate that the feisty young victim was not intimidated by the bullying police office and wanted to continue home. She rebuffed his advances, fought back, and threatened to report him. Her righteous outburst and rage were met by overwhelming force as the lecherous murderer with a badge smashed a flashlight against her skull and strangled her to death—*sexual assault plus murder*.

Facing the problem all murderers encounter—what to do with the body—the CHP's officer put the lifeless body on the hood of his car like a slaughtered deer. It was speculated that he didn't want any trace evidence to be found in his patrol car. His police training kicked in, but it was too late, trace evidence was on him and his victim. Prosecutors alleged that Peyer calmly drove to a familiar remote area and threw the body over an abandoned bridge near the isolated Mercy Road off-ramp into the bushes of a dry creek bed 65 feet below. Frantically driving to a nearby service station, he cleaned up and resumed his routine police duties, even writing a traffic ticket to a young man hoping to establish an alibi. The time he wrote on the ticket put Peyer miles away when Cara Knott was murdered.

Cara's sister and brother-in-law found Cara Knott's car at dawn the next day. The passenger door was locked, and the driver's window was half down, the keys still in the ignition. They drove to a pay phone and called the San Diego police who found Cara's body in their search of the area. Cara's father, who was also searching for her, came on the scene about the same time as the police. He said when he saw Cara's car with the keys still in the ignition he started crying. "I slowed down my car," Knott said, "I knew. I knew" (Warren, May 31, 1987).

The discovery set off a wave of terror among women living in the region. In an attempt to ally women's fears, CHP's Officer Craig Peyer appeared on local television giving safety tips to women who traveled alone. He told the women watching, "You never know whom you may meet along the road" and added emphatically, "You could even get killed." The calloused murderer appeared on TV complete with fresh scratch marks on his face. His TV appearance prompted a number of women to call in with unexpected comments. The concerned women reported that the same security conscious CHP officer on TV had stopped them and kept them for long periods of time engaging in bizarre behavior such as gently stroking their hair and shoulders, making them feel uncomfortable. As is common in police agencies, his fellow officers were aware of his bizarre antics.

Peyer's known reputation for stopping young female drivers raised the hackles of suspicion among his peers. At roll call several mornings after the murder, one of his fellow officers "jokingly" asked if he had killed Cara Knott, all eyes turned to Peyer, and the room went silent. He did not say a word. Prior complaints against Peyer were dismissed. He was considered a good officer. Known as "hot pencil," he averaged 250 tickets a month. His silly sex peccadillos were overlooked.

Peyer's feeble attempt at an alibi blew up. Investigators checking tickets written on that road the night of the murder discovered a ticket Peyer wrote that had 9:20 p.m. on top of a scratched out 10:30 p.m. The seventeen-year-old young man said Peyer stopped him at a 10 p.m. and wrote 10:30 p.m. on the ticket before changing the time to 9:20 p.m. Investigators sensed a deliberate attempt to create an alibi—the Knott's girl was killed between 9 p.m. and 10 p.m. The 9 to 10 p.m. period for her time of death was established through the habits of a usually cautious young girl who kept her family informed of her whereabouts. Cara Knott had called her family to let them know she was heading home and she stopped at a gas station at 8:27 p.m. to purchase gas and was never seen again.

Two witnesses reported they saw Knott's empty white Volkswagen in the Mercy Road area at 9:45 p.m., 3 tenths of a mile from where her body was found. It was painfully obvious who was the "likely" for the murder of Cara Knott—a cop. Evidence gathering began. Investigators took Peyer's uniform to the police laboratory and searched his home and locker.

Circumstantial evidence mounted. Tire marks found at the scene came from a law enforcement vehicle. The television footage showing the scratch marks on his face required an explanation. Peyer said the scratch marks resulted from slipping on a gas spill and falling against a CHP parking lot chain-link fence. However, a service station attendant reported that Peyer stopped the night of the murder to get gas and he "seemed nervous, disheveled and he had scratches on his face." She said he had come to the station between 9:30 and 9:45 p.m. The scratches were bright and red as if recent. This was hours before he claimed to fall into the fence. California Highway Patrol Officer Craig Peyer was arrested for the murder of Cara Knott and placed in the San Diego County Jail on January 17, 1987.

Following his arrest, bond was set at $1 million. Close friends and family mortgaged their homes and other valuable property to raise the minimum $100,000 cash bond. Although stripped of his law enforcement officer powers, he collected his $33,000 a year salary and continued to pay his bills. That ended when he was fired in June 1987. A trial date was set for September 1987. Friends rallied to help him in his time of need.

Even before the murder tail began, Knott's father filed suit against the California Highway Patrol saying that the law enforcement agency knew that Craig Peyer had the habit of stopping women motorists and had a known drinking problem. In support of the allegations, the complaint cited evidence presented at the April preliminary hearing where several women testified that Peyer had pulled them over and detained them for excessive lengths engaging in uncomfortable conversations and inappropriate touching. His drinking problems supposedly led to outbursts of ungovernable temper (Frammolino, August 14, 1987). This civil suit would not be resolved until after Peyer's trial on criminal charges, resulting in a settlement for $2.7 million settlement.

Expert witness testimony at the April 1987 preliminary hearing revealed fibers recovered from one of Knott's hands matched fibers from Craig Peyer's California Highway Patrol jacket. Fibers from Knott's sweat suit were found on his gun belt. Spots of blood matching Peyer's blood type were found on the young victim's sweatshirt. A slam-dunk case for sure.

The trial began on January 18, 1988, with a jury of nine men and three women before a packed courtroom of Peyer supporters. The prosecution called to the stand nearly two-dozen women who testified that Peyer had pulled them over for a variety of minor "chicken crap" violations, including faulty lights. All the stops occurred on or near the isolated Mercy Road off-ramp in 1986 where the body was found. The trace evidence—fibers, blood spots, etc.—was introduced. The abundance of circumstantial evidence was immense. Witnesses who had seen the scratch marks the night of the murder took the stand. Then, reasonable doubt raised its ugly head. The first signal that the case was not a slam dunk came when a San Diego police criminalist testifying for the prosecution said he did not find any traces of blood or skin under Knott's fingernails, calling into question the origin of the scratches on Peyer's face. Further clouding the source of the scratches was testimony from an off-duty San Diego police officer who said he was in the service station when Peyer pulled up and did not see any scratch marks on the CHP officer's face.

On February 17, 1988, the trial ended with closing arguments. Van Orshoven, the prosecutor, often with his voice quivering, described Cara Knott's stop by CHP Officer Craig Peyer. The impassioned prosecutor emphasized that the extremely cautious young woman trained in self-defense would not stop for just anyone, but she would stop for a policeman in uniform driving a marked police car. That policeman, he said, was Craig Peyer, a rogue cop with a history of stopping young women on deserted roads. He detained the young woman, the prosecutor continued, until she became anxious and exploded, scratching the face of her assailant in an attempt to get away. Threatening to report and expose her abductor, the young girl struggled until the assailant in blue, fearing exposure and job loss silenced her. The prosecutor, pointing at Peyer, roared: "He silenced Cara Knott by basing her skull with his flashlight and then strangling her."

Defense attorney, Robert Grimes, countered by calmly informing the jury there was room for doubt in the state's case. He reminded the jury that reasonable doubt dictated that his client should be acquitted. The defense attorney did not challenge the blood and fiber evidence. He dismissed the supposed evidence as all circumstantial, again reminding the jurors of reasonable doubt. Jurors began their deliberations.

The prosecution team expected a quick conviction, but it was not forthcoming. The jury became hopelessly deadlocked. Five jurors were unshaken in the belief that the prosecution did not show a clear motive or sufficient evidence that Craig Peyer killed Cara Knott. One juror went so far as to say that even though the CHP officer had a propensity to stop good-looking gals that didn't prove anything. He discounted the twenty-something women who testified Peyer stopped them. Fear of exposure was discounted as a motive because some jurors believed a veteran police officer could certainly handle that. He would have just put handcuffs on someone who had an outburst like the prosecutor suggested several jurors put forth. One juror did not give much weight to the blood and fiber evidence because it was not conclusive. After seven days of deliberation, the trial ended with a 7-5 deadlock for conviction. A mistrial was declared. Round two began when the state decided on a retrial.

Former California Highway Patrol Officer Craig Peyer was free on bail for almost a year when his second trial began before a six-man, six-women jury in May 1988. More than 277 prospective jurors were quizzed over three weeks before arriving at the 12-member jury. Excessive publicity and strong opinions of guilt and innocence complicated the selection. Deputy District Attorney, Paul Plingst, the prosecutor for the state, replaced Deputy DA Joseph Van Orshoven. Defense attorney Grimes was satisfied that the jury looked like "a group of reasonable people," and he was comfortable with their selection. Grimes did suffer a setback when the trial judge limited the defense's fiber expert in the second trial. His testimony had contradicted the prosecution's fiber expert, but his credentials and techniques were criticized.

The second trial had a new and damaging witness. Women came forward after the first trial ended in a deadlock and said she and her fiancé had seen a CHP car pull over a light-colored Volkswagen occupied by a lone female between 8 and 9 p.m. on I-15 the night Cara Knott's disappeared. The defense could not shake the witnesses' resolve. She saw what she saw. The service station attendant who had seen Peyer with fresh "claw marks oozing blood" on his face when he pulled in to clean up added that Peyer retrieved a flashlight and nightstick from the trunk of his cruiser and cleaned them off with a red grease rag. A supervisor had written an injury report on Peyer's alleged fall against the chain-link fence and said it was inconsistent with a person falling against it. This was not allowed into evidence because the judge ruled it to be hearsay evidence. The judge ruled that if the chain-link fence testimony were to come in Peyer would have to take the stand and give testimony. The defense called 27 witnesses to the stand, including Peyer's wife to rebut the prosecution's witnesses. Craig Peyer did not take the stand. No chain-link fence testimony. No deadlocked jury.

After 16 hours of deliberation, Craig Peyer was convicted of the on-duty murder of Cara Knott, with the presiding judge stating he was "absolutely convinced to a moral certainty" that "Mr. Peyer killed Cara Knott" (Reza, August 4, 1989). He was sentenced to 25 years to life for the murder. At Peyer's sentencing hearing, the judge heaped scorn on the CHP officials who had not acted on prior complaints about Peyer's conduct in stopping female drivers. Newspaper accounts quote the judge as rebuking the California Highway Patrol agency for allowing the rogue officer "to continue taking young women to the off-ramp, even after receiving complaints" about his bizarre behavior. He emphasized his point by saying if they had acted on the complaints instead of dismissing them "Cara Knott would be alive and Craig Peyer would not be on his way to state prison" (Reza, August 4, 1989).

The graying grandfather, Inmate number D93018, sits in his prison cell at California Men's Colony in San Luis Obispo, proclaiming his innocence. Peyer lives in the medium-security prison among the general population still maintaining there was nothing wrong with his forced personal chats with young women. He has been denied parole three times, each time telling the parole board "I have no idea how it happened." He will have another parole hearing in 2027 if he lives that long. He did tell one parole board that he had read the self-help book *Men Are from Mars, Women Are from Venus*, twice. In 2007, Peyer was given a chance to prove his innocence when the District Attorney's Office requested a DNA sample (DNA testing was not available at the time of his trial) for the Innocence Project. At the time, the D.A.'s office was reexamining old cases to ensure that justice had been served. Peyer declined to provide a sample without explanation.

## Florida Highway Patrol Trooper Timothy Scott Harris—1990

You don't want to have to go to your six-year-old daughter and say Mom's never coming home again, because Officer Friendly killed her.

Rick Hendricks, husband of the murdered woman on *ABC 20/20*, October 24, 1997.

Florida State Highway Patrol Trooper Timothy Scott Harris is the first Florida State Trooper to be arrested for murder committed while on duty. The eight-year veteran worked for two small Florida police agencies, Sebastian and Melbourne Village, before becoming a trooper. The television crew of *ABC 20/20* discovered what the Florida Highway Patrol (FHP) should have in their background investigation—if one was done. While employed with the Melbourne Village PD (MVPD), the future trooper had been suspended once. When he resigned in 1982, Harris had three serious allegations of misconduct pending against him. Timothy Scott Harris was a "Gypsy Cop" allowed to resign in lieu of charges being filed and then moved on to another law enforcement agency. The Melbourne Village director of public safety described his former employee to *20/20* as "totally incompetent" and "not fit to be a policeman." The MVPD wanted to get rid of their problem employee and send him on his way, so he left, as too often happens with a glowing recommendation stating "He is trustworthy, intelligent, and has a high sense of responsibility toward his profession as a police officer." He would be some other agency's problem.

The Florida Highway Patrol would not learn until it was too late that Harris had come to them with a well-developed habit of stopping women, taking down their personal information and then pursuing them. He had the *inclination* for sexual misconduct. He also perfected the technique of sitting along the highways with his car pointed in the direction of oncoming traffic to pick out attractive women to stop—*hunting victims*. Harris had other disgusting habits, described by his lawyer as referring to women as "sluts" and yelling sexual comments as he drove by them. He flicked his tongue at women, often with other police officers in the car with him. He was a known problem officer. He wrote lewd comments on traffic tickets and hung obscene cartoons in his patrol car. In keeping with the sexual machismo attitude of his colleagues in blue, no one turned him in. This provided a low-risk setting for his sexual misconduct. A captain with Vero Beach Police Department became disturbed by Trooper Harris's off-duty behavior following the breakup of his marriage, such as appearing in public unkempt, and living in parking lots and rest stops and wrote a letter to the Florida Highway Patrol. Nothing happened. The inevitable and predictable sad culmination of Harris's bizarre behavior came to an end on March 4, 1990.

A woman traveling south on Interstate 95 in Indian River County at approximately 10:00 a.m. looked up to see an FHP vehicle behind her with his blue lights flashing (Sellers, April 16, 1990). She wondered why she was being stopped—she was not speeding—as she pulled onto the shoulder of the road. The woman sat still as Trooper Tim Harris, age 32, approached her driver's window. The trooper peered in the window and asked to see her license. The woman later recounted that the officer had stared at her very pregnant stomach. The trooper wrote the woman a warning ticket for going 6 miles over the speed limit and sent her on her way. The unborn child in her womb had, in all probability, saved her life. The next woman Harris stopped that day would not be so lucky.

According to court documents, an hour later Lorraine Hendricks, an extremely attractive former model, age 43, a devout Catholic, and mother of a six-year-old daughter, was driving the same Interstate 95 in Indian River County. In a note of irony, Lorraine Hendricks had once appeared as a model in the Florida Highway Patrol's Arrive Alive publicity campaign. The hapless victim would soon be raped, tortured and strangled by a Florida Highway Patrol Trooper. She would not arrive alive. Speculation is that she saw the FHP vehicle with his lights flashing in her rearview mirror and pulled to the side of the road. The burly 6 foot three inch 200-pound dark-haired trooper came to her window.

Lorraine Hendricks disappeared and was never seen again until her badly decomposed nude remains were discovered five days later covered with pine needles in a thick stand of trees and palmettos. Her silver Honda Accord had been found earlier less than a mile away from where the body was found. The car, when found, had no indicators of car trouble or a struggle. Her possessions, minus her driver's license, and car registration were in the abandoned car. Investigators immediately sensed she had stopped for someone she trusted like a police officer or someone pretending to be a police officer.

Trooper Harris brought in for questioning admitted running radar in the area where the abandoned car was found. After sustained questioning, he admitted he stopped Lorraine Hendricks and took her to a secluded stand of pines where they had consensual sex—a common defense. The questioning continued, and finally, a calm but teary-eyed Timothy Harris admitted he had raped, tortured, and slowly strangled the resisting woman as she pleaded for her life. He blamed the murder on his mental breakdown from being estranged from his wife. Harris pleaded no contest to the charge of first-degree murder in exchange for a life sentence carrying a mandatory term of 25 years. Technically, he will be eligible for parole after serving 25 years, but there is little chance of parole.

# References

Anonymous. (1994, June 26). Ex-CHP officer gets 90 years. *Daily Breeze.*
Frammolino, R. (1987, August 14). Agency "know of problems": Peyer, CHP sued by victim's father. *Los Angeles Times.*

Healey, J., Beauregard, E., Beech, A., & Vettor, S. (2014). Is the sexual murderer a unique type of offender? A typology of violent sexual offenders using crime scene behaviors. *Sexual Abuse, 28*(6), 512–533.

Higgs, T., Carter, A. J., Stefanska, E. B., & Clorney, E. (2015). Toward identification of the sexual killer: A comparison of sexual killers engaging in post-mortem sexual interference and non-homicide sexual aggressors. *Sexual Abuse, 29,* 472–499.

James, J., & Prouix, J. (2016). The modus operandi of serial and nonserial sexual murderers: A systematic review. *Aggression and Violent Behavior, 31,* 200–218.

Leaf, A. (2014, December 27). The tragic story of Cara Knott, murdered by CHP Officer Peyer in San Diego. *United Against Police Terror.*

Reza, H. G. (1989, August 4). An emotional judge gives Peyer 25 years for killing Cara Knotts. *Los Angeles Times.*

Sellers, L. (1990, April 16). A woman is slain, a trooper confesses, a fear festers. *Orlando Sentinel.*

Stefanska, E. B., Higgs, T., Carter, A. J., & Beech, A. R. (2017). When is a murder a sexual murder? Understanding the sexual element in the classification of sexual killer. *Journal of Criminal Justice, 50,* 53–61.

The FBI Files. (2008). *Above the law.* DVR-The First Season: Discovery Channel.

*U.S. v. George W. Gwaltney,* 790 F.2d 1378 (9th Cir. 1986).

Warren, J. (1987, May 31). Family, boyfriend describe search for Knott the night she disappeared. *Los Angeles Times.*

Wikipedia. (2019, May 7). Murder of Cara Knott. Accessed June 4, 2019.

# Part I

## Concluding Remarks

## PSM Causal Equation: Inclination + Opportunity + Real or Perceived Risk = PSM

The Illustrative Examples fit within the **PSM Causal Equation** and represent the second category, rape plus murder, of Type 1-Sex-Related Criminal Homicides. Gerard John Schaeffer was a true "rotten apple" who would never have been a police officer if someone had paid attention to the red flags in his twisted and sordid past. Any reasonably competent background investigator could have quickly discovered them. A psychological examination had already found him unfit for police work, but the sheriff did not take the effort to find that out and hired the serial killer. Failure to conduct adequate background checks, or conducting none at all, is a contributing factor in many of the examples we discuss. It is well known among police professionals that "crazy people" want to be cops. They want to carry a gun and tell people what to do and not do.

It appears that evidence of known questionable behavior toward women was present in the background of CHP officers, George M. Gwaltney, and Craig Peyer. Their police sexual misconduct, was low-risk behavior until they made the flawed rational decisions in choosing their targets and murdered the victims to conceal their misconduct. The California Highway Patrol, knew or should have known and taken some decisive action before they killed on the job. Their fellow officers should have reported their bizarre behavior. Civil suits filed after both murders, alluded to past transgressions by Gwaltney and Peyer. Gwaltney's civil suit claimed one woman avoided a traffic ticket by having sexual relations with the officer and also alleged that he kept file cards on women in his CHP locker, as well as female underwear. The suit claimed there was a spirit of sexual machismo among the CHP officers in Barstow adding to a feeling of *low risk for on-duty sexual misconduct*. Adding support to this claim is the sordid history of Gwaltney's commanding officer Captain Jim Carl Burchett. Captain Burchett retired in 1983. After retirement, he served a prison term in 1993 after being convicted of attempted lewd conduct with a child. Then in 1995, he pleaded guilty in US District Court in Los Angeles to one count of conspiracy to distribute and receive pornography and seven counts of child pornography, (Gorman, January 12, 1996). In 1996, a highly decorated CHP sergeant, also an Officer of the Year, who had served 17 years in the Barstow CHP office committed suicide after being charged with the rape of a woman he picked up while in uniform (Gorman, January 12, 1996). We see the same pattern of sexual machismo leading to inaction and toleration of officer's misconduct repeated in many of the PSM types.

# Part II

## Sexual Predators in Blue: Rapists, Extortionists, and Harasshers

## Introduction

Murder is always a possibility whenever a victim resists or threatens an armed aggressor. That heinous outcome is exacerbated when the aggressor carries a badge and is equipped with numerous weapons of violence. The victims in this chapter are lucky they survived. The police sexual predators and rapists go beyond sexual gratification. Victims are objects to satisfy the sexual predator's desire and discarded—throw away sex objects. Victims are chosen from a vulnerable pool of perceived "perfect victims." The law enforcement perpetrators have the *inclination* for sexual abuse. They choose their victims from work-related settings—*opportunity*, and operate under a *real or perceived low risk*. Violence—implicit and explicit—is a characteristic dimension of the law enforcement perpetrator. Serial sexual assaults are other dimensions along with the possibility that some have committed unknown assaults plus murder.

# 4

# Type 2: Violent Rapists and Sexual Predators

The police sexual aggressors in this type share the same characteristics. They target male and female victims and lack the self-control to curb their impulsive sexual inclinations. Victims usually are selected opportunistically during a "hunt" for victims who are seen as throwaway sex objects. Violent rapists and serial sexual predators are the most dangerous police sexual aggressors except for serial sexual offenders. They are considered to be "rotten apples", even in departments known for other forms of police misconduct, mainly for the irrational nature of their crimes that lead to extensive media attention. However, in many instances the police peer group was aware of their sexual misconduct before the bizarre incident that exposed them.

## Violent Rapists

Violent LEO rapists are "outliers," even in "bad" or rogue police departments. Particularly, troubling is that many were known or knowable problem officers and their reign of terror could have been prevented. The victims are lucky to be alive. In one case, there are two alleged

© The Author(s) 2020
T. Barker, *Aggressors in Blue*,
https://doi.org/10.1007/978-3-030-28441-1_4

murders. In the other two Illustrative Examples, the disturbed behavior of the Violent Rapists indicates the possibility of sexual assault plus murder. The first I.E. is an off-duty officer, but he is included in this discussion because of the progression of his sexual inclination that began on duty and culminated after he finished his shift. The police officer's bizarre behavior is extremely violent and confused, leading to the conclusion that he may have been an unidentified sexually motivated serial killer or on the path to being one like David Middleton.

## NYPD—Michael Pena—Let Me Finish

Eyewitnesses called 911 and yelled for him to stop.
"I'm almost done," Officer Pena yelled back.
**Trial Testimony.** (Buettner, March 15, 2012)

According to newspaper accounts and court documents, Officer Michael Pena, a three-year NYPD veteran, drunk and off duty approached a petite 25-year-old woman on a residential street in Upper Manhattan (Zanoni et al., August 19, 2011; Ross and Mcshane, June 21, 2012; Doll, March 30, 2012; Crimesider Staff, May 7, 2012). It was 6 a.m. on August 19, 2011, and the excited young woman waited for a ride to her first day of school as a teacher. She was hired the night before by a charter school to teach second grade. The principal lived nearby and offered her a ride to the school. She waited outside his house as Pena approached. Unknown to her, the drunken off-duty NYPD officer spent the night drinking in a frustrated search for sex after he finished his shift He began drinking at a nearby bar around midnight while watching strippers perform. He called a woman he met the night before, but she did not respond. More drinks and he hit on the waitress—struck out again. Somewhere around 5 am he called several escort services, but they did not return his call. The drunken Michael Pena left the bar and began trolling the neighborhood for a sex object—impulsive *inclination*. He spotted the soon-to-be second-grade teacher—*opportunity*.

Pena asked the pretty young woman for directions to a subway stop and suggested she accompany him. Declining his offer, the helpful target started giving directions to a subway stop. The encounter turned bad as Pena grabbed her, showed her a gun, and warned, "Shut your f_____ mouth, or I'll shoot you in the f_____ face." "You're coming with we," he said. Pena pulled the stunned and frightened woman three blocks to an alley between two apartment buildings—*a perceived safe setting*. Once in the alley, he began brutally sodomizing and raping her. She screamed for help. Her screams alerted nearby witnesses who looked out their windows. One dialed 911 and leaned out her window and yelled for him to stop the brutal assault. The callous rapist continued and yelled "I'm almost done" and continued the sexual assault.

Within minutes, two uniformed officers were on the scene. The shaken victim worried about the officer's safety yelled: "He raped me; be careful, he has a gun." The grinning Pena stood with his pants down and said, "I'm a cop," pointing to his pants as if "being on the job" would somehow protect him from arrest. The uniformed officers found Pena's NYPD identification and badge in his pocket. Pena's 9-millimeter Glock pistol lay on the ground beside him. The disgusted officers arrested him and called an ambulance for his brutalized victim.

Pena showed little or no concern for his victim. He was consumed with self-pity. He asked a sergeant, "how am I going to call her [his girlfriend] when I got arrested for cheating with another girl?" Pena complained about being in custody and asked if his case could be "fast-tracked," because of his police status. He whined about the handcuffs being too tight and feeling dizzy. "Will my car be impounded?" He asked an arresting officer. "Do you know what the sentence is?" He asked a lieutenant. He expressed no remorse for the victim. The officers investigating the assault were disgusted with his attitude and feared he was a repeat offender—*a real possibility*. One unnamed law enforcement officer was quoted as saying "I think if you throw out the fact that he is a cop, and you have a cop who would rape a woman, a stranger like that—you have to think it is not a one-time thing" (Daily Mail Reporter, September 21, 2011).

Michael Pena's bizarre trial began on March 16, 2012, with the defense argument that Pena did assault the woman, but he didn't technically rape her. The admission was an attempt to avoid a rape conviction that carried a life sentence. The most serious charge—rape—required vaginal penetration. Therefore, the defense conceded Pena did assault the victim and he deserved punishment but not life in prison. There was, the defense contended, no DNA evidence or eyewitness testimony to show vaginal penetration. Pena's DNA was found on the victim but not in the victim.

On March 17, 2012, the jury returned a split verdict. The jurors unanimously found Pena guilty of three counts of criminal sexual assault—involves touching—and three counts of predatory sexual assault—possessing a weapon during the sexual assault which carries a maximum of life in prison, but were deadlocked on two rape counts which requires vagina penetration. Five lawyers on the 12-person jury may have influenced this strict interpretation, including one with 40 years experience as a prosecutor, defense attorney, and law professor. Jurors revealed the lawyers debated legal elements of the crimes for an inordinate amount of time. The victim left the courtroom in tears after the verdicts were announced. She could not understand. She testified he penetrated her and it hurt. Many jurors believed her. Newspaper accounts reported one juror's feelings: "I think she came away thinking, how could people not believe me. I wish she could know that there were people in the jury room who absolutely believed her, about the whole story" (Dwyer, April 3, 2012). The jury felt empathy for the victim and considered her courageous because she started teaching a few weeks after her brutal "rape." The judge left with no choice declared a mistrial on the rape charges. The prosecution declined to comment on a retrial but promised to request the maximum sentence of 25 years to life in prison at sentencing.

On May 7, 2012, Michael Pena, although he escaped the rape convictions, was sentenced to 75 years to life in prison. The legal technicality of penetration for rape did not avoid a life sentence. The judge gave him the 25-year maximum on each charge, to run consecutively. The judge declared Pena had assaulted the victim "in the most brutal and degrading manner possible." His victim beamed with a wide smile and hugged friends, family, and law enforcement officers. Pena apologized saying, "I have no explanation for what happened that day." Pena will not be eligible for parole until after his 100 birthday. He later pleaded guilty to the two rape charges with no effect on his sentence. He claimed he did so to spare his family the pain of another trial.

## Hartford, Connecticut—Julio J. Camacho—Violent Rapist and Possible Murderer

On October 24, 1997, four-year-old Rosa Marie Camacho walked with her mother Rosa Delgado to a nearby store to buy groceries. The 38-pound Hispanic female, nicknamed Rosita, was never seen again (Kovner, October 12, 2000; May 1, 2001), Rosa's mother disappeared with her, but she was seen again, and at least, her remains were seen again.

In November 1997, a headless and handless woman's body was found floating in three feet of water in western New Jersey about 180 miles from where the child and mother disappeared. The condition of the corpse—headless and handless—was an apparent attempt to thwart the body's identification through dental records and fingerprints. The nameless "Lady of the Lake" lay in the morgue unidentified until the FBI lab identified her as Rosa Delgado in 1999. The last person to see three-foot Rosa and her mother was the baby's father and the mother's former boyfriend Julio J. Camacho, a ten-year veteran of the Hartford, Connecticut Police Department. Camacho was a police officer with a checkered past who could not stay out of trouble.

According to published newspaper account (see above), Camacho was a problem officer before he completed his first year on the job. He was fired in January 1989 after an arrest for third-degree assault, accused of striking his ex-wife during a domestic dispute. For some not explained reason, a month later he was reinstated with the termination changed to suspension. The Harford Police Department (HPD) would regret that decision. Repeated infidelities with women he met on the job marred his second marriage to another Hartford police officer. In addition to fathering the missing Rosa Camacho, he was the father of a child with another woman that he met on duty. Officer Camacho met her sitting on her front steps while patrolling her neighborhood. She gave birth to Julio Camacho JR the next year. He was paying $752 a month child support for Rosita and $600 a month for Julio Jr. Also, he paid child support for a child from his first marriage. Combined, his child support payments totaled nearly $1600 a month, a real strain on his second marriage, and later alleged to be a motive for murder.

As disturbing as Officer Julio Camacho's private life and on-duty sexual activity was, it paled in comparison with what a 2001 federal grand jury's investigation of police corruption in the Hartford, Connecticut Police Department (HPD) revealed. The HPD was a rogue police department with numerous accusations of sexual abuse (Kovner, May 1, 2001, see also *Yolanda v. City of Hartford; Hartford Police Department; Officer Julio Camacho*). The grand jury indicted seven officers, including Julio Camacho for sexual offenses, including forced sex acts ranging from oral sex to masturbation with a police nightstick. All victims were known as prostitutes or exotic dancers—*vulnerable pool of victims.* One woman was allegedly forced to perform oral sex on police officers seven different times over a three-year period. While on duty and in uniform, two Hartford officers allegedly took four women who worked as topless dancers at a local strip club to a motel and forced them to perform sex acts on each other. One officer used a department Polaroid camera to take nude pictures of the women. All the officers were convicted and received sentences from probation to ten years.

At Julio J. Camacho's bail hearing for the two rapes disclosed during the sex scandal investigation, the federal prosecutor dropped a bombshell to prevent his release. In open court, the prosecutor revealed Camacho was the prime suspect in the beheading of Rosa Delgado and the disappearance of Rosita Camacho (Kovner, October 12, 2000). He outlined the circumstantial evidence found to support the allegation including possible murder weapons—a garrote-like wire with a loop on one end and a handmade hatchet. A search of his car revealed the trunk lining had been removed and the metal trunk bottom had been sanded clean. The search of his home found a New Jersey map with notes tracing the route to the spot where Delgado's body was found. Also found was a macabre library of books on serial killers and committing a perfect crime, including chapters on decapitation and concealing the identity of a corpse. The prosecutor said they were waiting on more evidence to charge Camacho. He went to trial on the rapes.

Julio J. Camacho received 10 years for raping two known prostitutes while on duty and in uniform. The pattern was the same for each woman. The women were not breaking any laws; at the time, he handcuffed them, pushed them into the back seat, and drove to a secluded area and raped them. He pleaded guilty on the condition the government would not pursue charges made by other women—at least four—against him. His public defender asked why the two women victims had not filed complaints when the alleged rapes occurred. The prosecutor quickly fired back "Who are they going to go to? They had no confidence that if they went to HPD, their complaints would be heard. It was only after this investigation began that they gained confidence that the system would treat them fairly" (Kovner, May 1, 2001).

Camacho has been released after serving his sentence, but he remains a suspect in the murder of Rosa Delgado and the disappearance of his daughter (Wagner, January 13, 2016). The FBI dug up the yard of his former house in 2016 looking for evidence. At the time, Camacho was incarcerated for failure to pay child support from previous relationships. There is no statute of limitations on murder.

## Miami, Florida—Michael Ragusa—Kidnapper and Rapist

Thirty-one-year-old Michael Ragusa's three-year career with the Miami, Florida Police Department came to an inglorious end on March 20, 2007, with his arrest by the Miami Beach police for kidnapping and attempted rape (Christensen, April 5, 2012). Even the state prosecutor admitted that Ragusa was a serial rapist who misused his police position to commit rape on numerous occasions (Matos, April 29, 2010). Sadly, his violent sexual assaults could have been prevented. Court documents revealed that the abduction and attempted rape should never have happened. Officer Michael Ragusa should never have been in a marked Miami PD police vehicle targeting vulnerable targets. He should never have been hired as a police officer. According to published reports, the city psychologist who interviewed him warned, "This is not somebody you'd want to hire." Other police agencies—Broward County Sheriff's Office and Miami-Dade PD, North Miami PD, Fort Lauderdale PD, and Cooper City PD—had rejected him. Furthermore, he did not attempt to disclose his sordid past and personality defects. Ragusa wrote on his Miami PD application that he paid for sex with strippers and prostitutes, stole cash from restaurants he worked as a waiter, and had a fiery temper. A cursory examination of his background and employment history would have quickly documented his unsuitability for police work. Why was this discredited applicant hired.

The police background investigator's, Willie Bell, history at the time was worse than Ragusa's (Christiansen, April 5, 2012). The Miami PD had disciplined Bell an unbelievable twenty-six times in his career. Those disciplinary actions included using unnecessary force, neglect of duty, improper discharge of a firearm, and theft. The background investigator had been arrested for battery, falsifying police records, and official misconduct, but the criminal charges were dropped when he agreed to attend an anger management program—*failure to deal with a known problem officer creates a low-risk perception in the police agency*. An assistant city attorney declared, "He is the most disciplined officer in the history of the city." The Miami Police Department moved him into the background investigators position to get him off the street, hoping to reduce the opportunity for him to get in trouble. This same *moving the trash syndrome* regularly occurs in police agencies and will be present in other types of police sexual misconduct. I have personally observed it in other police agencies and had it confirmed by other working and former police officers at all levels of government.

A new police chief came in as a reform agent the year after Bell was appointed background investigator. The new chief pledged to restore confidence in a department rocked by the scandals in the 1980s and 1990s. At that time—the 1980s and 1990s—the Miami PD went on a "hiring frenzy" to raise the number of minority officers on the street, pledging to hire 56% of the new hires from minority groups, including women. A laudable objective, except lax background checks, ignored psychological profiles; speedy training and rushing them onto the streets, combined with faulty supervision, insured the best minority applicants were not hired. Instead, the quest for minority candidates in a hurry ignored questionable backgrounds and deviant practices. The resulting scandals, corruption, misconduct, criminal activities, including robbery and murder, rocked Miami, made national headlines, and called for reform. The mess needed to be cleaned up, hence a new chief.

The new reform chief as part of his "Blueprints for the Future" declared his focus was "not on how to improve the quality of the men and women on the MPD, but the urgent need to increase their quantity." This undue pressure to hire led, as it had before, to putting officers like Michael Ragusa in uniform (Christiansen, April 5, 2012).

Published accounts and court documents reveal the events surrounding his 2007 arrest. Ragusa was off duty and riding around in uniform in his Miami PD take-home vehicle when he spotted a suspected illegal immigrant getting off a bus in Miami Beach, a few blocks from Ragusa's Miami Beach apartment. The 31-year-old single mother was a recent immigrant and single mother returning home from her 10-hour shift as a waitress. According to the police report, Ragusa dragged her into the car by her arms. He then drove three blocks to an unlit park where he exposed himself. Ragusa forcefully removed the crying woman's pants and started to penetrate her. The quick-thinking woman claimed to have a venereal disease. He stopped the assault and drove her home after getting her phone number. He later sent her a text message and called on her phone. The women, fearing other contacts, complained to the Miami Beach PD, who notified the City of Miami PD. He was arrested and charged with kidnapping and attempted rape.

The arrest for sexual assault by a police officer and its publicity usually trigger additional complaints. A second woman, a self-described prostitute, told investigators a slightly inebriated Michael Ragusa in uniform pulled her into a marked city of Miami police vehicle in Miami Beach and drove to a nearby unlit lot and forced her to perform oral sex. The investigation revealed Ragusa was off-duty and driving his take-home police vehicle. The State Attorney at a news conference remarked other victims were possible and "There may be evidence that suggests he was preying upon the most vulnerable, which is probably known prostitutes," she said. "They're afraid to go to the police, they're afraid no one will believe them" (Watcher, March 21, 2007). A third woman came forward and complained of forcible kidnapping and rape under the same circumstances.

His police history confirmed that Ragusa was "bad to the bone" with four lawsuits for using excessive force in his brief police career. Ragusa was a problem officer, and it was evident. He was sentenced to 10 years after pleading guilty to sexual battery, kidnapping, and kidnapping with a weapon. The 31-year-old victim that led to his arrest received a $550,000 settlement from the City of Miami and left the United States. The background investigator retired, and the reform chief moved on. The Miami Police Department resumed business as usual until another police misconduct scandal erupts. Miami PD is one of a handful of US police agencies with a cyclical history, roughly every twenty years, of scandal and corruption. New York City PD, New Orleans PD, Chicago PD, Los Angeles PD, Miami PD, Philadelphia PD, and Baltimore PD are other police departments with a storied history of police scandal, misconduct, and corruption (Barker 2011).

The next type of police sexual aggressors we discuss is not generally as violent as the impulsive rapists described above, but they can be.

## Serial Sexual Predators

The following Illustrative Examples of police sexual aggressors who use physical force on occasion. What we know from the published reports is that they primarily use threats of physical force to achieve their sexual acts. They are armed and represent a deadly threat if resisted or threatened. Therefore, there is always the possibility that further research will find little difference between the two categories. However, at this time they distinguish themselves from Type 3—Sexual Extortion by the threat of force not arrest or citation, and their acts are more repetitive. Nevertheless, these serial offenders exhibit the *inclination* for police sexual misconduct and select their victims—male, female, and same sex—from *an opportunistic pool* of vulnerable persons with credible issues.

Finally, the police sexual aggressors act in a setting of *real or perceived low risk*. And, their acts are repetitive.

The first Illustrative Example describes the most egregious known example of a law enforcement serial sexual predator in recent US history. It was his outrageous behavior that ignited the current interest in PSM. Daniel Holtzclaw is the epitome of those incidents that elicit an "I can't believe he did that" reaction from the police community and the public. That reaction is the foundation for most law enforcement sexual misconduct—the failure to recognize that PSM is a perennial police problem and taking appropriate action to prevent it. In the end, a three-pronged approach is necessary to identify the possibility of problem officers, reduce the opportunities, and insure that PSM is a zero tolerance—high-risk—behavior. Police organizations must be held accountable for the occurrence of Law Enforcement Police Sexual Misconduct.

## Oklahoma City, Oklahoma—Daniel Holtzclaw-Racist Sexual Predator Rapist

Daniel K. Holtzclaw on paper was the epitome of a modern professional police officer—a police recruiter's dream (Wikipedia, May 23, 2019). He came from a police background; his father and brother-in-law are police officers. The father is a 17-year veteran of the Enid, Oklahoma Police Department. Young and physically fit with a bachelor's degree in criminal justice what could be wrong? Well? Daniel K. Holtzclaw, aka The Claw, nickname when he was a star football player—Freshman All-American from the Football Writers of America—at Eastern Michigan University majoring in Criminal Justice is a serial sexual predator. He went on trial November 2, 2015, for 36 felony counts including rape, rape by instrumentation, sexual battery, forcible oral sodomy, burglary, indecent exposure, and producing lewd exhibition.

The young officer with three years on the job faced life in prison for sexually assaulting 13 black women over a 5-month period—February 2014 to June 2014. The victims ranged in age from 34 to a grandmother of 58—*black females with credibility issues*. These *safe targets*—middle-aged lower status black women who had reason to fear the police and credibility issues because of outstanding warrants, drug issues, or a prostitution background. The acts occurred under the veil of darkness during his 2 pm to 4 am duty shift. Without a doubt, the white police officer racially profiled his vulnerable victims.

He chose his victims randomly as the *opportunity* presented itself; some women walked the street, one became a repeat victim, and some were pulled over in the classic sex or arrest technique, whatever worked he used. The prosecutor stated at his arraignment: "He identifies a vulnerable victim that without exception except one have an attitude of What good is it gonna do? He's a police officer. Who's going to believe me? (Testa, September 5, 2014)." His predatory behavior would have continued, except he deviated from the pool of vulnerable safe targets and selected a credible middle-class black woman driving through, but not from, the run-down neighborhood he patrolled. Following her sexual assault, the woman went home and told her daughter what happened. They immediately reported it. The investigation revealed a history of sexual assaults.

On February 27, 2014, Holtzclaw's first known sexual assault occurred in the Culbertson East Highland neighborhood, one of Oklahoma's poorest census tracks where fifty percent of the population (80% black, 10% white) lives in poverty (Testa, September 5, 2014; Garcia, December 11, 2015). Just past midnight, his victim sat in her car in front of her house with her children and a friend. Two police cars pulled in behind her and blocked her in without explanation. The suspicious cops ran her friend's license and found no warrants. One officer left, and the other, Holtzclaw, remained. He ordered the children and friend into the house. He checked the victim for warrants and found three outstanding warrants. He said he needed to search her and for her to "play by the rules."

Holtzclaw's rules required lifting her shirt, so he could fondle her exposed breasts. His sexual urges satisfied, and he set her up for future contacts by saying he could help her with city warrants if she needed and drove off. The victim knew it could have been worse. Holtzclaw left the scene confident he was safe.

Two weeks later on March 14, a black woman walked down a dimly lit street among the vacant lots and abandoned properties in the same area. Holtzclaw stopped her and made her expose her breasts. She later told investigators she didn't report him because police officers could cause a lot of problems for her like "telling a drug house she was a snitch," a possible death sentence among her crowd.

Following two more contacts and fondling the women, his behavior escalated. The next victim, a black female, walked alone at night when Holtzclaw stopped her. The woman confessed she had a history of prostitution and drug addiction. She admitted smoking crack earlier. He searched her purse and found a crack pipe. The woman testified Holtzclaw drove to her house five blocks away and took her into the bedroom. Holtzclaw told her to sit on the bed as he "unzipped his pants and put his erect penis in her face." After forcing her to perform oral sex on him, he sodomized and raped her.

Two weeks after this brutal attack, Holtzclaw was at it again, picking up another woman walking and then sodomizing her in his patrol car. He then drove to an abandoned school, parked behind a building, and raped her. The sadistic rapist drove away telling the woman to "have a good night." The very next day Holtzclaw sodomized another black woman in the back seat of his patrol car. His attacks became more frequent and aggressive, as he felt safer in his depravations.

In the early morning of June 18, 2014, Holtzclaw's reign of terror ended. He stopped a 58-year-old grandmother driving home after playing dominos with a friend. During the preliminary hearing on September 5, 2014, investigating detectives described Holtzclaw's actions (Testa, September 5, 2014). He stopped her and proceeded up to the driver's side window. The woman identified as J.L. could not lower the broken window. She opened the door a few inches to talk to the approaching officer. The burly six feet three two hundred and sixty pounds officer opened the door wider and moved closer to J.L. J.L. recounts her inner radar went off as she felt this night would not end well. Holtzclaw directed the apprehensive woman to the rear seat of his patrol car and asked if she had been drinking. J.L. replied no and said the Styrofoam cup in her front seat was filled with Kool-Aid. He told J.L. he had to check her out and to lift her shirt. She raised her shirt, not high enough to expose her breasts. Not satisfied, Holtzclaw told the frightened woman to lift her shirt and bra, shining his flashlight on her exposed breasts. J.L. reported Holtzclaw started playing with his penis and told her to stand up and pull down her pants. She complied but left her underwear on as Holtzclaw shined his flashlight on her "vaginal area." She felt his erect penis on her face. She begged him to stop. J.L. told the investigator she kept thinking "OK, this is a police officer, and if he's gonna do this, he's gonna kill me. And I'm not gonna make it out of this alive" (Testa, September 5, 2014).

The attack continued. He put his penis in her mouth for about ten seconds, pulled it out, and stopped, telling her "I'm gonna follow you home." J.L. went back to her car and drove into what she thought was a driveway and did a U-turn. Holtzclaw pulled his patrol car around her and unexpectedly drove off. The shaken and bewildered woman drove home and told her daughter. The victim and her daughter went to a nearby police station and reported the sexual attack. She was told to go to the hospital for a sexual assault medical forensic exam. The on-call Oklahoma City Sex Crimes detective met her there.

The police had a previous complaint of sexual assault by a uniformed officer in the area but were unable to link it to Holtzclaw until the June 18 victim came forward. He was placed on leave the day of the June 18 victim's complaint. The media picked up the allegation, and other claims of sexual assaults by Holtzclaw were reported. Holtzclaw was arrested on August 21, 2014, after GPS records from his patrol car put him at the scene of the sexual assaults—*use of technical assist*. His bond was set at $5 million. On August 28, 2014, the outraged Oklahoma NAACP sent a certified letter to Attorney General Eric Holder asking for an investigation into a Hate Crime Violation(s) of Racial Profiling by Oklahoma City Police Officer Daniel Holtzclaw. The Oklahoma NAACP applauded the actions of the Oklahoma City police but wanted an expanded investigation.

On September 5, 2014, Holtzclaw had his bond reduced to $500,000. The prosecutor argued against bail reduction, insisting he was a danger to the community. Family and friends rallied behind Holtzclaw and raised the money. His release had a number of conditions: He was under house arrest living with his parents, fitted with a

GPS monitoring device, and forbidden to have any contact with his alleged victims.

There was a bizarre twist to media coverage of the alleged sexual assaults that raised the fear of other police sexual predators in Oklahoma. Within two weeks of Holtzclaw's release on the reduced bond, two other Oklahoma police officers were arrested for multiple sexual assaults, creating a media circus of calls for reform and investigations. The first arrest occurred on September 14 when an Oklahoma Highway Patrolman was charged with kidnapping and rape after three women alleged he assaulted them. The first woman claimed the highway patrolman stopped her, asked sexually explicit questions, and then drove her to a secluded spot and raped her. The second and third victims made similar accusations. All three women claimed the trooper turned off his uniform video camera before the sexual assaults—*failure to use technical assist.* The next day a Tulsa County Deputy Sheriff was arrested for sexually assaulting two women by exposing himself and inappropriately touching them following a call to their home. Newspaper accounts reported authorities to expect to receive at least five more complaints on the deputy. Holtzclaw regained the media's attention.

Not able to stay out of trouble, in October 2014, he was ordered to serve 14 days in jail and have his bond increased to $609,000 for going to his doctor's office without reporting it—a technical violation. In August 2015, after a second bond violation, the insurance company securing the bond pulled out. The revoked bond cost the Holtzclaw family $50,000, and they could not raise the entire bond amount. He remained in jail until his trial.

The trial began on November 2, 2015. He was tried before a jury of eight men and four women, all white, raising troubling questions given the racial dynamics of the case, especially when the defense would center on the victims' reputations. The victim's reputation became a central issue when one accuser was not allowed to continue testifying because she tested—judge called for testing—positive for PCP, prescription drugs, and marijuana. Later, the woman told the jury "I'm not going to lie. Before I came here, I smoked some marijuana and a blunt stick laced with PCP" (Schwab, November 13, 2015). Destroying the credibility of the witnesses was the primary strategy of the defense.

The expected and common defense in police rape cases was not successful. Daniel Holtzclaw was convicted of 18 counts of sexual battery, rape, and other offenses and sentenced to 263 years in prison. He cried at his sentencing but never expressed remorse for his crimes.

## Anchorage, Alaska—Anthony Rollins

The local agency that helps sexual abuse victims, *Anchorage's Standing Together Against Rape*, reported a 13-year veteran African-American Officer Anthony Rollins, in uniform and on duty raped a woman. The Anchorage, Alaska Police Department (APD) command structure reacted in stunned disbelief (Grove, March 3, 2012). Not Tony Rollins? He was married to Sgt. Denise Rollins, APD's supervisor of the School Resource Officer Program. Anthony Rollins was a member of APD's Honor Guard. The decorated model officer received a Meritorious Conduct award two years earlier for assisting in anti-bullying programs in Anchorage schools, earlier in the year he was awarded the department's highest recognition, the Medal of Valor, for rescuing a man from a burning building. Following department protocol, he was placed on paid leave until the matter was resolved. Everyone in the department assumed the allegations were false. What was found was unexpected.

The three-month investigation revealed the model officer was a sexual predator that assaulted at least six women over the past three years—2006 to 2009. Equally disturbing, the investigation revealed the APD's lax attitude toward police sexual misconduct created a culture among officers that contributed to the burgeoning scandal—*perceived safe setting for PSM*. Furthermore, model police officer Anthony Rollins married to an APD sergeant was known to engage in "consensual" sex acts on duty and in uniform (Anonymous, March 3, 2012).

On July 15, 2009, a grand jury indicted Officer Anthony Rollins on four counts of Sexual Assault 1, six counts of Sexual Assault 2, Criminal Use of a Computer 4 counts, and six counts of Official Misconduct. He was placed in the Anchorage Jail with a cash-only bond of $100,000.

After numerous delays, the trial began on January 20, 2011. Court documents revealed all six victims testified to sexual assaults—sex acts or inappropriate touching. One woman testified Rollins forced her to perform oral sex while he processed her at the police station for a drunk driving arrest, and another claimed Rollins picked her up at an alcohol sleep-off center and raped her. The other victims were walking or driving when stopped and sexually assaulted. They were all in their late teens or early 20s. In an unusual and risky move, Rollins took the stand. Rollins testified he only had sex with four of the victims, and it was consensual. He claimed he was an adulterer but not a rapist. Readily admitting the sex acts were on duty and in uniform, he claimed many APD officers had sex on duty—*everybody does it defense.* Another APD officer testified officers had sex on duty, just not as much as Rollins said.

On February 20, 2011, Rollins was convicted of 18 of the 20 counts. The judge said Rollins was "a rapist in blue with a badge" (Grove, April 12, 2012). A year later, Rollins was sentenced to 87 years in prison. It was not the end. A civil lawsuit filed by his victims revealed Rollins engaged in a pattern of sexual misconduct long before he was brought to trial and the Anchorage Police Department knew it and did not take proper action to prevent future acts—*organizational and peer group support.* The department knew or should have known he was a threat to women. There was a pattern and history to his sexual misconduct (Anonymous, March 3, 2012). The first investigation into his sexual misconduct occurred in 2001 with a report that a woman performed oral sex on him in an apartment hallway. The woman and Rollins denied the accusation, and it was deemed unfounded. Two years later, a prostitute claimed Rollins threatened her with arrest if she did not have sex with him. Sensing a "bad" cop, the APD and the FBI ran a sting. He made several flirtation remarks to an undercover officer, but no sex or arrest solicitations. The sting revealed he spent a lot of time at the home of a woman member of his church while on duty. Called in, Rollins admitted to 20 sexual encounters, adding he listened to the police radio at her house and answered all the calls he received. The disciplinary reaction was a negative review and a transfer. He should have been fired for this gross violation. The prior pattern of sexual misconduct was clear. Anchorage, Alaska Police Department failed to supervise and discipline an officer known to engage in police sexual misconduct. It was predictable he would become a sexual predator. The lawsuit was settled for $5.5 million. Following a review by the International Association of Chiefs of Police, the Anchorage Police Department instituted a zero-tolerance policy for sexual misconduct (Strom, October 6, 2012).

## West Sacramento, California—Sergio Alvarez

Officer Sergio Alvarez, a five-year veteran of the West Sacrament CA PD, was arrested on February 25, 2013, and charged with 35 felony offenses for sexually assaulting six women between October 2011 and September 2012 (Anonymous, February 26, 2013; Walsh and Stanton, October 22, 2015). The disturbing charges included rape, oral copulation against will, and kidnapping. His victims—ages 20 to 47—were selected from a vulnerable pool of women living on the edges of society in area known for prostitution activity—*safe targets*. A deputy assistant attorney described them as: "These people [women] were down and out, hardcore dope users and alcoholics but they were victims and vulnerable because of a combination of being homeless, prostitutes, drug addicts, and afraid of the police" (Bordon et al. 2014). Alvarez stopped them while he was on routine patrol and forced them into performing oral sex on him.

One of Alvarez's victims had the courage to call the female shift commander of the precinct where Alvarez worked, and she initiated the investigation. The investigation discovered five more victims willing to register a complaint and Alvarez was indicted and fired. Alvarez pleaded not guilty and took the stand in his defense, claiming he did not know some of the women accusers and those he knew had engaged in consensual sex—*common defense*. The jury after nine days of deliberation found him guilty on 18 counts, including rape, oral copulation against will, and kidnapping. He was sentenced to 205 years in prison.

# Fort Worth, Texas—Daniel Lopez and the Iron Sergeant

In February 2010, Daniel Lopez, a 20-year veteran of the Fort Worth, Texas PD, pleaded guilty to 5 sexual assaults of women between August and November 2010 and received a twenty-year sentence (Anonymous, February 29, 2012). Lopez used well-known police techniques to identify targets for his sexual depravations—pretext stops and record checks. Checking their criminal records after stopping them, Lopez discovered their vulnerability—intoxication, no license, equipment violations, or warrants, combined with a history of drug or prostitution arrests. Marginalized women with credibility issues were his preferred targets—*safe victims.*

Lopez made a critical error—one of his victims was not a safe target. She reported him to the sheriff's department. The investigation began, and another complaint was made. The Tarrant County Sheriff's Department alerted the Fort Worth detectives to a woman reporting a rape by a uniformed Fort Worth officer. The woman said she was walking down a city street when an FWPD patrol car pulled up. The officer asked for her name, handcuffed her, and then put her in the back seat of his car. He drove to a park and brought up her prostitution history. "The officer told me to give him oral sex, or I'd go to jail." Feeling threatened she complied. A third victim reported she was jaywalking when a uniformed officer stopped her. He checked her criminal record and found outstanding warrants. The sexual predator drove to a nearby park and forced her to perform oral sex on him.

Lopez confronted with the complaints admitted contact with the victims but claimed he detained them briefly to question about drug activity. Lopez was aware the detectives could establish a connection with the women through his GPS tracking—*technical assist.*

Fort Worth PD savvy detectives retrieved the GPS records for Lopez's vehicle the date of the complaints. Fort Worth PD, like some US police departments, equips patrol vehicles with GPS recording devices mounted in the trunk. Known as "Iron Sergeants" or "Skunks in the Trunk," they keep track of the car during the shift and record its travels, that is, useful for officer's safety and dispatching purposes; GPS tracking is also used for accountability purposes making sure patrol cars stay on their beat, do not spend too much time at a particular location, or were or were not at a complaint location. Cops hate them.

The detectives confronted Lopez with the radio transcripts showing his checking women for outstanding warrants and the GPS record showing his patrol car in the area described by the victims. Officer Lopez's pattern of checking criminal records before sexually assaulting victims was obvious. They contacted women whose records he checked. Two more sexually assaulted victims filed complaints. However, the detectives suspected other victims among those contacted unwilling to make a formal accusation. In any event, the evidence against Lopez was enough to convince him to plead guilty to the five rapes and receive a twenty-year sentence. A technical supervisory assist like "The Iron Sergeant" proved its usefulness.

## Houston, TX—Abraham Joseph—Legal Immigrant Victimizing Illegal Immigrants

On January 2, 2011, Houston, Texas Police Officer, Abraham Joseph, born in India and a naturalized US citizen, stopped outside a southwest Houston cantina where an illegal immigrant from El Salvador in her early twenties who spoke little English worked as a waitress. It was 3 am, and she was taking a break and talking to a Hispanic man. Officer Joseph without explanation handcuffed both and put them in his patrol car. He drove to an isolated area where a business surveillance camera filmed him taking the man's handcuffs off, letting him go, again without explanation. He was a cop, why explain to these illegals—*he was safe*. Joseph drove to an unlit park in southwest Houston, where he brutally raped the still handcuffed victim multiple times, including once on the trunk of his patrol car. Finished, he let her go, and the troubled young woman made her way home on foot (Daily Mail Reporter, September 4, 2012).

The victim recounted the ordeal to her aunt and uncle. As she relayed the details of her savage kidnapping and rape, they noticed bruise marks on her wrists, arms, and legs. At first, they could not believe the incredible tale. They never believed a police officer would do such a thing. Finally, the hysterical victim persuaded her relatives to drive back to the park and look for evidence. They found tire tracks, indications of a struggle, and what appeared to be body fluids. Conflicted, they debated calling the police. They feared the police would come, accuse the victim of lying and have her deported. Finally, after heated arguments, they called the police. The uncle waited at the crime scene for the police while the aunt and the victim went to the hospital.

The Houston PD detectives, contrary to the family's expectations, believed the victim. The crime scene investigation and witness interview by HPD's elite Special Crimes Division and Internal Affairs Division found cause to relieve Joseph of his police duties that day. He was subsequently indicted and fired. During the pre-trial investigation and publicity, four women came forward with allegations of similar rapes by Officer Abraham Joseph. The new victims were all illegal immigrants, working in nightclubs in the southwest section of Houston. He threatened them with deportation if they complained. One victim claimed Joseph raped her twice, telling her each time she had outstanding warrants and would go to jail and be deported if she did not have sex with her. She became pregnant and aborted the pregnancy. At trial, the prosecutor told the jury Joseph targeted women in the country illegally stating, "These Hispanic women are trash to him. They don't even belong. He can rape them and dispose of them, and they wouldn't dare tell. He's a Houston police officer" (Daily Mail Reporter, September 4, 2012).

Joseph miscalculated with his last victim and paid for it. After a month-long trial, former Houston Police PD Abraham Joseph was convicted and received the maximum sentence of two life sentences. Joseph cried at his sentence, and his wife collapsed. His last courageous victim sat on the front row with a huge smile on her face. She later said through an interpreter "I want to thank God, first of all, the district of attorney, the jurors. And all the people that believed me because I just told the truth. And I am very pleased because justice has been made" (KHOU Staff, October 9, 2012).

# NYPD Wilfredo Rosario—Community Policing Gone Awry

"The truth will come out," Wilfredo Rosario told NY Supreme Court Justice Daniel Fitzgerald.

"Mr. Rosario, the truth did come out," Justice Fitzgerald fired back. "You've stained the reputation of every decent, hardworking police officer on the force." (Eligon, August 6, 2010)

This exchange took place after the second conviction for a series of sexual assaults committed by former NYPD Community Affairs officer Wilfredo Rosario. Rosario's first conviction took place in January 2010 for an official misconduct and attempted coercion complaint lodged against Rosario in 2002. The eight-year hiatus occurred because the 2002 complaint was not acted upon until another woman complained in 2008.

In 2002, Rosario, a 10-year NYPD veteran, father of five, and Marine veteran of Desert Storm, and his partner approached a car parked after hours in Riverside Park. The victim, then 18 years old, and a male friend were in the car. After separating the two, officers questioned each. Rosario began by asking the girl routine questions, age, name, address, and phone number, before switching to personal questions, "Were you going to make out? Were you going to have sex? Are you a Virgin?" Then, he asked the shocked teenager would she perform oral sex on him. If she did, he wouldn't have to tell her parents, and he would throw away the summons he was writing. Recognizing the dangerous situation she was in, she devised a strategy.

She promised to comply at a later date and engaged him in conversation. Eight years later, she testified, "I just wanted to keep him talking," she told jurors, "I'm so used to television shows and movies that when you keep them talking, you're safe." She asked his name. He said his nickname was Buddha. Feigning a bad memory, she asked him to write it down. He complied misspelling it in block letters—BUDDAH—on a scrap of paper. She gave the scrap of paper to NYPD investigators later. The same scrap of paper was introduced into evidence eight years after the incident. She and Rosario agreed to meet the following day.

Instead, the young girl reported him to the Civilian Complaint Review Board (CCRB) several days later. Her complaint of solicited oral sex was not acted upon, probably because she admitted on cross-examination eight years later she had left it out of her email to the CCRB. She had also not mentioned in her first taped interview with detectives that Rosario promised to tear up the summons in exchange for oral sex, the key element in a sexual coercion charge. Rosario was convicted on the 2002 charges and immediately fired, however; sentencing was delayed until the outcome of his second trial.

May 18, 2010, was not a good day for the NYPD, former NYPD officer Wilfredo Rosario convicted of official misconduct and attempted coercion the past January was on trial in Manhattan for sexually assault-ing two women (Sulzberger and Eligon, May 18, 2010). Across the bridge in Brooklyn, NYPD Narcotics Detective Oscar Sandino was arraigned in federal court for violating the civil rights of two women by using the threat of arrest to coerce them into sex acts. In February 2010, the 13-year veteran narcotics detective arrested a woman and her boyfriend on drug charges following a raid. At the precinct, Detective Sandino told her she would lose custody of her children unless she had sex with him. She complied. After her release, Sandino told her he expected her to continue having sex with him and began calling her. She called the NYPD's Internal Affairs Division, which began an inves-tigation. The investigation revealed two more allegations of coerced sex. One involved the cousin of a man Sandino arrested on drug charges in 2006. He told the cousin if she didn't have sex with him, her cousin would receive a "lengthy sentence." On September 7, 2010, Sandino pleaded guilty to federal misdemeanor charges, was suspended from the NYPD, and agreed not to fight the dismissal proceedings.

In Manhattan, Wilfredo Rosario's second trial began. One woman testified Rosario had approached her on the street and began a conversa-tion. She told him she wanted a job as a school crossing guard, and she wanted to get her son into after-school programs. Rosario told her since he was a Community Affairs officer he could help. He got her name and address. The next day he appeared unannounced at the woman's apartment, claiming to have application forms for her to fill out. She let him in, and he began fondling her and then raped her. After he left, he called her from the precinct and threatened her if she reported the sexual assault. According to court documents, "I know where you live. Don't' tell anybody what has happened," were his exact words. A second victim claimed Rosario lured her into his car with promises to help her find work. He then drove to a secluded area, touched her breasts, forced her to kiss him, and touch his erect penis while his pants were unzipped.

At trial, Rosario denied the accusations and claimed the NYPD was trying to frame him because he was part of a successful racial discrimination suit against the department. The prosecution countered this. The prosecuting attorney citing the possibility of additional victims called Rosario a "selfish, narcissistic predator." He went on to say "He thought he could victimize them without consequence," and added. "He thought they were people who would never report what happened to them, or no one would believe even if they did." The jury convicted Rosario, and he was sentenced to five years in prison. The conviction for the 2002 incident was included in the sentence. The police officer miscalculated in choosing victims and one where earlier department action might have prevented further misconduct.

## Pittsburg, Pennsylvania—Adam Skweres—Consequences of Failure to Act

Pittsburg PD Officer Adam Skweres was arrested in 2012 and charged with bribery, coercion, official oppression, and indecent assault for a series of sexual assaults that occurred as early as 2008. The time lag between complaint and charge led the executive director of the Pittsburg Citizen Police Review to opine that it was a very unsettling situation. "That time frame is concerning." Equally disturbing is Skweres first attempt to join the PPD when the city's psychologist deemed him "not psychologically suited for police work" (Harding, February 23, 2012).

The psychologist determined he was unfit after reviewing Skweres background investigation file, which included what neighbors, and others said about him, his financial history, and a personal interview. He also examined the results of a polygraph exam and the results of a written psychological test. Skweres appealed the psychologist's findings and his rejection to the civil service board. The city appointed another psychologist who found him suited. The city's psychologist, who had examined Pittsburg police candidates for 20 years, declined to comment to press inquiries, other than to say he was disappointed. Events would show that the original rejection was the correct finding. Careful vetting is an absolute necessity in the police hiring process. Identifying and dealing with problem officers are also necessary. The Pittsburg Police Department, in Skweres's case, disregarded both of these essential practices and paid dearly for their actions or inactions.

Officer Skweres, an Iraq war veteran, honorably discharged as s staff sergeant, had five years on the Pittsburg PD at the time of his arrest. However, he was a known problem officer. Skweres had 18 months on the job when the first complaint against him was made. His victim was driving to work when a motorcyclist hit her car. Officer Skweres arrived, and she admitted to no insurance and a suspended license. He pulled her aside and told her she was in a lot of trouble, but he could fix it and made several sexual advances. Claiming she was late for work and had to go, Skweres let her go with a threat: "If you say anything about this I'll make sure you never walk, talk, or breath again." He then wrote his cell phone number, work phone number, extension number, and badge number on a piece of paper from his police notepad. She told her boss what happened, and he convinced her to report the sexual advances it. She contacted the police and met with a detective and female officer and took a polygraph test. The results were inconclusive. The victim never heard from the police until Skweres's arrest in 2012.

A second complaint, also in 2008, occurred when a woman was in court testifying as a victim in one of his cases. Skweres called her outside the courtroom to talk privately. He told the women he knew she and her husband were having child custody problems and he could help her out. Help came with conditions. He would write a positive letter to the county's Office of Children, Youth, and Families if she would give him oral sex. A negative letter would be sent if she turned him down. The woman filed a complaint with the Pittsburg Police Department but never heard from them.

A third complaint was filed against Officer Skweres in December 2011. The rogue officer appeared at the victim's house and offered to help her boyfriend who had been recently arrested. In order to receive his help, the woman had to strip and perform oral sex. She declined and offered to expose her buttocks to him "in order to satisfy him" she wrote in her complaint. The fourth complaint and the one resulting in his arrest occurred on February 11, 2012. Skweres had arrested a woman's boyfriend several months earlier. He promised to help him out if she performed oral sex. She resisted and Skweres unclipped his holster to frighten the woman. She performed oral sex on him, and then he cleaned himself with a paper towel and left. The distraught woman reported her sexual assault to the FBI. An outside agency was now involved (Gurman and Ward, February 17, 2012). This complaint from an outside government agency prompted a full-scale investigation by the police department. Five days later, Skweres was fired.

The city defended their inaction on the other complaints by saying that it wasn't until the fourth complaint that there was enough "hard evidence" to make an arrest and take him off the street. Dr. Samuel Walker, a national expert on police misconduct, commented on the city's inaction: "Common sense would say if you have suspicions about this person's conduct, you take [him] off the street, period. If there were two [complaints] back in 2008, that raises the significance of it even further. There should have been something done" (Fisher, August 14, 2014).

Skweres spent almost a year under house arrest with electronic monitoring before he appeared in court. An additional woman came forward, raising Skweres's "known" victim count to five. He pleaded guilty to all counts and received a sentence of 3 ½ years to 8 years in prison and lifetime registration as a sex offender. Whether or not this punishment fits his crimes in open to debate.

## Broward County, Florida Jonathan Bleiweiss—Same-Sex Sexual Predator

Eight months before his ignoble arrest, Deputy Sheriff Jonathan Bleiweiss was nominated for Employee of the Year by supervisors and faced 15–20 other nominees for the prestigious award (Anonymous, August 8, 2009). He finished first on the secret ballots. He responded by saying "I think it shows how far we've come in the world when a police worker, an openly gay officer, could achieve an award like this." He pointed out things had changed since he became a Broward County Sheriff's Office—BSO—employee in 2002 and endured a sergeant making jokes about him, calling him a "sex offender." He was touted in newspapers as a pioneering openly gay police officer. Bleiweiss and the BSO did not know a tsunami of condemnation was coming.

At the time the award nomination and selection process were going on, Deputy Sheriff Jonathan Bleiweiss was stalking illegal immigrants, stopping them and performing sex acts with them and demanding their phone numbers and other contact information to set up future liaisons. The men were chosen because Bleiweiss knew they would not report him—*safe targets*. They feared not being believed and retaliated against by being deported. He also knew shame and embarrassment would come from their peers in the Hispanic community (Mayo, February 16, 2015). This was a vulnerable pool and Bleiweiss knew it. He was safe; at least, he thought he was.

In April 2009, an investigation was opened after complaints came to the sheriff's office from an attorney saying a BSO deputy was sexually abusing undocumented immigrants from El Salvador and Mexico during traffic stops (Anonymous, August 8, 2009). In July, eight victims made a positive identification of Bleiweiss from a photo lineup. In August, he was arrested on 14 charges, including three counts of sexual battery by a person in authority, four counts of battery, and one count of stalking. There was a pattern to his sexual depravations.

Victims were fondled during early morning traffic stops. He coerced most of the men and one minor to engage in oral sex with him with the possibility of deportation. Some were forced to give cell phone numbers and agree to future sexual encounters. They complied because they feared reprisal. One illegal Mexican immigrant told investigators he had five separate sexual incidents with the deputy. He pleaded for Bleiweiss to stop because he only liked women. Another man, also an undocumented Mexican immigrant, reported assaults on three occasions. The minor, a teen from Mexico, said Bleiweiss fondled and masturbated him on two occasions.

Bleiweiss was held without bond in protective custody awaiting trial. The State's Attorney fearing victims would not testify if their names became public requested identifying information be excluded from trial and a gag order imposed on what the lawyers could say about the victims. His unnamed victims had already been humiliated on Spanish language TV. The judge denied the request, stating, "I don't see any reason for imposing any special restrictions or closings in this case."

After a state habeas corpus hearing, Bleiweiss was granted bail in January 2010 and moved to Oregon living with his father while awaiting trial. In 2013, he moved to San Francisco. When the cases went to trial in February 2015, most of his victims had been deported. Those remaining in the United States were reluctant to testify and many witnesses could not be found. Most of the civil suits filed against Bleiweiss and Broward County were dismissed. The end result was predictable, a plea deal. Bleiweiss pleaded guilty to 14 counts of false imprisonment, 15 counts of battery, and four counts of stalking. His deal involved five years imprisonment and no sex offender status and 10-year probation after finishing his sentence. The prosecutor declared, "After six years, it was the best and the most just and fair resolution that the state could come up with." Probably so, Deputy Sheriff Jonathan Bleiweiss' careful selection of victims saved him from being labeled a sex offender the rest of his life and spending the rest of his life in prison—victims refused to testify.

## San Diego, California—Anthony Arevalos—Known Sexual Predator

San Diego, California, is considered to be one of the nations safest city—a low crime and victimization rate. Safe unless you were a female partying in the popular downtown Gaslamp Quarter from 2009 to 2011 and encountered the officer known by his peers as "The Los Colinas Transport Unit"—Los Colinas Detention Facility (jail). San Diego PD Officer Anthony Arevalos, 18-year veteran, married and father of two, was well known for targeting attractive female drivers and arresting more women than any of his peers. It was known that he took lewd pictures of women he stopped and showed them to fellow officers (Stickney, November 14, 2011). Those allegations included pictures of women giving him oral sex in the back seat of his police vehicle. He showed off women's driver's licenses like trophies.

Court records revealed several officers refused to work with him or assist him in arrests because they feared his sexual misconduct would get them fired. Yet he was never formally reported or investigated—*peer group support for police occupation deviance*. The knowledgeable officers had the prescience to know that sooner or later Arevalos was going down hard. That happened on November 17, 2011, when a jury found him guilty of eight felony charges of sexual battery, assault, and soliciting sexual bribes from five women. He was sentenced to eight years and eight months in prison. His trial and conviction was the inevitable result of his known pattern of sexual misconduct and the police department's failure to take appropriate action. His pattern of behavior fits into the characteristics of police sexual predators.

Officer Arevalos worked a special unit in the San Diego PD traffic division, a proactive unit patrolling for drunk drivers, paying extra and overtime. Working alone, he picked and chose who and when to stop a suspected drunk driver. San Diego's party district, Gaslamp Quarter, was like shooting fish in a barrel. He offered attractive women a way out of arrests. He was assigned to this special unit even though, or some allege because, his supervisors knew of his bizarre sexual habits—*known disturbed inclination*. In 1998, he admitted to flirting with a woman with mental disabilities in the backseat of his patrol car. The officer assisting him on the call testified in a civil suit that Arevalos' behavior beyond flirting (Moran, March 29, 2013). He testified Arevalos took pictures of the nude woman as she masturbated with a police baton in the back seat of a police vehicle. "He had his Polaroid out and when I got there the female was in the back seat naked with her handcuffs in front of her and she had the baton" he said. The officer reported Arevalos to his supervisor who gave Arevalos a verbal warning for an obvious firing offense—*bureaucratic cover-up of known police sexual offender creating a real or perceived low risk for such deviant acts*.

His next PSM violations were similarly mishandled. In 2007, Arevalos was caught viewing pornography on a department computer on duty. The same year, a father also complained of the way Arevalos handled the traffic stop of his 16-year-old daughter. She was returning from the beach dressed in a bikini top and short skirt. Arevalos stopped her to inform her that her registration tags were going to expire soon, "chicken crap" pretext stop (police argot). Arevalos made her bend over in front of him. The girl said the experience "creeped" her out. Arevalos was issued a verbal warning for both transgressions. However, as a result of these complaints, Arevalos was transferred to the traffic division as punishment—a common practice in departments where the traffic division is considered a lessor assignment than patrol. Within two years, he was working the special DUI unit that expanded his opportunities for predatory sexual abuse among a larger pool of vulnerable victims. Buoyed by the department's inaction toward his sexual misconduct, he continued his aberrant behavior.

At trial, a 26-year-old female bartender testified that in September 2009, she closed up a Gaslamp Quarter restaurant, slammed down several drinks, and drove off. She inadvertently drove the wrong way on a one-way street and was stopped by Officer Arevalos. He took her to the station for a breath test. She read double the legal limit (Stickney, November 14, 2011). Instead of booking her he drove back to the woman's car, all the while pressuring her for sex in exchange for letting her go. She didn't promise anything. He said he would come to her restaurant and collect on what she owed. She reported the contact to a detective friend who said she should call internal affairs. She did not report it again until Arevalos was arrested. When asked to comment on the detective's failure to report Arevalos' complaint, an assistant chief demurred and said it was unclear whether the detective's inaction violated department policy.

In February 2010, Arevalos arrested a woman for drunken driving after she was involved in a single-car crash. She testified in a civil suit deposition that he took her to the Las Colinas jail. On the way to the jail, he stopped his car and sexually assaulted her by inserting his hand in her vagina. The woman filed a complaint that night. Two days later, she called to check on the status of her complaint and was told there was no record of it. After Arevalos was arrested in March 2011, departmental officials told newspaper reporters her complaint was investigated and turned over to the District Attorney's Office, which decided not to file charges. Another missed opportunity to end Arevalos' sexual depravations. His sexual assaults continued.

In October 2010, Arevalos stopped a suspected DUI driver. He asked about her private body parts, touched her breasts, and put his hand down her pants. He told her if she flashed her breasts, he would let her go. The woman flashed him, and he put his hand in her pants and moved it from front to back. Arevalos called her a cab and let her go. The next month, Arevalos stopped a 20-year-old San Diego State University student at 1:30 a.m. as she left a Gaslamp Quarter bar. Following her arrest, he made improper suggestions of things she could do to get out of the arrest. Then, in January 2011 Arevalos arrested a young female coming out of a nightclub. After he handcuffed her, the women testified he asked her twice what she had to "offer" him. He added that sometimes women offered things to him to help himself. She did not offer him anything to "keep my dignity." Two months later, Arevalos predatory sexual behavior finally came to an end.

March 8, 2011, was the night of Mardi Gras in the Gaslamp Quarter. Arevalos following his usual pattern stopped a thirty-one-year-old woman leaving a nightclub for failure to use a turn signal, a "chicken crap" pretext stop. The woman tested over the legal limit for blood-alcohol content. He asked her what she would do to make the DUI arrest go away and suggested she give him her panties. She agreed and Arevalos took her to a bathroom of a nearby 7–11 convenience store. They both entered the bathroom—captured on surveillance tape—where the woman removed her panties and Arevalos digitally penetrated her vagina. Arevalos conducted another breathalyzer test, and the woman tested under the legal limit. He allowed her to leave. Then the incident turned bizarre.

An hour after letting her go Arevalos sent the woman a text message: "This is officer Anthony....let me know when you get to work safely...then you can erase this and I will contact you at the end of the month;" The woman responded-OK. The next day the victim filed a complaint with the San Diego PD (SAPD). The investigating detective and the victim set up a recorded phone call to Officer Arevalos (Kemp, February 5, 2014). The phone call contained the following incriminating statements:

> *Victim to Arevalos*: "You're a cop, you're a little intimidating, it's a little overwhelming. I was standing there with no panties on."
> *Officer Arevalos*: "I know that. You're a grown woman. You handled it very well."
> *Victim*: "What did you like best?"
> *Arevalos*: "You know what I liked the best? When the shirt came up and the pants went down, I didn't expect your body to be as nice and wonderful as it was."

On March 11, 2011, Arevalos was arrested and charged with the sexual assault and the SAPD put his picture in the paper and asked for other victims to come forward. They did.

On November 17, 2011, Arevalos was found guilty on eight felony charges, acquitted on eight charges, and a mistrial declared on one count where the jury could not reach a unanimous vote. He was also found guilty of four counts that were reduced to misdemeanors. During the trial, the defense argued that the women were too intoxicated, emotional, and vengeful during the traffic stops to accurately know what happened. Obviously, why Arevalos chose them. He was sentenced to eight years and eight months in prison. Thirteen women filed suits against the City of San Diego claiming that the City and police department knew or should have known he was a danger to women and failed to take action against him. The police department countered that the complaints never reached the top; however, they settled and promised to deal with the issue. Twelve of those suits were settled for a total of $2.3 million. The remaining suit, involving his last victim, was settled right before trial for $5.9 million (Sklar, October 28, 2014).

The City reacted by appointing the city's first female chief of police—the current chief abruptly resigned—and asked for a Department of Justice review of the San Diego Police Department (Watson, March 24, 2014). The federal audit made 40 recommendations to improve recruiting, hiring, training, and supervision all aimed at identifying problem officers more quickly. Eighteen DUI arrests made by Arevalos were vacated. New SAPD policy required two officers to accompany females in custody. A mandatory reporting policy for police misconduct was implemented. The new female chief began testing the wearing of body cameras, and all patrol officers were to be equipped with body cameras by the end of 2015. Body cameras are a useful, but not perfect by itself, technical supervisory assist in preventing police sexual abuse. They like digital audio recorders must be turned on to be useful.

## Fullerton, California—Albert Rincon—Digital Audio Recorder—Technical Supervisory Assist

Fullerton, California, a city with a checkered past when it comes to allegations of police misconduct, had policies in place to deter or prevent police sexual misconduct. Police department policy stated that "whenever practical" pat-downs of detained persons should be done by an officer of the same gender as the person being searched. If not possible to have a same-sex officer to do the pat-down, a witness officer is to be present. Court testimony revealed a second department policy required officers to wear a digital audio recorder (DAR) and turn it on whenever they made contact with a suspect (Staff, September 30, 2011). Officers were required to transfer audio files from the DAR to the City's computer at the end of each shift. The DAR is a valuable tool that provides unobtrusive ear evidence to law enforcement citizen interactions. It, like a body camera, provides evidence to support the officer's or complainant's version of a hostile/disputed incident. The DAR tells the truth. The DAR is also less expensive than body cameras—less than one hundred dollars.

However, policies are of no effect if individual officers do not adhere to them and supervisors do not enforce them. They are often all show for public relations purposes. This was the case in Fullerton's police department. Officer Albert Rincon admitted in five years with the Fullerton PD he never called for a female officer to pat down a female he detained, creating a *real or perceived low risk for PSM*. No one ever checked. Rincon also turned off his DAR at some time during female detentions. The investigating officer testified at deposition: "I know that in dealing with this case, there always seemed to be a point where [the DAR] would go off." Judge Guilford, the federal judge at the summary judgment hearing, pointed out that turning the DAR off rather than forgetting to turn it on indicated, "Rincon chose to leave no audio recording of the arrest" (Bode & Nastashi v. City of Fullerton et al. SACV 1-835 AG [MLGx]). Thus, deliberate attempts to hide the nature of the encounters. Rincon offered no explanation for turning the DAR off. A simple audit—routine risk management—would have put the brakes on Rincon's predatory sexual abuse. This demonstrates organizational indifference to a known police problem.

Fullerton PD Officer Albert Rincon was never criminally charged with any of the alleged sexual assaults; therefore, we rely on information contained in the successful civil suit filed by two of his victims to describe the alleged depravity of his behavior. Court documents detail the complaints against Officer Rincon starting with an incident on August 1, 2008 (Bode & Nastashi v. City of Fullerton et al. SACV 10-835). Officer Rincon allegedly entered a bar where a female bartender worked and asked if she was on probation. She replied yes, and he searched her purse and the surrounding area. He claimed to have found a small amount of illegal drugs in the surrounding area and handcuffed the female and placed her in the back seat of his patrol car. He then, according to testimony, proceeded to pat down the woman by running his hands over her breasts and running his hands over her legs and cupping her groin area. He put the seat belt on the woman, exposing her right breast and refusing to cover it. He then made comments on her "nice" breasts. On the ride to the station, he asked the woman for oral sex in exchange for releasing her. She refused. At the station, Rincon allegedly grabbed the handcuffed woman and cupped her groin and digitally penetrated her vagina with his middle finger. After her release, Officer Rincon allegedly repeatedly harassed the woman at her workplace and asked to be her friend and engage in sex acts. The woman was interviewed by an Internal Affairs detective in November 2008, booked, and appeared at a preliminary hearing where all charges were dropped for insufficient evidence for a criminal trial. This was the basis for the civil suit.

Officer Rincon pulled over the second plaintiff in the civil suit on November 14, 2008, for allegedly driving with her headlights off—a "chicken-crap" offense. Rincon administered several field sobriety tests. According to testimony, the tests indicated the woman was sober and Rincon called another officer to administer an additional alcohol test. In spite of the evidence to the contrary, Rincon arrested the woman for DUI and put her in his police vehicle. During the pat-down search in the back seat, Rincon allegedly groped the woman and digitally penetrated her vagina. In putting the seat belt on his victim, Rincon allegedly forced the woman's shirt and bra over her chest, exposing the woman's breasts. Rincon allegedly offered to drop the charges if he would arrange a date with her daughter who had been in the vehicle when she was stopped. She refused. The woman was booked and appeared at a preliminary hearing where the Orange County District Attorney dropped all charges for lack of sufficient evidence to file a criminal complaint.

The City of Fullerton contacted the Orange County District Attorney's Office on November 17, 2008, and asked that one of their investigators examine the sexual abuse allegations against Officer Rincon and determine if he should face criminal charges. The City placed Rincon on administrative leave pending the outcome of the investigation. The investigator decided to review other women arrested by Rincon in 2008. He was able to identify twelve women and interview seven of them. The seven women alleged Rincon had sexually violated them in some way. Five of the seven women were never prosecuted for their arrests.

A similar pattern of sexual misconduct became evident. Officer Rincon would detain or arrest women and make sexual propositions or inappropriately touch them or both. There was never a female officer or a witness during any of the pat-downs. Finally, Rincon would turn his DAR off at some time during the arrest or detention. The results of the investigation were sent to the District Attorney's Office who, for some unknown reason, decided not to seek criminal charges.

The City of Fullerton conducted its own disciplinary investigation, listing all seven allegations of sexual misconduct against Officer Rincon. The City found that there was "no evidence of improper conduct" in six of the seven allegations. Instead of firing Rincon, he was given two reprimands for violating the DAR policy, one reprimand for violating the pat-down policy and one reprimand for misplacing one of his victim's drivers license. He was ordered to receive training on pat-downs and the importance of using gender assistance and keeping his DAR activated during searches. The handling of the Rincon allegations led the federal judge in the civil suit to conclude: "At the end of the day, the City [Fullerton, CA] put Rincon back onto the streets to continue arresting women despite a pattern of sexual harassment allegations. A reasonable juror could conclude, based on the facts, that the City did not care about what its officers did to women during arrest" (Bode & Nastashi v. City of Fullerton et al. SACV 10-835).

The City of Fullerton settled the civil suit for $350,000. Although Albert Rincon was never charged with any PSM offenses, he no longer works for the Fullerton PD. The city did take action to prevent any more real or alleged police sexual misconduct. In 2014, the Fullerton City Council approved $650,354 to purchase body cameras for all its police officers. The body cameras would replace the DARs and record all public contacts, including use of force incidents. In February 2015, the Fullerton PD became the first police department in Orange County, California, to equip all its officers with body cameras that record video and audio.

# Rogue Police Department—Maywood, California—Serial Sexual Predators the Norm?

"The Maywood Police Department has failed to consistently follow generally accepted hiring practices in evaluating applicants for the position of police officer and has failed to screen out and disqualify individuals who are not suited to perform the duties of a police officer."

*In the Matter of the Investigation of the City of Maywood Police Department.* California Attorney General's Final Report 2009.

The Attorneys General's investigation followed a scandal revealing the MPD towed and impounded 17,773 vehicles during the time period under investigation. There was a quota system in effect, 2-car minimum each shift per officer. Targets for the city's revenue-generating campaign were Hispanic, poor, and undocumented immigrants. Adding fuel to the clamor for an investigation was an unsuccessful recall of three of the five City Council members, including the Mayor and Vice Mayor. There was a good reason for the recall vote. The three council members voted to hire, a new chief of police without a background check, according to the state investigation.

The investigation revealed the chief in question was a former Maywood police officer that was convicted of falsifying overtime records while employed by the Los Angeles Police Department—*gypsy cop*. The new chief had also been a college instructor until terminated for acts of dishonesty. The chief in question replaced a chief who resigned after allegations of domestic violence. Several months after his hiring, the newly selected chief resigned following allegations of sex on duty. Enough was enough. California's Attorney General announced a "top to bottom" review of the police department after the towing and hiring scandals and accusations of sexual misconduct, racism, and brutality among the officers in this small suburb southeast of Los Angeles. Maywood was a troubled city with a sordid history.

Maywood, California, was known as the last resort for California's Gypsy Cops. Maywood PD's sorry reputation resulted from the departments hiring practices, poor supervision, absence of training, no early warning system to identify problem officers, nonexistent complaint system, and no personnel directive system of policies and procedures. Maywood Police Department was a rogue police department, a refuge for misfit police officers.

The rogue police department hired police officers that could not be hired by another agency because of their questionable backgrounds or poor character (Glover and Lait, April 2, 2007). Examples included a Los Angeles deputy sheriff terminated for abusing jail inmates, a LAPD officer fired for intimidating a witness, and a former Huntington Park, California officer charged with negligently shooting a handgun and driving drunk. One officer had been terminated by the Los Angeles

County Sheriff's Office for "bizarre behavior and unprofessional conduct." Another officer rejected by 25 other police departments was hired by the Maywood Police Department. A third of the police force had troubled pasts with other police agencies. Their hiring was justified by a Maywood police chief with a checkered past of domestic violence as "Its OK to give a person a second chance if you learn from your mistake." Their behavior did not improve in Maywood after their "second chance" as the Gypsy Cops built up a history of misconduct and crime. Why would a police department engage in such egregious hiring practices?

In order to save money, MPD conducted superficial, or no, background checks. Certified police officers were allowed to laterally transfer without MPD checking to see if charges were pending. This was a boon to the agency, no reason to send an already certified officer to the academy, a significant saving in money and lost time. Another cost-cutting measure dispensed with the requirement of pre-employment polygraph examination. Does the practices save money? In the long run, hiring Gypsy Cops ends up being costly to the agency in terms of criminal and civil liability. According to published reports that happened, when Maywood, California Police Department hired Ryan Allen West. West had just resigned amid allegations of misconduct from the Brawley, California Police Department.

West wasted no time getting back into trouble. In 2006, he was accused, along with two other Maywood officers of handcuffing two students outside a bar and using a Taser gun on their genitals. No action was taken against him or the other officers. Later, in March 2008, he was charged with 12 felonies, including rape, assault by a public officer, burglary, and multiple accounts of sexual assault. One victim claimed West approached her and threatened to arrest her because of an outstanding warrant unless she met him at a local hotel. West admitted meeting the woman at the hotel but said the encounter and sex were consensual. The investigation led to other victims and West was fired. At the time of his appearance in court in June 2013, West had been charged with sexually assaulting five women on duty in 2006 and 2007. He pleaded no contest to five felonies, two counts of rape, and three counts of penetration with a foreign object and was sentenced to 19 years in prison (AP, June 4, 2013). Civil suits are pending.

In 2010, the city finally gave up its efforts to reform it police department when its liability insurance was canceled because of excessive civil damages paid. The California Joint Powers Insurance Authority terminated general liability and workers compensation coverage because the city posed too high a risk. The city had no choice but to disband its police department. As one councilman put it, "We have no alternative. Nobody will insure us, not as long as we have the police department" (Vives, June 17, 2010). The city of Maywood disbanded its police department and contracted with the Los Angeles Sheriff's Department (LASD) for police services.

The LASD is the largest sheriff's department in the world employing 18,000 deputies (www.lasd.org). The LASD contracts with 42 cities within the county for police services, patrols 130 unincorporated communities, and provides services such as jails, laboratories, and academy training for smaller cities in the county. There are numerous small cities in the United States that would benefit from disbanding their police departments and contracting with a larger agency for police services.

# Conclusion

### PSM Causal Equation: Inclination + Opportunity + Real or Perceived Risk = PSM.

The chapter once again points to the consequences of poor or nonexistent accepted police hiring practices—no or lax background checks of prospective police officers. This allows individual's with the *inclination* for sexual misconduct to enter the *policework* occupation. We saw the disastrous consequences of Gypsy officers who are allowed to continue their deviant sexual behavior in other agencies. The identified pool of vulnerable pool of targets—*opportunity*—includes same-sex victims. The *real or perceived low risk* for PSM was shown to be exacerbated by the organizations culture—code of silence and peer group support—and failure to identify and disciple malefactors. It is clear that sexual inclination and racial, ethnic, and status, profiling coupled with aggressive reactive policing strategies leads to law enforcement sexual misconduct under real or perceived low-risk conditions. We will see these conditions and combination of conditions in the following chapters. This chapter also introduced the existence of *technological supervisory assists* such as body and dash cameras and GPS devices in the discussion to prevent, control, and punish PSM.

# References

Anonymous. (2009, August 8). Broward deputy charged with sexually assaulting illegal aliens. *Examiner.com.*

Anonymous. (2010, January 11). Timeline of Marcus Jackson case. *WBTV.*

Anonymous. (2012, March 3). Report says Alaska Department knew cop had sex on job. *Officer.com.*

Anonymous. (2013, February 26). California officer accused in rash of on-duty sex. *The Sacramento Bee.*

AP. (2013, June 4). LA-area police officer pleads no contest to 5 on-duty sex assaults gets 19 years in prison. *Associated Press.*

Barker, T. (2011). *Police ethics: Crisis in law enforcement* (3rd ed.). Springfield, ILL: Charles C. Thomas.

Bordon, A., Chin, T., Golnzales, K., & Law, N. (2014). Trial begins for officer accused of sexual assault on duty. *DavisVanguard.org.*

Buettner, R. (2012, March 15). Facts conceded at officer's rape trial. *The New York Times.*

California Attorney General. (2009, March). In the matter if the investigation of the city of Maywood Police Department. *California Attorney General.*

Christensen, D. (2012, April 5). Miami cop Michael Ragusa raped dozens, new documents show. *Miami New Times.*

Crimesider Staff. (2012, May 7). Michael Pena. Former NYPD officer gets 25 years for sex attack. *CBS News.*

Daily Mail Reporter. (2011, September 21). Drunken police officer says he didn't rape teacher, but he was "cheating on his girlfriend". *Daily Mail.*

Daily Mail Reporter. (2012, September 4). Cop 'handcuffed waitress, drove her to secluded park and repeatedly raped her on trunk of his police cruiser'. *Daily Mail.*

Doll, J. (2012, March 30). A Jury's strange reason for refusing to convict on rape charges. *The Atlantic Wire.*

Dwyer, J. (2012, April 3). Juror's doubts outweighed their empathy. *The New York Times.*

Eligon, J. (2010, August 5). Judge sentences ex-officer to 5 years for sexual assault. *The New York Times*.

Fisher, J. (2014, August 21). Should cops accused of crime by citizens remain on duty. *Jim Fisher True Crime*.

Garcia. (2015, December 11). 13 black women on how an Oklahoma City police officer terrorized their neighborhood. *VOX*.

Glover, S., & Lait, M. (2007, April 2). Maywood police reforms promised. *LA Times*.

Grove, C. (2012, March 3). Report says Alaska Department knew cop had sex on job. *Anchorage Daily News*.

Grove, C. (2012, April 13). Rollins sentenced to 87 years in prison. *Anchorage Daily News*.

Gurman, S., & Ward, P. R. (2012, February 17). In complaint, cop says: Just let me have sex with you. *Pittsburg Post-Gazette*.

Harding, M. (2012, February 23). Would-be officer's psych exam appeal may have altered hiring policy. *Pittsburg Tribune-Review*.

Houston, F. (2007, March 20). Miami police officer arrested for kidnapping and attempted sexual assault. *Miami New Times*.

Kemp, J. (2014, February 5). San Diego cop who traded tickets fro sexual favors hoping to have conviction overturned as one lawyer claims corruption. *New York Daily News*.

KHOU Staff. (2012, October 9). Jurors sentence ex-HPD cop to life in prison for Raping waitress. *KHOU*.

Kovner, J. (2000, October 12). Former officer tied to killing evidence is revealed in court. *Hartford Courant*.

Kovner, J. (2001, May 1). Ex-city cop sentenced to 10 years. *Hartford Courant*.

Matos, M. (2010, April 29). Prosecutor says cop was serial rapist. *Courthouse News Service*.

Mayo, M. (2015, February 15). Why no sex offender for guilty cop? *Sun Sentinel*.

Moran, G. (2013, March 29). Victim: Misbehaving cop struck before. *The San Diego Union-Tribune*.

Rodriguez, I., Ortega, J., & Marino, J. (2009, August 5). Defenders, prosecutors review cases. *South Florida Sun-Sentinel*.

Ross, B., & Mcshane, L. (2012, June 21). Michael Pena, ex-NYPD cop, admits raping woman months after jury failed to convict him. *New York Daily News*.

Ruettner, R. (2012, May 7). Ex-officer sentenced to 75 years in prison for sexual assault. *The New York Times*.

Schwab, K. (2015, November 13). Holtzclaw trail delayed until accuser sobered up. *The Oklahoman.*

Sklar, D. L. (2014, October 28). Costly end to shameful episode: $5.9 M settles police sex case. *Times of San Diego.*

Staff. (2011, September 30). Federal judge calls Fullerton Police Department's handling of allegations of sexual misconduct by an officer 'shocking.' *OC Weekly.*

Stickney, R. (2011, November 14). Trouble behind the badge—Timeline: Anthony Arevalos sex assault trial. *NBCSanDiego.com.*

Strom, P. (2012, October 5). In wake of Anthony Rollins, Anchorage Police Department implements new policies. *Stromlaw.com.*

Sulzberger, A. G., & Eligon, J. (2010, May 18). 2 officers, 2 courts and charges of eliciting sexual favors. *The New York Times.*

Testa, J. (2014, September 5). How police caught the cop who allegedly sexually abused black women. *BuzzFeed.*

Vives, R. (2010, June 17). Maywood to disband police department. *Los Angles Times.*

Wagner, M. (2016, January 13). FBY digs for evidence at former Conn. home of ex-.cop suspected in daughter's 1997 disappearance, girlfriend's death. *New York Daily News.*

Walsh, D., & Stanton, S. (2015, October 22). West Sacramento to pay $2.8 million to victims of rapist police officer. *The Sacramento Bee.*

Watcher. (2007, March 21). Officer Michael Ragusa charged with attempted rape & kid. *PoliceCrimes.com.*

Watson, J. (2014, March 24). Feds probe San Diego police misconduct. *AP Online.*

Wikipedia. (2019, May 23). Daniel Holtzclaw.

*Yolanda v. City of Hartford et al.* (2004, August 2). Civil Action 3:00CV2386. US District Court: District of Connecticut.

Zanoni, C., Weiss, M., & Fractenberg, B. (2011, August 19). Off-duty cop accused of gunpoint rape in Inwood. *DNAInfo.*

# 5

# Type 3: Sexual Extortion aka Sexual Shakedowns

## Introduction

The evidence suggests that the most numerous form of police sexual abuse occurs when a law enforcement officer enters into a quid pro quo sexual relationship during "normal" routine duties. The sexual events are, for the most part, opportunistic and not the trolling or hunting incidents found in serial sexual predators, although pretext stops are in play in that type also. Pretext stops are common in contemporary, proactive aggressive police actions described as zero tolerance, stop and frisk, and quality of life policing. They are also a common complaint in over policed minority communities. Supposedly, in a pretext stop the officer has reasonable suspicion to suspect a crime has occurred or about to be committed. However, police sexual predators misuse pretext stops to find victims and engage in discriminatory police action. This is true in police agencies outside the United States.

Pretext stops during proactive police strategies are a real concern in UK police agencies where their misuse has been called into question as discriminatory or abuse for sexual purposes. Beginning in July 2017, all police forces in England and Wales must begin publishing a yearly

© The Author(s) 2020
T. Barker, *Aggressors in Blue*,
https://doi.org/10.1007/978-3-030-28441-1_5

analysis of their stop and search statistics and provide an explanation for any disproportionality. This yearly analysis is no silver bullet cure for police sexual encounters or discriminatory stops and searches, but pretext stop reform as proposed by the UK is a move to a solution. Such actions could identify problem officers and rogue police departments where "We can settle this" quid pro quo sexual shakedowns without the use or threat of violence become common practice, such as our first Illustrative Example.

## Irwindale, California—Sexual Shakedowns in a Rogue Police Department

The City of Irwindale, California, is one of 88 cities located in the San Gabriel Valley of Los Angeles County. In 2013, Irwindale's 24-person police department was known as a rogue police department where "a sizable number, if not the majority, of the police officers engage in corrupt activities and other forms of misconduct, including police sexual abuse" (Barker 2011: 81). From 2013 to 2015, there were 14 internal investigations underway, and three police officers were on administrative leave for multiple sexual abuse allegations: sexually assaulting women during traffic stops—Type 3, and inappropriate sexual relations with Police Explorer Scouts, and sexually harassing a female police cadet—Type 10 (Favot, October 22, 2013).

Community members called for the City Council to disband the disgraced police department and contract with the Los Angeles County Sheriff's Department for police services as was done in Maywood, California. Community action groups pointed to three patterns of police sexual abuse in the 2013—2015 time period—sexual shakedowns, sexual harassment, and police sexual abuse in police/community sponsored programs. Multiple patterns of police sexual abuse misconduct will not surface at the same time unless the police agency has a real ethical crisis (Barker 2011). The specific examples demonstrate the actions of a rogue police agency.

## Sexual Shakedowns—Type 3

In March 2014, Irwindale PD Sergeant David Paul Fraijo, 36, was arrested and charged with five felony counts including kidnapping to commit another crime, forcible oral copulation, oral copulation under color of authority, sexual battery by restraint, and assault under color of law (Anonymous, March 12, 2014). The allegations arose from a traffic stop Sgt. Fraijo made on a female newspaper delivery person in the early morning hours on October 20, 2012. Sgt. Fraijo asked for her driver's license. When she told him she didn't have one, he ordered her to drive to a parking lot where he sexually assaulted her. He fondled the woman's breasts and then forced her to touch, kiss, and orally copulate him. He pleaded not guilty to the charges and claimed consensual sex.

In January 2015, following plea bargain negotiations Fraijo pleaded no contest to one count each of oral copulation under color of authority and sexual battery by restraint (Anonymous, January 12, 2015). He was sentenced to 9 years in prison and to register as a sex offender for life. The city paid the victim $400,000 to settle her multi-million dollar civil suit.

## Sexual Abuse in Police/Community Sponsored Programs—Type 10

Officer Daniel Camerano, 27, an eight-year IPD veteran and adviser to the department's Police Explorer Program pleaded no contest to three felony counts: using a minor for sex acts, oral copulation of a person under 16 and contact with a minor for sexual offense (Anonymous, December 5, 2015). The charges related to sexual relationships with two teenage girls in the Explorer program. He had sexual relations with a 14-year-old girl between May 2009 and December 2012 and sent suggestive text messages to a 17-year-old girl in November 2012. He was sentenced to two years and eight months in prison and to register as a sex offender for life.

A civil suit filed on behalf of the 14-year-old girl alleged that Camerano molested the girl during "ride-alongs" where she and Camerano worked alone overnight in a patrol car. The suit alleged he molested the young girl in the station house "where other officers and supervisors knew or should have known" about the abuse—*peer group support.*

## Sexual Harassment—Type 7

A police cadet who worked at the Irwindale Police Department for four years sued Lt. Mario Camacho for sexual harassment (Flories, January 3, 2013). The alleged victim began working at the department as a police cadet in 2008. Lt. Camacho began holding her hand, kissing her, and groping her while they were on duty in his office and in patrol cars. At first, she rebuffed his advances, but he began treating her "mean" and created a "hostile work environment." When she relented, he promised her a permanent position and showered her with gifts. She alleged he lent her money and rented her a condo below market value. Lt. Camacho made her move out when her boyfriend moved into the condo. She resigned from the department and filed suit.

## Multiple Police Departments: Matthew Leavitt—Sexual Shakedowns and Gypsy Cop Merry-Go-Round

Matthew Leavitt is the poster example of "passing the trash" and its effects. Matthew Leavitt was a Rogue Police Officer and a Gypsy Cop; it was evident but ignored. On March 15, 2008, it was alleged in a civil suit that two Cedar Grove, West Virginia officers, Matthew Leavitt, and R. Curry, detained the plaintiffs without cause and then arrested a female and sexually assaulted her. Leavitt allegedly told the woman she would not have to go to jail if he had sex with her or she gave him oral sex. When she refused, she was taken to jail and again subjected to repeated sexual assaults. According to a timeline posted in the *Charleston Gazette* (Anonymous 2009), his background prior to this incident indicated the Cedar Grove PD or any police department should not have hired him—*poor vetting*. From November 2000 to June 2001, he was employed at the South Central Regional Jail. While working at the jail, he was arrested and fired for driving under the influence—June 25, 2001. Leavitt then joined the Army—December 2001 to December 2004. He was disciplined for drinking on duty in the Army. In spite of his firing from the jail and Army discipline, he was hired by the Cedar Grove PD in March 2005.

In April 2006, while a Cedar Grove officer, Leavitt was charged by the Charleston, West Virginia PD for assault during an off-duty bar fight. He left the Cedar Grove PD, reason not given, and was hired by the Madison, W.VA PD—*Gypsy Cop*. While at Madison PD, he was accused of harassing a woman, her boyfriend, and daughter after answering a call for service-June 13, 2006. Leavitt resigned August 2006 from the Madison PD and was hired by the Smithers W.VA PD—October 2006. One month later, November 6, 2006, the Mount Hope, W.VA PD, hired him. Eighteen days later, November 24, Leavitt left the Mount Hope PD and within five days—November 29—was hired by the Gauley Bridge W.VA PD. In January 2007, Leavitt was fired from the Gauley Bridge PD and hired in the same month by the Montgomery W.VA PD.

As a Montgomery PD officer, Leavitt was involved in at least three incidents involving excessive force and the use of racial epithets, one incident involved stopping a mixed-race couple and hitting the male on the head with a blackjack-a forbidden weapon-and spraying him in the eyes with pepper spray at close range. The victim's wife was subjected to improper sexual touching, licking on the neck and saying "Little whore, you know you like it like that." He was suspended for this incident and later fired. He was charged and convicted of federal law violations for this complaint.

It is difficult to comprehend the police work history of Matthew Leavitt, because he worked full-time at one department and part-time at another during the same time period, a common practice among small police departments in rural areas. However, it is clear that his behavior was erratic and involved repeated acts of sexual misconduct and brutality. He was a rogue police officer. The fragmented American system without national hiring and firing standards will always work against police sexual misconduct and other forms of police crime reforms.

The charges against his first victim when he was a Cedar Grove were dismissed, and she filed a civil suit against Leavitt and the department. On the second offense at Montgomery PD, Leavitt was sentenced to two years in prison after a guilty plea for using excessive force, intentional use of blackjack on a male suspect and unlawfully arresting his wife for DUI. They have filed a civil lawsuit against the city and the police department.

## Delcambre, Louisiana Officer Ernest Billiot—Sexual Shakedowns & Gypsy Cop

The town of Delcambre and the city of Jeanerette in Louisiana are small municipalities. Jeanerette has a police department of 26 sworn officers, and Delcambre PD has 5 sworn officers, including the chief. Delcambre Police Officer Ernest Billiot worked for both police departments. He was fired from the Jeanerette PD in 2005 after 10 years service when the mayor asked an outside consultant to review the police department and its operation. The outside consultant pointed out that Lt. Billiot was not able to carry a gun because he had pled guilty to a simple assault charge in 1999 (Randal, November 15, 2008). He was fired.

Billiot filed suit against the city of Jeanerette, claiming he was fired for arresting the mayor's grandson. He was hired by the Delcambre Police Department while the lawsuit was pending. According to court records, he stopped a female in the early morning hours as she drove through Delcambre on February 17, 2008. He told her he was taking her back to the police to administer a breath alcohol test—the department did not have a machine. At the station, he allegedly ordered the woman to undress for a strip search, while engaging in sexual comments. Billiot then drove the woman back to her car, kissed her, and asked for her phone number. She gave him a false number, which he wrote on his hand. He then let her go without charges.

The victim immediately called the state police and reported her sexual assault. Billiot was arrested and charged with sexual battery and kidnapping. He was fired immediately after a grand jury indicted him. He was convicted of second-degree kidnapping and sexual battery and sentenced to 10 years in prison. The victim sued Billiot, the police department, and the city, citing their indifference to his previous history as a contributing factor in her victimization. It is hard for a city or police department to defend against this charge when they knew, or should have known through a background check, not to hire a Gypsy Cop.

## El Cajon, California William Robert Taylor

William Robert Taylor was a three-year veteran of the El Cajon Police Department when he was arrested for sexually abusing seven women. The women all gave vivid accounts of his perverted sexual behavior. He forced them to perform sex acts on themselves, undress for him, or let him fondle them while he made lewd sexual comments. One woman, whom he arrested for shoplifting, testified he had her undress and masturbate with his baton in the back seat of his patrol car (Huard, February 27, 2007). Her DNA was found on the tip of his baton. To add insult to injury, he stole two knives from the woman before turning her loose. He allegedly forced an 18-year-old woman to undress while he masturbated. He was investigating the theft of two scooters at the time. He was accused of fondling several other women he stopped or arrested.

At trial, Taylor was convicted of five charges, petty theft for taking two knives from the woman he arrested and forced to masturbate with his baton—he was acquitted of that charge, two counts of requesting or receiving a bribe, sexual penetration under color of authority and sexual battery. He was sentenced to five years in prison. He was certainly a serial sexual predator, but he was not included in the previous chapter because no physical violence was alleged in his perverse acts.

## Wayne State University Gregory Gladden—Campus Police Sexual Shakedown

Gregory Gladden, a black 38-year-old Wayne State University police officer, pulled over a 22-year-old female on May 25, 2011. She was not a Wayne State University or employee. The events of that encounter are described in the court documents of his appeal from a 16–30 years sentence after his conviction for first-degree criminal sexual conduct (*People v. Gregory Alan Gladden* Wayne Circuit Court. LC No. 11-006508-FH).

\* \* \*

....On May 25, 2011, the victim was traveling in her car, turning from Trumbull onto Warren when she blew a tire after riding over the curb. She was driving on the rim when two separate police cars stopped her. Their lights were on, but the sirens were not activated. She thanked the officers for stopping and asked if one of the officers would follow her home, which was just a block away. Defendant [Gregory Gladden] who was one of the officers offered to escort her home. Once the other officer left the scene, defendant asked if she had been drinking; he told her he could smell it on her breath. The victim admitted she had. The victim did not have her license and offered her passport. Defendant did not ask her to perform any field sobriety tests. Defendant asked her to turn off her vehicle and step out of the vehicle. "[H]e said he was going to take me to a holding cell, call his boss and see if he could get me a deal." The victim was afraid an arrest record would "shatter my ability to pursue my career aspirations here in the city." She shared these concerns with the defendant. She got into the back of his SUV and did not think she had any choice. Defendant identified himself as "Derrick" from the Detroit police. He had a gun and a badge.

Defendant drove around for a while and eventually went to Manoogian Hall [on Wayne State campus]. The victim had not been there before. Defendant told her he was looking for a holding cell. He used a swipe card to access the locked building. They took an elevator to the fourth floor where there was a lounge. They both sat down on a couch. Defendant ordered the victim to stand up saying "I need to check you for weapons." The victim laughed and said, "I'm not even wearing any underwear." She was wearing only a sundress and flip-flops. She explained that she was trying to keep it light. "I wanted to get out with the least amount of confrontation possible and no brutality." The victim stood in a "T" position. Defendant ran his hands over her body and lingered at her breasts. The victim knew this was not a normal pat-down. Defendant told the victim he needed to remove her dress. Again, she did not feel like she had a choice and she complied. The victim was trying to figure out "what was going on." She asked the defendant if he wanted to have sex with her. It was not an offer. Defendant said "no." She asked if he wanted a "blow job" and he responded "yes," the victim put her dress back on. She told defendant that her mouth was too dry. She walked over to the sink where she filled an Absopure water bottle with water. The victim asked defendant how she would know if he had any sexually transmitted diseases. He said he was disease-free. The victim told defendant "if I do this you won't bring it up again." Defendant "shook on it." Defendant unzipped his pants and pulled out his penis. The victim put her mouth on it. "He held the back of my head, pushed it down, said choke on it b****." After approximately 30 seconds, defendant ejaculated in the victim's mouth. She spits the ejaculate into the water bottle. She stood up, capped the bottle, threw it away, and followed the defendant back to the SUV......

\*    \*    \*

The defendant drove the victim back to her car, and she drove off. She was afraid of being pulled over again, so she left her car in a parking lot and walked to a bar where she knew her best friend and her boyfriend were playing pool. Her friend convinced her to call the police. The police took her back to Manoogian Hall and the lounge to do a walkthrough of the assault. While they were there, Officer Gladden walked in, and the victim said: "Holy s****, that's him." Gladden was arrested and charged with the assault. Gregory Gladden's appeal was unsuccessful and his sentences of 16–30 years for criminal sexual assault, 2–5 years for misconduct in office and 345 days for neglect of duty were affirmed. There is no evidence of known prior sexual assaults by this officer.

## Immigration Officer Isaac R. Baichu—Sexual Shakedown by a Federal Police Officer

The Department of Homeland Security (DHS) is one of the many federal agencies that came into existence to enforce mala prohibita laws passed by Congress. *The Guardian* reports that there are 55,000 law enforcement officers within the DHS, making it the largest police force in the world (Franco and Shah, November 19, 2015). Along with its creation, DHS opened up a new police misconduct opportunity structure for newly created law enforcement officers. This new opportunity structure includes police sexual abuse.

Allegations of sexual misconduct have plagued the Customs and Border Patrol (CBP)-agency within the DHS in recent years. Thirty-five incidents of CBP agents sexually assaulting women and children immigrant detainees were reported between 2012 and 2014 (Franco and Shah, November 19, 2015). Two incidents of coerced bribes—one money and the other sex—had been reported from the same Citizenship and Immigration Services Office in Garden City, New York.

A Columbian woman married to an American citizen recorded Isaac Baichu, an Adjudication Officer at the US Citizenship and Immigration Services office in Garden City, New York, demanding sex in exchange for a green card. She gave in one time because he threatened to hold up her application and deport her relatives (AP, March 21, 2008). He was recorded—mobile phone hidden in a purse—saying, "I want sex. One or two times. That's all. You get your green card. You won't have to see me anymore." Even though she was recording the conversation, she gave in to his request for oral sex. The victim told her story to *The New York Times* and called the Queen's New York District Attorney's office. She met with the officer again, this time prosecutors for the DA's Queen's office listened in and arrested Baichu.

In a note of irony, Baichu was an immigrant from Guyana, becoming a US citizen in 1991. He had been employed with DHS for three years and handled over 8000 green card applications. One can only speculate on the number of vulnerable victims he processed and coerced into sex. His victim was certainly vulnerable. She came to the United States in 2004 on a tourist visa and overstayed. When she married an American citizen in 2007, she was allowed to "adjust" her illegal status, but she needed a green card to visit relatives in Columbia and return. She faced deportation if her application for a green card was denied.

The former federal immigration officer pleaded guilty to coercing oral sex and was sentenced to 1½–4½ years in prison.

## San Antonio, Texas—Multiple Officers Engaged in Sexual Shakedowns

In 2011, the Texas Civil Rights Project (TCRP), a non-profit community-based foundation, that "promotes racial, social, and economic justice through education and litigation" (TCRP 2011), published a report on *Police Misconduct in San Antonio*. There were four reports of on-duty sexual abuse cited in the report; three were directly related to sexual shakedowns.

## SAPD Officer Craig Nash

Officer Craig Nash, a six-year veteran, allegedly picked up a transgender woman prostitute in February 2010, handcuffed her, put her in his patrol car, and drove her to a secluded area and forced her to perform oral sex on him (TCRP 2011). He also allegedly raped the victim. After his arrest, a man also reported that Nash had sexually assaulted him in the summer of 2008 (Anonymous, March 6, 2010). The transgender victim immediately reported it and Nash was arrested. Nash entered into a plea agreement where he pleaded guilty to a misdemeanor charge of official oppression and a one-year sentence. Prosecutors dropped the felony charge of sexual assault by a police officer that carried a maximum sentence of life in prison. Was the victim's deviant status—transgender—a factor in the "light" treatment by the criminal justice system?

## SAPD Officer Gregory Mickel

On June 26, 2009, SAPD Officer Gregory Mickel, a four-year veteran, made a traffic stop on a truck. The passenger in the truck was a 46-year-old psychiatric patient with two prior prostitution arrests. Mickel allegedly ordered her to sit in his patrol car and told the man to leave. Mickel told the woman he would arrest her again for prostitution unless she had sex with him. The complaint alleges that he drove to a secluded parking lot and had sex with her in the back seat of the patrol car. He let the woman out, and she called 911 and requested an ambulance and reported an SAPD officer had raped her. Mickel responded to the call and cancelled the ambulance. He tried to cancel all other responding officers by claiming that the victim had mental problems. Mickel admitted to having sex with the victim but said it was consensual. He was arrested and charged with felony sexual assault. He pleaded guilty to official oppression and violation of civil rights and gave up his Texas certification without jail time. Again, is this a pattern of "light" reaction and treatment?

## SAPD Officer James McClure

In September 2008, SAPD Officer James McClure conducted a traffic stop of a female driver. According to published newspaper accounts, he noticed a bulge in her pants and called for a female officer to search her. No female officer was available. McClure allegedly took the woman to the rear of a building and ordered her to strip naked, which she did. He found a bag of marijuana in her pants, but he did not arrest her. He allegedly fondled the victim, gave her back the marijuana and let her go. He was indefinitely suspended, in effect fired.

# Denver, CO. Officer Hector Paez—Chose the Wrong Victim

Officer Hector Paez, a four-year veteran of the Denver, Colorado Police Department stopped a woman, a heroin user with a lengthy rap sheet, on May 16, 2010. He ran a check on her and found an outstanding warrant—false reporting to a pawnbroker. Paez allegedly drove the woman to an isolated area and forced her to perform oral sex on him or go to jail. He miscalculated her vulnerability and reluctance of the victim to report her victimization. She reported him. Following an investigation by the Denver Police Department's Internal affairs Bureau, he was arrested for second-degree kidnapping, sexual assault, and attempt to influence a public servant (Roberts, October 18, 2010). The latter charge came from lying to the Internal Affairs Bureau about the sexual assault.

At trial, Paez took the stand and testified about his encounter with the victim. He said he did pick her up and took her to a secluded location to get intelligence from her about narcotics sales. Choosing the secluded location and not taking her back to her car was done so she would not be seen talking to a police officer (Fender, October 14, 2012). His bizarre explanation did not impress the jury. Jurors asked if he had made any notes of his interview with the victim, and he was unable to produce any. The prosecutor asked why he had not given the narcotics detectives any of the information he had obtained. Paez, according to newspaper account, said he had been arrested and forbidden to go to police headquarters before he could report what he had found out. Paez was convicted of sexual assault and kidnapping and sentenced to eight years in prison followed by 10 years to life of sexual-offender probation.

# Indianapolis Metropolitan Police Department (IMPD)

According to news accounts, IMPD Police Officer Anthony S. Smith, a 37-year-old officer, had been on the department for a little over a year when he made a foolish move. He allegedly stopped a 19-year-old female driver early in the morning of August 15, 2008. He discovered that the young driver had an outstanding warrant. Telling her, he did not want to put her in jail; he allegedly proposed a solution; and ride around with him for an hour. She agreed and was with him as he answered several calls. The frightened female called her boyfriend and told him what was happening and how scared she was. Then, Officer Smith allegedly told her he would take her to jail unless she had sex with him. When her "ride along" was over, the victim reported the incident. Smith, at first, denied the event, and then during questioning gave the standard defense saying the sex was consensual.

It was easy for the investigators to match up Smith's path from the car's GPS with the victim's description of where they had traveled—*technical supervisory assist*. It was revealed that Smith kept condoms in the trunk of his patrol car—suggests *inclination*. He was fired and arrested and charged with rape, criminal deviate conduct, two counts of sexual misconduct, three counts of official misconduct, and two counts of intimidation.

## Hamilton County Tennessee—Willie Greer—Lateral Hire of Known Sex Abuser

Willie Marshay Greer, a 33-year-old black male was a probationary deputy with three months on the job for the Hamilton County Tennessee Sheriff's Department when he was arrested for allegedly raping a woman during a traffic stop (Berger, January 9, 2014). He was a lateral hire from the Chattanooga State Community College Campus Police when he came to the sheriff's department. Two of the three examiners with the sheriff's department recommended that he be hired, and he received glowing reviews from his references during the background check. One of his references, a lieutenant with the Forrest City, Arkansas Police Department had known him since he was a baby. He said Greer was a hardworking, dependable, restrained, and calm individual that he would hire immediately. Greer was hired and put to work as a road deputy working by himself. Then it all went bad.

January 5, 2014, just after 1 a.m. a 26-year-old woman said Deputy Greer stopped her speeding car and forced her to perform a sex act on him. She described the events of that night for investigators. After stopping her, the woman alleges he ran a background check on her and found open warrants and told her she was under arrest. Greer handcuffed her and told her "I could let you go, but you'd owe me." When she replied that she did not know what he was talking about, he took the handcuffs off and told her to get in her car and follow him. She followed him to a secluded area where he pulled over. She stopped and got out of her car. Officer Greer put the handcuffs back on and seated her in his patrol car. She said he then pulled his penis from his pants, grabbed her by the back of the head, and forced her to perform oral sex (Anonymous, January 10, 2014). He then allegedly asked if she was thirsty and gave her a fruity drink in Wendy's cup when she said she was.

The woman reported the sexual assault and investigators checked with Wendy's in the area where the stop took place and found one where the employees said a black officer had ordered a fruit punch from the drive-thru earlier that evening. They brought Greer to the station, and the victim picked him out of a line-up. Greer admitted the sex act and claimed it was consensual. He was arrested and fired. Greer was indicted by a federal grand jury and charged with civil rights violations "for sexually assaulting the victim, which violated her constitutional due process rights to bodily integrity, kidnapping, carrying a firearm during a sexual assault and possessing a firearm in furtherance of the crime (FBI, September 24, 2014)." He is awaiting trial.

## LAPD Officer Russell Mecano

According to court documents, the strange saga of Los Angeles Police Officer Russell Mecano began on October 20, 2007 (*The People v. Russell Mecano*. Court of Appeals, Second District, California-B233401). Taylor P. an 18- or 19-year-old homeless girl was living on the streets of Santa Monica with her boyfriend Eric when a woman approached Eric and Taylor slapped her. Two officers were called to the scene, one of those officers was Russell Mecano, both Taylor and Eric were taken to the police station. Taylor was alone in the booking cell when Officer Mecano allegedly approached and told her he could get her released on her own recognizance, O. R'd, but she would owe him if he did. After she was booked, Mecano approached her out of view of his partner and began asking questions and making sexually suggestive remarks.

Eric was booked on warrants and Taylor was "O. R'd." Officer Mecano went to the station's ATM and withdrew $200 in $20. He gave the money to Taylor and allegedly told her to go to a nearby Holiday Inn, take a shower and wait for him to get off his shift. He is reported to have told her he would be "fucking pissed" if she burned him for the money." He called a taxi and told the driver to take her to the Holiday Inn. When Taylor got in the taxi, she told the driver she was afraid of the policeman and told him to take her to the beach. He did. Mecano called the taxi company three times trying to find out where they took Taylor. Taylor approached two officers at the beach and told them what had happened. One, a Homeless Liaison Police Officer, told her to report the incident. Taylor did not report the incident until March 16, 2008.

Even though Officer Mecano's alleged technique was not successful with Taylor P., he allegedly tried it again. On May 18, 2008, an 18-year-old girl, Alex, was at the Pacific Palisades Park with several of her friends. Some of the group smoked marijuana. At least one was arrested. Mecano allegedly pulled Alex off to one side and asked what was going on. She told him she had marijuana and a marijuana pipe in her purse. He left the marijuana and the pipe in her purse and took her driver's license. He allegedly asked if she would hook up with him if he let her go; he then reportedly asked if she had money, and if she would get a motel room and wait for him to get off his shift. She said she would, but had no intentions of meeting up with him.

Mecano allegedly said he wanted to make sure she was for real and walked Alex toward a building and pushed her up against a wall. He allegedly kissed her and put his hands up her shirt and touched her breasts. Officer Mecano allegedly unzipped her pants and put two fingers in her vagina. Alex stopped him by saying they could do that later.

According to published account, Mecano told Alex he would keep her driver's license until they met later and asked for her cell phone number. Alex left without receiving a citation.

Once she left the scene, Alex called the 411 number of the Pasadena police and told them what had happened. Then, she called her mother and told her. While she was on the phone to her mother, Mecano called and left a voicemail. When she got home, they called the LAPD, and they sent detectives to her home, and the investigation began.

In March 2011, Russell Mecano went on trial for sexually assaulting Alex and soliciting sex from Taylor P. The jury, after four hours of deliberation found him guilty of one count of misdemeanor solicitation and one felony count each of sexual battery and penetration with a foreign object by a public safety official and penetration with a foreign object by force or duress. He was sentenced to 8½ years in prison and to register as a sex offender for the rest of his life. The appeal of his sentence was denied.

## Lexington, Kentucky Police Sergeant Robert D. Brown—Sad Ending for Police Hero

Sgt. Robert Dale Brown, a ten-year highly decorated, Medal of Valor, officer with no prior disciplinary action was charged with one count of first-degree misconduct and two counts of second-degree misconduct after allegations of receiving sexual favors from a woman he stopped on December 9, 2011 (Kocher, December 18, 2012). At first, the woman, who admitted to being high on Xanax when stopped, was quoted in a taped interview saying "I think he did try to take my pants off, but he didn't touch me in any way." Later at trial, and in a civil suit she claimed that Sgt. Brown stopped her and found a marijuana pipe in her possession and drove her to a secluded spot where "He started pulling my pants down. That's when he lay me down in the back seat, and he raped me." After the alleged rape, he dropped the woman off at her brother's house without charging her with any offenses.

The forensic examination did not reveal any evidence of a sexual attack; however, communication records showed an hour and 3-minute lapse in time from when the stop occurred, and the alleged rape occurred. Sgt. Brown had no contact with dispatch during that time period. Further discrediting Sgt. Brown's explanation, no contact in a secluded area, was a "geolocating" of messages and texts made by the victim while in the claimed "secluded" area. At trial, the jury found Brown guilty of all counts, and he was sentenced to unsupervised probation.

## San Diego, California PD Daniel Dana—Consensual?

The day after San Diego Police Chief William Landsdowne held a news conference to publicly apologize for a spate—nine—of allegations of police misconduct Officer Daniel Dana was accused of kidnapping and raping a 34-year-old woman while on duty (Perry, May 25, 2011). Dana was accused of raping a prostitute. The woman claimed that she had been forced to have intercourse and "orally copulate" the officer in his patrol car to escape being arrested for prostitution. The defense claimed that the officer and the woman had developed a friendship and the encounter was consensual. The five-year veteran officer, who was married and expecting his first child, at first pleaded not guilty but took a plea deal. He pleaded "No Contest" to one count of misdemeanor act and was sentenced to three years probation.

## UK

### Northern Ireland Police Officer

A married Police Service of Northern Island constable allegedly had regular sex with a young female crime suspect after he arrested her (Hudson, September 1, 2018). She told another police officer of the affair and he reported it to the Office of the Police Ombudsmen. The investigation recovered hundreds of text messages and images

## Avon and Somerset Police Officer—Domestic Violence Victim

A married police officer was dismissed for sending a picture of his penis to a domestic violence victim with whom he was having an affair (Matthews, March 21, 2017). The examining board found that the affair, although it may have been "consensual" was an abuse of his power and position. She was a vulnerable person and he knew that. Furthermore, he sent the lewd picture from a court restroom while he was on duty.

## London Metropolitan Police Detective—Year Long Affair with Student

A married Met detective was charged with carrying on a 10-month affair with a 20-year-old student from Albania he arrested in 2015. They had sex in the women's home, two hotels and the police station. At one tryst, they allegedly engaged in a threesome with another man at a spa. He pleaded guilty to misconduct in public office and guilty to appearing in court late drunk. He was sentenced to four months in prison (*PoliceOracle.com*, May 4, 2017).

## Bedfordshire Police Detective—Blackmail

A Bedfordshire Police was dismissed and convicted of gross misconduct for attempting to blackmail a man for using a prostitute (Garrod, September 20, 2017). He wrote a letter to the man demanding money to stop him from telling his family, friends, and work colleagues of his visit to the prostitute.

# Conclusion

The Illustrative Examples presented all fit the pattern of quid pro quo sexual shakedowns where an on-duty police officer with the *inclination* for sexual misconduct encounters a vulnerable victim with credibility problems—*opportunity*—under what is a *real or perceived low-risk* setting. Several of the I.E.'s indicate that the officers involved could be serial sexual predators, but the secondary data does not provide proof of physical violence and documented multiple victims. We once again see police agencies that fit the definition of rogue police departments— *"rotten barrels" not "rotten apples."* We also see the tragic effects of hiring Gypsy Cops.

# References

Anonymous. (2009). Cops break the laws, change departments. *Charleston Gazette.*

Anonymous. (2010, March 6). New allegations surface against San Antonio officer Craig Nash, accused of assaulting trans woman. *Examiner.com.*

Anonymous. (2014, January 10). Woman says county deputy forced her to perform sex act after traffic stop. *The Chattanoogan.com.*

Anonymous. (2014, March 12). Former Irwindale police officer pleads not guilty to sexually assaulting woman during a traffic stop. *CBS Local Media.*

Anonymous. (2014, December 5). Former Irwindale cop pleads no contest to sex charges involving 2 teenage girls. *CBS Local Media.*

Anonymous. (2015, January 12). Ex-Irwindale cop gets 9 years in prison for sexually assaulting women after traffic stop. *CBS Local Media.*

AP. (2008, March 21). Immigrant agent charged with demanding sex for green card. *The Associated Press.*

Barker, T. (2011). *Police ethics: Crisis in law enforcement.* Springfield, IL: Charles C. Thomas.

Berger, B. (2014, January 9). Hamilton County Tennessee—Willie Green— Lateral Hire of Known Sex Abuser. *Time Free Press.*

Favot, S. (2013, October 22). Some Irwindale residents call on city to disband police department. *San Gabriel Valley Tribune.*

FBI. (2014, September 24). Former Hamilton County Deputy Sheriff Indicted for Sexual Assault While on Duty. U.S. Department of Justice. Office of Public Affairs. Press Release.

Fender, J. (2012, April 24). Woman: Fear led her to comply with Denver cop's sexual demands. *The Denver Post.*

Fender, J. (2012, October 14). Accused Denver cop says he sought narcotics intel from woman, not oral sex. *The Denver Post.*

Flories, A. (2013, January 3). Ex-Irwindale police officer cadet charged sexual harassment by lieutenant. *Los Angeles Times*.

Franco, M., & Shah, P. (2015, November 19). The Department of Homeland Security: The largest police force nobody monitors. *The Guardian*.

Garrod, A. (2017, September 20). Detective who demanded hush money for prostitute use jailed. *PoliceOracle.com*.

Huard, R. (2007, February 27). Woman tells of sex act in patrol car. *U-T San Diego*.

Hudson, R. (2018, September 1). Suspect claims long affair started after her arrest. *Police Oracle*.

Kocher, G. (2012, December 18). Accuser testifies in Lexington officer's misconduct trial. *Herald-Leader*.

Matthews, A. (2017, March 21). Married policeman, 36, who sneaked into a courtroom looks to send a picture of his penis to a domestic abuse victim while on duty is sacked. *Daily Mail*.

Miller, E. (2014, October 14). Deputy took oral sex in exchange for not arresting woman. *Sun-Sentinel*.

Perry, T. (2011, May 15). In San Diego, not your typical police scandal. *Los Angeles Times*.

Police Oracle. (2017, May 4). Met affair with student. *PoliceOracle.com*.

Randal, S. (2008, November 15). Police Lt. Billiot wasn't supposed to have a gun, was fired, got a new job, now fired again after new charges. *The Daily Advertiser*.

Roberts, M. (2010, October 19). Hector Paez: Cop jailed for allegedly making woman perform sex act to avoid going to jail. *Westword*.

TCRP. (2011). *Police misconduct in San Antonio*. Austin, TX: Texas Civil Rights Project.

# 6

# Type 4: Betrayal of Trust

## Introduction

The police are by theory in our communities to serve and protect. That is often not true if you live in America's urban chaos cities or when the "officer friendly" you call sees you as an sex object. The police sexual aggressors discussed thus far, "hunt" or "troll" for victims' through proactive policing strategies such as the customary "rolling and patrolling" of uniformed officers in marked law enforcement vehicles at the local, county, state, and federal level. The primary purpose is to provide a visible presence to prevent crime or other breaches of social order. Police-citizen encounters are most likely to occur during proactive stops under valid suspicious circumstances. However, *proactive*, aggressive police actions known as zero tolerance, stop and frisk, and quality of life policing cause the most police-community relations problems in urban minority communities, raising the specter of racial, ethnic, and status profiling. We saw in the last chapter that sexually abuse inclined LEOs use people and traffic stops as a pretext to identify potential sex victims. Reactive policing actions result from officer initiated actions and call for help or assistance.

© The Author(s) 2020
T. Barker, *Aggressors in Blue*,
https://doi.org/10.1007/978-3-030-28441-1_6

For the most part, *reactive* policing strategies do not involve quid pro quo exchanges. The victim seldom gains anything by "submitting" to the sexual abuse. They are victims of a crime, some disturbance, or emergency, and they trust the police to help in some manner. However, some citizens' dial 911, expecting help and their "helper" turn out to be their worst nightmare. Vulnerable domestic violence victims are injured, psychologically and physically, when they report their victimization. Crime victims report their victimization and the unthinkable happens. They are groped, raped, and sodomized by the responding law enforcement officers.

Police sexual abuses during proactive calls are true exercises of abuse of power and the cruelest form of police sexual abuse. For example, a Toronto, Canada police sergeant is accused of two separate sexual assaults of women after offering them rides home late at night (Takema, May 5, 2016). These sexual assaults destroy trust in the police agency—*Betrayal of Trust*.

*   *   *

## Milwaukee, Wisconsin—Ladmarald Cates: Dial 911—Get a Rapist

"I called 911 for help," the 19 year-old mother of two said in court, "I didn't call 911 to be the victim." (Daley, January 19, 2012)

According to newspaper accounts and court documents, L.L., single mother of two, returned to high-school to better herself and improve the future for her and her young children. She received her high-school diploma and enrolled in the University of Wisconsin—Milwaukee majoring in Criminal Justice. She was on track to fulfill her dream of becoming a police officer or lawyer until she dialed 911 on July 16, 2010. Following her call for help, she became a severally depressed former college student contemplating suicide. Her responding officer allegedly sodomized and raped her (Barton, February 12, 2011 and US v. Ladmarald D. Cates—No. 12-870). Then, she received vile treatment by the Milwaukee Police Department (MPD). She was arrested and jailed for four days. Adding injury to insult the Milwaukee District Attorney's office declined to prosecute her rapist.

LL's version of the July 16, 2010 event began with neighborhood girls throwing bricks through her windows and yelling at her. She called 911 and officer Ladmarald Cates and his partner arrived. Instead of talking to the tormenting girls, the officers appeared intent on getting everyone out of the house except L.L. The officers urged her to call someone to get the young children. She did. Then Officer Cates's partner handcuffed the woman's brother, saying there was a missing person's report on him. The officer took him outside and placed him in the police car. Cates allegedly gave L.L.'s boyfriend, present on the scene, $10 and told him to go to a nearby store and buy some water. Cates declined water from the refrigerator because it "looked cloudy." Cates and L.L. were now alone.

Officer Cates followed L.L. to the bathroom where L.L. reached behind the toilet and retrieved a brick that landed there. When she turned around, Cates allegedly stood with his pants down and an erection. He demanded oral sex, according to L.L. and she complied out of fear. He then had sexual intercourse with her and let her go.

L.L. ran outside, screaming, "He raped me. He just raped me." Her excited cries drew a sympathetic crowd. Her 15-year-old brother, who had been let out of the police car with the handcuffs removed, shouted at the two officers, demanding they take action. Officer Cates allegedly told L.L. to shut up and threw her to the ground, increasing the crowd's agitation. The growing crowd and its loud objections to L.L.'s treatment led the jumpy officers to put in an urgent "officers need assistance now" call.

Ten officers responded. L.L. told a responding officer she had been raped by Officer Cates and needed to go to the hospital, "He cracked up laughing," L.L. alleged (Barton, January 16, 2011). The officer added, "You're not going to the hospital. You're going to jail. Quit lying." She was arrested and transported to jail.

At the jail, the booking officer allegedly did not believe her accusation of rape by a police officer and refused her request to go to the hospital. While she was in her cell L.L. alleges, Officer Cates came in and told her "You better tell them you made it up." If she didn't "he and his partners will be coming for me." L.L. asked to speak to a supervisor. A sergeant came to her cell and told her she would not get out of jail by lying. L.L. again says she repeated her request to go to the hospital. Twelve hours later an Internal Affairs (IA) detective came to see her. He sent her to the hospital for treatment and collection of evidence. The detective interviewed L.L. at the hospital and returned her to jail, two days later she was released without being charged.

The IA detective interviewed Officer Cates, and allegedly he gave different stories of what happened. First, he said that he did not have any sexual contact with L.L. the day of the incident. However, he added he had consensual intercourse with her when they first met nine months ago. At that time, he stopped L.L. for a traffic violation, and they exchanged telephone numbers and had sex in his car two weeks later. The next day Cates changed his story and admitted he had oral sex and intercourse with L.L. on the day of the call. He admitted he let his sexual arousal get the best of him and it was a stupid mistake to have sex on duty—an act prohibited by regulations. Finally, Cates, according to published sources, admitted the earlier story of consensual sex nine months earlier was false.

Cates's back and forth contradictory explanations of the events provided ample justification for his dismissal. He was fired, and the results of the investigation were forwarded to the Milwaukee County District Attorney's Office for prosecution. Following two months of review, the Milwaukee County District Attorney's Office Sensitive Crimes Team declined to prosecute. The letter to the police chief from an Assistant District Attorney cited the reason/s for declining prosecution: "After completing my review as outlined above, I determined that the sustainability of criminal charges depended on the credibility of the victim and citizen witnesses. While I find the victim's version of events credible, I do not believe that her testimony would be strong enough to successfully prosecute Officer Cates (Hall, July 16, 2010)." Not satisfied with this inaction, L.L. decided to search for other remedies.

L.L. searched the Internet for an attorney and found Robin Shallow. Shallow convinced an Assistant US Attorney to prosecute Ladmarald

Cates for violating L.L.'s civil rights. Cates was indicted on two federal counts: Count one stated "while acting as a Milwaukee police officer [Cates], deprived a woman [LL] of her due process right to bodily integrity by sexually assaulting her in violation of 18 U.S. C. 242. Count two charges Mr. Cates with using and carrying a firearm in relation to and in furtherance of a crime of violence...."

At trial, Ladmarald Cates took the stand and described a bizarre case of consensual sex, where the victim flirted with him and engaged in three acts of oral sex and one act of sexual intercourse. The trial lasted for three days before the jury, after three hours of deliberation, returned a guilty verdict on count one and not guilty on count two, using a firearm in a crime of violence. The federal judge sentenced him to 24 years in prison. His sentence was enhanced by two years for lying under oath. L.L. filed a civil suit against Ladmarald Cates, the city of Milwaukee and the Milwaukee Police Department. The lawsuit alleged the City of Milwaukee knew that Cates had a history of violent assaults on women.

L.L.'s suit points to a frequent occurrence in police sexual abuse cases, prior indications of aberrant behaviors that were ignored or mishandled. The police chief at the time of Cates's arrest admitted an "obvious pattern" of serious allegations was overlooked. He should have been fired years before the rape of L.L. Ladmarald Cates was accused of breaking the law at least five times in his 13-year police career, according to published reports, three of those allegations involved sexual abuse. The first obvious sex-related incident calling for termination involved a domestic violence charge.

In 2000, Cates was suspended for two days for sexual battery. His victim was a girlfriend, also a Milwaukee, police officer. He choked and shoved her during an argument. Domestic violence conviction is a career ender for police officers; federal law prohibits anyone convicted of domestic violence offenses from carrying guns. The Lautenberg Amendment (1996) to the Gun Control Act of 1968 prohibits anyone convicted of misdemeanor domestic violence from possessing firearms and ammunition.

The Milwaukee PD found a way around this prohibition with a charge and conviction on a lesser but related crime. Women's groups, including the National Center for Women and Policing, have complained for years that police officers have high domestic violence rates—2 to 4 times higher than the general public (womenandpolicing.com/violence); however, police departments treat officers differently when handling domestic violence cases. According to published reports, Cates was allowed to avoid domestic violence charges through a one-year prosecution diversion program. He kept his police job if he refrained from committing any criminal activity, avoided criminal contact with the victim and underwent counseling.

According to newspaper reports, the manner in which Cates domestic violence incident was handled by the Milwaukee Police Department was typical Milwaukee Police Department reaction (Barton, October 30, 2011). In 2001, a Milwaukee PD officer was arrested for battery, domestic violence and battery, and misconduct in public office. The charges could have resulted in 5½ years in prison and barred him from possessing a gun for the rest of his life. An internal investigation concluded the domestic violence charges were true and resulted in administrative action, six days suspension. Barton (October 30, 2011) reports that in 2010 the wife of a high-ranking commander in the Professional Performance Division, the Internal Affairs Division that investigates police misconduct, called 911 because she was in fear of violence from her husband. No report was taken, and there is no recording of the 911 call. Another MPD officer was convicted of disorderly conduct after fighting with his wife and choking her cousin, a common technique to downgrade the charge from domestic violence to avoid the Lautenberg Rule. A MPD sergeant received deferred prosecution, same as Cates, for the charge of domestic violence. He got treatment for depression and alcohol abuse, and the charge was dismissed. The newspaper analysis revealed five current Milwaukee officers accused of domestic violence had received deferred-prosecution agreements.

The domestic violence incident is not the only firing sexual abuse offenses Ladmarald Cates committed before the rape of L.L. (Barton, October 30, 2011). In 2005, Cates, working as a head jailer, was accused of having an inappropriate sexual relationship with a female prisoner. He was given a six-day suspension. In 2007, Officer Cates was accused of having sex on duty with a 16-year-old girl. The investigators sent this incident to the prosecutor's office, and they declined to prosecute. There is a clear pattern of police sexual abuse misconduct in this officer's history. He should have been terminated years before the July 16, 2010, rape.

## Iredell County, North Carolina—Richard "Ben" Jenkins: Domestic Violence Victim Abuser

"Finding dates working with victims of domestic violence is like *shooting fish in a barrel.*"

Deputy Richard "Ben" Jenkins. (Italics supplied. Wick & Mangiardi v. Redmond 2013). US District Court No 5-12-cv-00052-RLV'DSC. (2013-P.5)

The quote from Iredell County Deputy Richard Jenkins comes from court documents filed in a civil suit against him and the sheriff for sexual harassment. The plaintiffs, two women, went to Jenkins, the department's domestic violence (DV) investigator, to file violence charges against their husbands and seek protection. Instead, Deputy Jenkins allegedly made lewd comments and continually propositioned and stalked them on and off duty. Investigator Jenkins allegedly treated domestic violence victims as his special cache of sexual partners. However, he was no bad apple; the barrel was rotten.

His perverted behaviors were emblematic of the more significant problem in the Iredell Sheriff's office, prompting a federal judge to conclude "Here, the evidence shows that there was a custom of male ICSO [Iredell County Sheriff's Office] deputies and officers using their positions to sexually harass females over whom they had power" (Wick & Mangiardi v. Redmond 2013). There were multiple victims.

Court records reveal Victim 1 was married to an alcoholic who subjected her to psychological and physical abuse. In December 2008, the husband in a drunken rage began strangling their son, and she intervened. He punched her in the face, breaking her jaw. In January 2009, she confronted her husband with an affair he was having with a co-worker, and he viciously attacked her. The adulterer pulled her by her hair into a walk-in closet and kept her confined there for four hours.

He pointed a loaded gun at her head threatening to shoot her, while she cowered in a corner. He punched a hole in the drywall and fired a shot into the drywall before she escaped.

The woman fearing for her life and the safety of her children consulted an attorney who advised her to file charges. Her husband was arrested, and she was referred to the Iredell Sheriff's department domestic violence unit (DVU) and met Detective Sergeant Richard "Ben" Jenkins—a really bad day for an abused woman seeking help.

Court records describe Investigator Jenkins's relentless efforts to force Victim 1 into a sexual relationship. He frequently called Victim 1 off duty and after work hours, engaging in salacious conversation, such as asking the color of her panties and beseeching her to come to his house. In one particularly vulgar call, he told the victim that "his balls were three times their normal size and asked her to lick them and take away the pressure," adding, "he shaved his balls so that they would not prick her in the face." During other calls, Jenkins, according to court records, made comments about having an erection, masturbating, and wanting her to come to his house and "finish him off." He continually bragged about being a great lover. In a discussion in his office on a Sunday, he repeatedly asked her to go to the bathroom and take pictures of her vagina. He offered to take photos of himself and give them to her. She said she feared he would violently sexually assault her. His cruelest threat came when he told Victim 1 that if she continued to rebuff his demands he would have the charges against her husband dropped and she knew what would happen to her and her children if he were released.

Court records show Victim 1 reported the lewd conversations and threats through her attorney to the Iredell Sheriff's Department. Two high-ranking officers were assigned to investigate the complaint. In a perfunctory investigation, Jenkins admitted to several sexual harassment incidents, including asking for pictures of Victim 1's vagina, asking her to help him with his "swollen balls," and asking her to come to his house. The investigator's failed to interview any of the witnesses Victim 1 supplied and one investigator blamed the victim saying, "I think she's kind of leading him on as well.... I believe she is partially to blame" (Wick & Mangiardi v. Redmond 2013). The investigators concluded

Jenkins had sexually harassed Victim 1 and reported their results to the chief deputy. This same chief deputy was later accused of sexual harassment of female employees.

The investigators allegedly never considered termination and recommended on the spot to reassign Jenkins to a mid-level jailor position at a higher salary. The sheriff's department made no attempts to determine if Jenkins had sexually abused other domestic violence victims. The matter was closed, or so they thought.

Victim 2 did not come forward until Victim 1's complaint became public with the civil suit (Sheldon, May 1, 2012). She worked as a mediator at the Iredell County Court House in frequent contact with Jenkins. That contact was amicable until she approached the ICSO Domestic Violence Unit (DVU) for help and obtained a temporary restraining order against her abusive husband of seven years. Now, as a domestic violence victim, she became another fish in Jenkins's barrel of potential victims. Jenkins allegedly in an effort "to help her" called her into his office, closed the door and gyrated his hips, grabbed his genitals, and asked her if she wanted "some of this." This terrified the woman, but her nightmare had just begun.

What followed was allegedly a year of sexual harassment and abuse. From then on, every time they passed in the courthouse Jenkins made sexual gestures imitating fellatio or cunnilingus. Allegedly, he would ask her if she wanted it, grabbing his penis. He began stalking her. In a Mexican restaurant, he slid in beside her in a booth, started touching her leg, saying, "Can I just put my hands up your skirt? Can I just get a feel?" (Wick & Mangiardi v. Redmond 2013). At work one day, he slid his hands inside the back of her skirt. These abusive groping behaviors occurred after Jenkins was moved to the jailor's position following Victim 1's complaint. She joined Victim 1 in the civil suit against Jenkins and the sheriff. Jenkins prior acts of sexual abuse of domestic violence victims and department inaction became public during the civil suit.

The investigation revealed in 2006 Jenkins began a sexual relationship with a woman who reported an abusive husband threatened to kill her. A deputy discovered the relationship and reported it to the sheriff and chief deputy telling them "if [Jenkins] wasn't already screwing her he would be" (Wick & Mangiardi v. Redmond 2013). The sheriff and chief deputy said nothing and told the whistle-blower to leave. Sometime later, according to the civil suit, Jenkins's wife found him at 2:30 a.m. in his mother's house asleep in his underwear with the same woman sleeping in his arms. Jenkins and his wife got into an altercation, leaving Jenkins with visible bruises. Jenkins self-reported the altercation with his wife and admitted the sexual relationship to his female DVU lieutenant. She took no action against Jenkins, and he continued his sexual pursuit of domestic violence victims—*departmental inaction created a real sense of low risk for PSM.*

The civil suit brought to light the department's history of sexual harassment and failure to act when it was reported. It was a rogue sheriff's department. Court records revealed the ICSO's chief deputy sexually harassed multiple female subordinates, causing several women to quit their jobs when complaints went uninvestigated (Wick & Mangiardi v. Redmond 2013). Numerous reported sexual relationships with subordinates were ignored. Court records revealed many sexual harassment victims failed to come forward because "they were afraid to talk." They kept it to themselves. Sexual harassment was so pervasive in the ICSO that victims ignored it. The federal judge in his ruling against summary judgment for the sheriff's department faulted the sheriff for his "boys will be boys" attitude toward sex-based harassment and cited a statement the sheriff made, "You have to expect this working with the guys."

The civil suit was settled for $425,000. Deputy Jenkins was promptly fired after the settlement. The sheriff announced he would not seek reelection. The ICSO announced it would revise its sexual harassment policy and provide sexual harassment training for staff members; there had never been any.

## Detroit Officer—Deon Nunlee

Standard police protocol when responding to domestic violence calls is to separate the "alleged" combatants until the preliminary investigation is completed. However, during this separation officers should not lose sight of their partner. Allegedly Detroit Police Officer Deon Nunlee ignored the second part of the protocol. He and his partner answered a 911 call where a boyfriend assaulted a 31-year-old woman (Damron, March 7, 2014). The officers arrived, and allegedly Nunlee took the woman upstairs to a bedroom. While they were upstairs Officer Nunlee allegedly sexually assaulted the woman. His partner downstairs questioning the boyfriend claimed he was unaware of the assault. Not believable, but possible. She reported the assault and Nunlee was placed on administrative leave. When the results from the rape kit came back, Nunlee was suspended without pay. His DNA was found on the woman. He was charged with three counts of second-degree criminal sexual conduct, and one count each of assault with intent to penetrate and misconduct in office. The six-year veteran officer entered into a plea deal, pleading guilty to misconduct in office and second-degree sexual conduct and sentenced to serve 18 months to 15 years in prison.

## Hickman County, Tennessee Deputy Sheriff—Kenneth H. Smith

In 2011, Deputy Sheriff Kenneth H. Smith pleaded guilty to violating the civil rights of two domestic violence victims (DOJ, 2011). He somehow convinced the gullible domestic violence victims to allow him to take nude pictures of them, including their private parts, as part of his investigation. He was sentenced to 24 months in prison.

## Shelby County, Tennessee Sheriff's Office—Deputy James Bishof

A woman, who had been arrested the night before for domestic violence—she struck her estranged husband and a woman he was with—went to the Downtown Memphis, TN office of the Shelby County Sheriff's Department to talk about her arrest (McKenzie, July 29, 2011). The Domestic Violence Detective, James Bishof, said he could help her. He allegedly convinced the woman that he needed to take photographs to support her case. They went to a private women's restroom where Bishof took photos of her breasts, buttocks, and private parts, even though there were no injuries. He allegedly then told the woman that he had a better camera at his home and made arrangements to meet her at her residence to take better photographs. He met her at her residence and allegedly had her strip naked, and he sexually assaulted her. She reported the assault and investigating detectives recovered the photographs from his work camera, and Bishof was arrested.

## Chicago, Illinois—CPD Officers Paul Clavijo & Juan Vasquez—Intoxicated Victim Raped

A common defense to sexual assaults is the victim consented even though intoxicated. That defense fails when the sexually assaulted victim cannot consent due to their intoxication. The woman, in this example, had a blood alcohol content of 0.38 percent—nearly five times the legal limit to drive. The victim was too intoxicated to give informed consent to the two Chicago police officers who offered their assistance then allegedly raped her. Published reports present the following scenario.

It was about 2 a.m. on March 30, 2011, when Chicago police officers Paul Clavijo and Juan Vasquez parked their marked Chicago PD Tahoe SUV in an unlit area in Chicago's Northside near Wrigley Field (Meiser, May 25, 2011). A 22-year-old female was coming down the dark street. She was crying and having trouble walking. She had spent the night drinking and arguing with a male friend. The officers drove forward and signaled the woman to approach the police vehicle. Sensing her distress, they offered her a safe ride to her destination. She accepted, after all, they were cops, and they wanted to help her.

Had her brain not been addled by liquor, she would have realized that the cops' next statement had evil intentions. She was told she was not allowed to sit in the back seat. She would have to sit in Officer Clavijo's lap in the passenger seat (Jane Doe v. Clavio, Vasquez & City of Chicago. US District Court Northern District of Illinois, Eastern Division—Complaint).

Their next move was brazen and demonstrates a feeling among the officers that there were no consequences for misconduct. Vasquez drove to a liquor store. He went in—in uniform—and bought a bottle of vodka. While Vasquez was in the liquor store, Clavijo allegedly sexually assaulted the intoxicated woman. The officers drove to the woman's apartment that was outside their assigned patrol area. The three of them played strip poker, and she had sex with one of the officers. They suggested a threesome, unnerving the woman. In fear, she began banging on the wall while screaming for help. She left the apartment and ran down the hallway screaming. The two officers fled the apartment; one naked, clothes in hand, the other dressed in his uniform. The hasty exit caused them to leave behind a cell phone and parts of a Chicago police uniform (Alverez, May 12, 2011).

Responding officers sent the woman to the hospital where her BAL was 0.38, five times the legal limit to drive. Extreme intoxication. DNA analysis showed that both officers had sexual contact with the woman.

The sexual abuse allegations evoked a strong reaction from city officials. The interim police superintendent said, "The offenses are insulting to hardworking Chicago police officers." The Cook County State's Attorney, Anita Alvarez waxed on indignantly, "Citizens are expected to follow the orders of police officers and to respect their authority. In these cases, these officers committed disgusting violation of that trust" (Alverez, May 12, 2011).

Both officers were relieved of duty and stripped of their police powers, and in May were charged with Criminal Sexual Assault (Class 1 Felony) and Official Misconduct (Class 3 Felony). Clavijo was also charged with Criminal Sexual Assault and Official Misconduct for a separate sexual assault of a 26-year-old woman three weeks earlier.

The prior assault happened under similar circumstances. Clavijo and Vasquez allegedly offered a ride to a woman waiting on a bus early in the morning. They drove the woman home and then asked to use her bathroom. Vasquez went to the bathroom, and Clavijo allegedly followed the woman into the bedroom, pushed her down on the bed and raped her. She says she did not immediately report the assault because she worked in the area and the officers know where she lived.

In May 2011, the victim of the March 30 assault filed suit against the city and the Chicago Police Department alleging that there was a "code of silence" among Chicago police officers and unwillingness by supervisors to investigate misconduct.

Clavijo and Vasquez resigned from the police department. In February 2014, both officers entered into plea agreements. They pleaded guilty to official misconduct involving battery and received two years probation. The previously indignant city officials did not put out any press releases after the sentencing. No public announcements. The second assault charge against Clavijo was dropped. In the plea arrangements, they did not admit any sexual offenses, escaping registration as sex offenders. However, because of the felony conviction, they cannot serve as police officers again. The victim received a settlement of $415,000, ending her civil suit with taxpayers ultimately paying for police misconduct.

## Wellford, South Carolina—Bennie Brandon Hand: Sexual Abuse of Mentally Challenged Woman

Wellford, South is located in Spartanburg County, South Carolina, and has a six-person police department. In 2012, the small town and the police department were rocked by the arrest of Officer Brandon Hand (Smith, May 13, 2013). The thirty-two-year-old 6-year veteran officer was arrested by SLED (South Carolina Law Enforcement Division) for misconduct in office, third-degree criminal sexual misconduct and abuse of a vulnerable adult. According to the arrest warrants, the 5'11"330-pound officer did engage "in a sexual battery [oral sex] with a person who he knows is mentally defective and suffers from a mental disease, which renders her incapable of appraising the nature of her conduct." The act/s allegedly occurred on several occasions between July 1, 2012, and January 1, 2013, while he was on duty and in uniform. He is currently in jail and awaiting trial.

## Sacramento, California—Gary Dale Baker: Rape of Stroke Victim

The judge sentencing Gary Dale Baker, a black 22-year veteran of the Sacramento Police Department (SPD), called his crimes "unspeakable" (Bernstein, November 11, 2015). The alleged events described in the arrest warrant and newspaper accounts are disturbing (Wilkinson, December 20, 2012; SPD Warrant 10-352728, September 19, 2012).

**First assault—November 24, 2010**—The 75-year-old stroke victim was suffering from Aphasia, a speech, and language disorder caused by damage to the brain, and recovering in a senior living complex when first approached in a driveway by an unknown black male between 35 and 45. She described him as being 5"6'–5"9" with a medium build and black hair. She told investigators that he could be a policeman, deputy sheriff, or security guard from the vehicle he was driving. She had a short conversation with the man, and he left. Later, the same man knocked on her door and forced his way into the apartment. He immediately started kissing her as she objected. He pushed her down onto a couch and attempted vaginal intercourse as she struggled. The assailant allegedly forced the woman to orally copulate him to ejaculation. The rapist fled, and the victim reached a medical alert and activated the alarm.

SPD investigators collected DNA at the scene and sent the victim to the hospital. The rape examination found evidence of a rape and bruising and tearing of the vaginal area. No DNA matches were found, and no suspects were identified.

**Second Assault—September 20, 2012**—Two years after the first assault, the victim reported that the same man returned and allegedly raped her and forced her to orally copulate him. The hospital exam confirmed the evidence of rape.

**Third Assault—December 11, 2012**—The same assailant returned to the victim's senior living apartment and allegedly attempted to force the victim into sex. The attempt was unsuccessful and investigating officers recommended the family install a motion detector camera in the apartment, which they did.

**Fourth Assault—December 18, 2012—**Seven days after the third assault, and one day after the installation of the camera, the rapist returned and sexually assaulted the elderly victim. The investigating detective viewed the film footage and recognized the rapist, Sacramento Police Officer Gary Baker

Baker was arrested and placed on administrative leave. Two days later after confirmation of a DNA match in all the sexual assaults, he was charged with nine counts, including rape, forcible oral copulation, sexual battery, and burglary. He was convicted at trial and sentenced to 62 years to life.

*   *   *

## Police Sexual Abuse of Domestic Violence Victims in England and Wales

We know of officers who develop inappropriate relationships with victims of domestic abuse. They have ignored their professional duty and their moral responsibility, and instead abused their position of power to exploit victims. We do not know the true scale of this, but everyone in this room knows it goes on far more than we might care to admit.—British Home Secretary in a speech to the British Police Federation, May 2016

According to Her Majesty's Inspectorate of Constabulary (HAIC), the UK government watchdog agency for England and Wales police forces, there were 430 reported allegations of abuse of force during 24 months (2015–2016). The victims came from the similar available pool of "perfect victims" domestic abuse victims, alcohol and drug addicts, sex workers, and arrested persons. Police sexual aggressors are a problem common to the occupational work setting no matter what country is examined. "It [police sexual abuse] is an exploitation of power where the guardian becomes the abuser," said the Inspector of Constabulary. Thirty-nine percent of the abuse of force allegations involved victims of domestic violence who had sought police help. Sixty-eight of these vulnerable victims, 16% of total, had "abused their authority to exploit them or develop an inappropriate relationship with them" (http://aa.com.tr/en/europe/uk–police-officers-accused-of-sexual-abuse).

This particular report originated as a result of an investigation by *The Guardian*, a British daily newspaper known for its investigative reporting. The original investigation was a result of the conviction and sentencing of a Northumbria police constable to life for the rape and sexual assault of women he met on duty. He sexually assaulted abused addicts, shoplifters, and a disabled teenager, demanding sex for help. According to the news report, they identified 59 officers from 25 police forces who raped, sexually assaulted and sexually harassed women from 2008 to 2012. The sexual predators ranged from constables and officers up to the rank of deputy chief constable. Particularly appalling were the officers who sexually abused domestic violence victims in safe women's refuges. The domestic violence women in these refugees were drug addicts, prostitutes, and women with no money and no home. As the newspaper reported, who would believe these women over a police officer? The obvious answer is—NO ONE. *The Guardian* concluded that police sexual abuse in England and Wales police forces was the result of "a lack of supervision, a failure to vet officers and the turning of a blind eye to the sexual exploits of male officers, in a still macho police service" (Laville, December 8, 2016).

## Conclusion

The last Illustrative Examples of the repeated rapes of an elderly stroke victim challenge the earlier assertion that PSM is, with the exception of sexually motivated serial killers the result of rational behavior responding to *inclination, opportunity, and real or perceived low risk*. From all appearances, the sexual aggressor was not "normal" or rational; however, we do not have the necessary information to make that determination. This points to the need for information and research on PSM. How did this person become a police is an unanswered question. The remaining I.E.s fits within the **PSM Causal Equation**.

# References

Agerholm, H. (2016, October 22). Police investigate 150 allegations of sexual misconduct by officers. *Independent.*

Alverez, A. (2011, May 12). Two Chicago police officers charged with sexual assault while on duty. *Cook County State's Attorney's Officer: Press Release.*

Anonymous. (2016, December 8). Hundreds of police accused of sexual exploitation. *BBC News.*

Barton, G. (2011, January 16). Fired milwaukee officer sentenced to 24 years in rape. *Journal Sentinel.*

Barton, G. (2011, February 12). Fired cop no stranger to inquiries. *Journal Sentinel.*

Barton, G. (2011, October 30). Police department ignores national standards for officers accused of domestic violence. *Journal Sentinel.*

Bernstein, S. (2015, November 11). Sentenced to life for raping a stroke victim. *Reuters.*

Daley, M. (2012, January 29). She dialed 911: The cop who came to help raped her. *The Daily Beast.*

Damron, G. (2014, March 7). Detroit officer charged with sexually assaulting woman while responding to a call. *Detroit Free Press.*

DOJ. (2011, October 7). Former Hickman County, Tennessee Deputy Sheriff sentenced to 24 months in prison for civil rights and false statement charges. *Department of Justice Press Release.*

Grierson, J. (2016, December 8). Hundreds of police in England and Wales accused of sexual abuse. *The Guardian.*

Hall, A. E. (2010, July 16). Letter to Chief Edward A. Flynn. State of Wisconsin v. Ladmarld Cates.

Laville, S. (2016. December 8). The police are still ignoring sexual abuse by officers: It's time for zero tolerance. *The Guardian.*

McKenzie, K. (2011, July 29). Shelby County Sheriff's detective faces charges of aggravated sexual battery. *The Commercial Appeal.*

Meisner, J. (2011, May 25). Lawsuit: Sex misconduct by Chicago cops not investigated by city. *Chicago Tribune.*

Sheldon, L. (2012, May 1). Second woman accuses deputy of sexual harassment. *WSOCTV.com.*

Smith, G. F. (2013, May 14). Wellford police officer charged with abuse of vulnerable adult. *South Carolina Patch.*

Takema, D. (2016, May 5). Toronto police officer faces second sex assault charge. *The Star.*

Wick & Mangiardi v. Redmond. (2013). Civil Action. No. 5: 12-CV-00052.

Wilkinson, K. (2012, December 20). Sacramento police officer arrested for rape of elderly woman. *Sacramento Press.*

# 7

# Type 5: Consensual On-Duty Sex

## Introduction

Consensual sex on-duty, thee most numerous type of PSM, has a long, sordid history in the *policework* occupation. Since the founding of the London Metropolitan Police in 1829, there have been "women of the night" and "loose virtue" ready to service the boys in blue (Smith 1985; Rawlings 2002). Sex with willing partners was considered an accepted perk for early American police officers. A New Haven, Connecticut Police Chief in the late 1960s described police cars as "traveling bedrooms" because of the amount of sleeping and sex that took place in them (Ahern 1972). This is still true in many police agencies. This biased and sexist view allowed a male-dominated police culture to develop and continue in police work worldwide. This misogynist view demeans women and perpetuates a "good old boys" defense to coerced sex with "less than willing" victims, "they got what they asked for." As we have seen, this defense is well known and used by police sex aggressors to justify their abusive behavior. However, there is a dark, dirty secret to this "consensual" sex defense. Many of the supposedly "willing" partners are less than willing participants. They are coerced victims in an unequal relationship (Barker 2011).

© The Author(s) 2020
T. Barker, *Aggressors in Blue*,
https://doi.org/10.1007/978-3-030-28441-1_7

Furthermore, consensual on-duty sex is unethical and outside the boundaries of acceptable law enforcement conduct. Police professional associations throughout the world and women's advocacy groups dictate that *on-duty sex* whether allegedly "consensual" or not should be prohibited. Consensual on-duty sex is official misconduct, unethical, and in some instances criminal. Consensual on-duty sex acts have victims and lead to management/supervisory problems, distrust of the police, and police-community relation's problems. Consensual sex in the workplace creates a hostile work environment conducive to sexual harassment. In some law enforcement agencies, it is a part of the organizational culture—*low risk and well known*. The following examples provide supporting evidence for this intolerant view. I expressed this view for seventeen years as a certified police academy instructor to rookies and advanced classes on Police Ethical Behavior. Consensual sex on duty demeans the officer, the willing and not so willing victims, the department, and the *policework* occupation. I believe that *policework* is not and never will deserve to be called a profession as long as police officers provide direct or implicit support for the unethical and criminal behaviors of their colleagues (see Barker 2011).

# Lakeland, Florida: Organizational Culture of Police On-Duty Sex

### Findings of Fact—Florida State Attorney's Report

1. As many as 10 sworn LPD [Lakeland Police Department] officers have engaged in sex acts and sexually suggestive behavior while on duty over the past seven years [2006–2013] with an LPD civilian employee. The sex acts occurred among other places, at the Lakeland Police Department, other City of Lakeland Municipal Buildings, in Lakeland Police Department patrol cars, in city parks, and on private property.
2. While there were also allegations of LPD officers engaging in sex acts with the LPD civilian employee off duty and in other jurisdictions, the focus of this investigation was for on-duty actions of the officers.

3. Of the ten current or former officers who engaged in sex acts or sexually suggestive behavior, five were supervisors and ranked members of the LPD.

4. Seven sworn members or former members, admitted, under oath, to the allegations of the LPD civilian employee. Two sworn officers partially admitted and partially denied, under oath, the allegations of the LPD civilian employee. One sworn officer denied, under oath, the allegations of the LPD civilian employee.

5. We question the credibility of three LPD sergeants, Bryan McNabb, Rusty Longaberger, and David Woolverton. I will not use their testimony pending the outcome of the internal affairs investigation…

6. Not only are the officers directly involved in this matter at fault. There were other LPD employees who knew about what was going during this time period but declined to get involved and stop it [fostering a *low-risk* setting for PSM].

   *Source* Letter to LPD Chief Lisa Womack from Florida State Attorney Jerry Hill-June 25, 2013 with accompanying report— *Investigative Report—Lakeland Police Department—SAO1012013-16.*

\* \* \*

Lakeland, Florida is a city of approximately 100,000 people halfway between Tampa and Orlando. The tourist city was stunned and thrust into the national spotlight by a police sex scandal that was revealed in a 59—page report issued on June 25, 2013, by Jerry Hill the Polk County's State Attorney (cited above). The city's mayor called it a "national embarrassment." The report was a damning indictment of the Lakeland Police Department and its culture of sexual misconduct. The State Attorney linked the culture of sexual misconduct to other LPD problems and shortcomings that surfaced before the report such as, questionable traffic stops and searches combined with botched investigations. He went so far as to say that some high-ranking police officials were more interested in having illicit sex than doing their jobs.

According to newspaper accounts, the sexual harassment allegations included asking for sex, unwanted touching, sexual innuendos, sharing sexual photos—photos of male and female sex organs, and coerced and consensual sex (Maready et al., June 26, 2013; Caulfield, June 25, 2013). Perverse sex acts were common and included the department's chief spokesman who was, a captain, and the patrol and training supervisor, sending a photo of his penis to a female employee (admitted during the investigation). A police officer and a civilian LPD employee—crime analyst, having on-duty sex in a church (admitted during investigation); and a fire inspector, sworn law enforcement officer, and reserve officer with LPD, and the same civilian LPD employee having sex in her car outside the funeral reception for a slain police officer (admitted during investigation). The report revealed that officers sent photos and videos of them masturbating to female employees.

The female crime analyst, at the center of the scandal, claimed a fire inspector sent her a photo of him having anal sex with a dildo and asked her to do the same to him. Another officer allegedly sent her pictures of him in women's lacy lingerie, stockings, and boots and claimed to wear woman's panties on duty. This same officer allegedly watched porn on his personal computer and phone while on-duty. A civilian employee, director of employee relations, allegedly pulled down the crime analyst's panties and clipped some pubic hairs and put them in an envelope, so he would have something to remember.

The report and court documents alleged female sexual harassment victims, and other female employees including an allegation that an LPD's victims advocate and a sex crimes detective were knowledgeable of the sexual misconduct with the crime analyst but did not report it out of fear of retaliation. Furthermore, the police department and its supervisory staff allegedly created a hostile work environment and culture where personal satisfaction was more important than professional law enforcement standards and goals (Caulfield, June 25, 2013).

According to the report and other sources, the sexual misconduct problem was not the result of "rotten apples." It was a "rotten barrel," causing the problems. The sexual misconduct first came to light from a "whistle blower." An LPD sergeant noticed suspicious activity on the part of an LPD officer and the crime analyst. He reported it and the recently appointed—March 2011—female chief of police turned the investigation over to Florida Department of Law Enforcement, resulting in the State Attorney's investigation and report. The reports findings were salacious.

Two female civilian crime analysts admitted to having consensual sex with LPD officers and were the repeated victims of sexual harassment by department members. One left during the 2.5 months Florida Department of Law Enforcement investigation. The principal complainant, seven years of on and off-duty consensual and coerced sex, was 37 years old at the time of the investigation. She was married and had two teenage sons. She told investigators she felt pressured to engage in sex with the officers out of fear of losing her job. She claimed that her prior history of sexual abuse, sexual molestation beginning at age and self-abuse and suicide attempts exacerbated her sexual promiscuity. Her known inability to say no and a reputation for sexual promiscuity made her a vulnerable target for police co-workers who sensed her weakness and took advantage of her.

Seven LPD officers admitted to a variety of sex acts on duty during the investigation (Maready et al., June 26, 2013). Three sergeants denied the accusations and declined to take polygraph exams. The state's attorney questioned their credibility. Many of the acts uncovered in the investigation were crimes—felony, and misdemeanor. However, they could not be prosecuted because too much time had passed. The investigators could not pinpoint specific dates of the alleged acts, and there was no physical evidence. Furthermore, the complainant's admission of consensual sex acts damaged her credibility.

Although there were no criminal charges, there were consequences for those caught up in the sex scandal. The captain mentioned above admitted making a photo of his genitals and giving it to the female crime analyst. He was given two options—retire or be fired. He chose to retire, saving his benefits and pension.

Two of the three sergeants mentioned in the report as having credibility problems were fired for Conduct Unbecoming of an Officer, Failure to Report Misconduct, and Neglect of Duty. A third female sergeant, allegedly involved in the cover up, resigned instead of termination. She was charged with neglect of duty, untruthfulness, and conduct unbecoming of an Officer for not reporting violations. The officer who allegedly had consensual sex with the crime analyst in the church, starting the investigation, resigned. The crime analyst at the center of the sex scandal was terminated for conduct unbecoming and untruthfulness. Although the sexually promiscuous "victim" considered herself to be a whistle-blower, Chief Lisa Womack disagreed.

The newly appointed female chief of police said the "victim" tried to cover up the acts and only went public when she faced termination. That is accurate, according to the State Attorney. The State Attorney's Report concluded the civilian crime analysis denied her relationship with the officer at the church in the initial investigation and only admitted to on-duty sex relations with him when faced with discipline and termination. Then, and only then, did she describe the other consensual and coerced sex encounters?

The Lakeland City Commissioners backed Chief Womack throughout the scandal until another LPD officer was arrested for on-duty sexual battery after the investigation was complete. This sexual abuse was on the chief's watch and her support crumbled. The final straw came when a majority of LPD officers and other police employees voted 152–123 as having no confidence in Chief Womack's leadership (Anonymous, January 24, 2014). She resigned two days after the no-confidence vote. The wreckage from the LPD sex scandal resulted in 27 LPD employees being disciplined, including about a dozen officers who resigned instead of termination and three who were fired. Also, the civilian crime analyst, victim, or reluctant whistle-blower, was fired and the chief was forced to resign.

## Rialto, California: Reform of a Rogue Department?

In 2010, the working-class city of Rialto, California located in San Bernardino County had a population of 99, 171 and a police department of approximately 160 sworn officers. Dr. Mark Kling D.P.A., a career police officer known for reforming police departments, was chief of police. He was appointed chief in August 2006, four months after the City Council voted to disband the police department and contract with the San Bernardino Sheriff's Department for police services.

The City Council and most of the community were fed up with the behavior of their police officers, individually and as a department (Dulaney, November 18, 2010; Winton, November 19, 2010). The RPD was plagued for fifteen years by allegations of racism, sexism, discrimination, brutality, and corruption, and the council saw little hope for reform. Changing their mind at the last moment, the City Council rescinded the disband order to try for reform one more time and hired Dr. Kling, the Chief of Police of Baldwin Park, California Police Department.

In 2010, Chief Kling was in the process of replacing officers who left the RPD, voluntary, and termination, after disbandment was announced. He was hard at work instituting needed reforms when 37-year-old Nancy Holtgreve burst into his office to report police sexual misconduct. The visibly outraged woman had a sordid tale to tell (Claim for Damages, July 30, 2010).

Holtgreve was a waitress at the local Spearmint Rhino strip club. She claimed she and several of her fellow workers engaged in on-duty sex with RPD officers. The spurned woman's complaint was specifically directed at Officer James Dobbs. Dobbs, who, according to Holtgreve, abused and threatened her after she demanded child support payments for a son resulting from their illicit relationship. She said they had sex three times the previous year and she became pregnant. The lovers allegedly agreed to keep the relationship secret from his ex-wife and his fiancée who was also Chief Kling's secretary. Dobbs allegedly promised to support her and the baby. After the baby was born, Dobbs reneged on paying child support. She reported this to the chief and claimed the sex took place after she got off work and while Dobbs was on-duty. The tryst, she alleged, occurred at the Rialto Police Benefit Association's union building. To make matters worse, Holtgreve added that other Rialto police officers were involved in alleged on-duty sex acts with her and her fellow waitresses at the strip club, individually and in a group.

The stunned Chief Kling promised to investigate her claims and asked her to keep the allegations out of the newspapers. The scorned woman wanted revenge. She went to the newspapers and other media outlets, embroiling the police department in a major sex scandal.

Chief Kling's investigation began as an inquiry into any improper police conduct within the Rialto Police Department with a promise to "Hold these officers accountable if these allegations are true. And if the allegations aren't true, we are going to do everything we can to clear their names" (Winton, November 19, 2010). Almost immediately, Officer Dobbs and three other officers were put on paid leave. Two other officers were suspected of improper behavior but were not put on paid leave for fear of compromising the investigation. The City Council threw their support behind Chief Kling, although some secretly regretted not disbanding, according to newspaper sources. The president of the Rialto police union emphatically denied he was aware of sexual activity between civilians and officers at the union hall.

The investigation revealed Holtgreve and her co-workers did meet with Dobbs and other police officers at a nearby 24-hour restaurant after they got off work. Officers did have sexual contacts with the waitresses, but it appeared that the only on-duty sexual contact was between Holtgreve and Officer Dobbs. Holtgreve and Dobbs did have sex in the union hall while he was on duty. All members of the union had keys to the union hall, and it did have a full mattress in it for officers to use after back-to-back or late shifts. The claim that Holtgreve had sex with on-duty narcotic officers in the department's narcotic's office was not substantiated. The Narc did have off-duty sex with Holtgreve but not on police department property. The allegation of group sex with on-duty police officers at the union hall was not substantiated.

Two officers quit before the investigation was finished; James Dobbs was one of them. The implicated officers resigned as the department was proceeding on their terminations. Four officers were found not to have had sex on duty but had engaged in other violation. According to the chief, they received "severe and appropriate punishments." California law prohibits disclosure of the punishments received. None of the violations were criminal.

Positive change occurred in the Rialto Police Department. The locks were changed on the union hall along with a better key control system. There is a surveillance camera in the lobby, and cots have replaced the mattress. All Rialto patrol vehicles have GPS devices in them so their locations can be recorded—*technical supervisory assist*. All patrol officers are equipped with body cameras—*technical supervisory assist.* Chief Mark Kling left police work and is now Professor Kling teaching undergraduate and graduate criminal justice classes at California Baptist University at Riverside, California, after 30 years in law enforcement.

## Yukon, Oklahoma PD—2005

Yukon, Oklahoma prides itself as a family-oriented community of approximately 25,000 people. In 2014, the city was ranked #1 in a newspaper study of safe Oklahoma cities (www.cityofyukonok.gov). The Yukon police department (YPD) has 34–37 members and the majority of the officers—52%—are female. To become a police officer the applicant must have a minimum of 60 hours college, prior military or law enforcement experience may be given as partial credit. Since 2012, Yukon Police Department, a longtime veteran YPD officer, John Corn, has led the department. Chief Corn has an Associates Degree in Criminal Justice from Oklahoma State University and a BA in Behavioral Science from Oklahoma City University. Chief Corn is also a graduate of the prestigious FBI National Academy. These laudatory accomplishments did not prevent an organizational culture of *low risk and peer support for consensual on-duty sex.*

Chief Corn was YPD's Assistant Chief of Police in 2005 when a man walked into a convenience store within sight of the police station and observed the store clerk engaged in oral sex with an on-duty Yukon police officer. The shocked interloper did his best "I didn't see nothing" imitation and walked out (Raymond and Kramer, July 3, 2005). Later, he told the storeowner.

The storeowner confronted the 23-year-old clerk with the accusation. The clerk gave a tearful confession, who then contacted the police. A detective interviewed the clerk, and she gave a statement detailing an entire year of sexual encounters with Yukon police officers. In a newspaper account, the clerk stated, "I would see one or two of them every month at least. It was like a circle...I never knew who was going to call" (Raymond and Kramer, July 3, 2005). Allegedly one officer introduced her to another, and she felt compelled to engage in sex with him and so on. She added that the officers warned her not to say anything stating, "I always felt like if I said anything, I would get in trouble. I didn't want to get in trouble. I'm not a bad girl." Once again, this points out that sex with an on-duty police officer, representing the power of the state, is not that "consensual." Citizens and police officers are not on equal footing in their extortionate encounters, police officers know that and some, like the Yukon police officers, take advantage of it.

Aftermath. The officer who engaged in oral sex with the clerk when the man walked in resigned after admitting his guilt. Two others resigned not admitting their guilt but saying they did not want to cause their families any more conflict. A fourth officer was given the option of being fired or resigned. He refused to resign and was fired. A sergeant received a two-week suspension and put on probation for a year. Another supervisor was reprimanded for knowing about a nude photograph of the clerk being taken and not reporting the violation. The department directed that all police officers, including supervisors, would receive ethics training and began tweaking their early warning system to identify problem officers. The clerk at the center of the sex scandal was not fired, but she left town.

## Phoenix, Arizona: Mayor's Son

In 2011, Officer Jeffrey Gordon, a six-year veteran of the Phoenix, Arizona Police Department (PPD), was accused of inappropriately touching a female employee and placed on administrative leave while the complaint was investigated (Anonymous, August 28, 2011; City of Phoenix—Internal Investigation—June 15, 2011). Officer Gordon was the son of the Mayor of the city of Phoenix, complicating the investigation. The city's police chief removed himself from the investigation to avoid any suggestion of a conflict of interest. Further muddling the probe was "inappropriate and unwanted touching" of a fellow worker is an example of sexual harassment and a form of sex discrimination. Things would get worse during the investigation as other sexual misconduct allegations were uncovered.

The department's Professional Standard's Division (PSD) conducted the investigation (see City of Phoenix, June 15, 2011). At the outset, the PSD investigation concerned itself with the "inappropriate and unwanted touching" of a city worker and expanded its purview when prior consensual sexual acts became known. Gordon admitted to giving the woman a massage to relieve her stress and said he could have inadvertently touched the top of her breasts during the massage. He was found to have violated department policy for giving the message and "not maintaining a professional approach to their [official] duties at all times." He was also accused of sending two pornographic texts to the city worker while they were both on duty. Gordon told the PSD investigators that he did not remember sending any pornographic texts, but if he did it occurred inadvertently when he forwarded them to the persons above or below her name on his phone contact list. Forensic investigation revealed the texts had been sent but could not determine whether Gordon or the woman were on or off duty when the texts were sent or received. The woman did not want any criminal prosecution. Therefore, the PSD found this complaint to be unresolved.

Two additional allegations of possible sexual misconduct surfaced during the investigation and were examined by the PSD—one complaint involved Officer Gordon "French" kissing an apartment-complex employee in 2007. Gordon admitted, according to newspaper reports, a relationship with the woman, at the time he was single, and "French" kissing her one time and kissing her on the cheek on another occasion. The PSD found him in violation of Operations Order 3.13.2. D—Employees will maintain a professional approach to their duties at all times. The second allegation involved consensual, on duty, sexual relations with an apartment-complex employee in 2007. The woman denied any sexual contact with Officer Gordon. Gordon, however, admitted to having mutual oral sex with the woman in a vacant apartment and consensual sex on another occasion. The PSD investigators found Officer Gordon in violation of Operations Order 3.13.6 (B)—Employees will not engage in sexual activity or contact at any time while on duty... This is considered Unprofessional Conduct: Consensual sexual conduct on duty, during a work shift, or at a police facility, and is punishable by one-day or more suspension.

The findings of the internal investigation were turned over to the Disciplinary Review Board (DRB) consisting of members of the public, peer officers, police commanders, and an assistant police chief, for review. The DRB recommended a 32-hour suspension to the acting police chief. He imposed a four-day suspension, a light punishment for consensual sex on duty, but it appears to be in line with the way on-duty consensual sex is viewed in many police departments—*low-risk sexual misconduct*. It is possible that being the mayor's son influenced his punishment.

The Arizona Peace Officer Standards and Training Board reacting to the allegations and their resolution suspended Officer Jeffrey Gordon's law enforcement certification for six months. Gordon was placed on administrative assignment pending appeal.

## Milford, Ohio—Consensual Sex—On-Duty Police Officer and the Mayor?

Milford, Ohio is a small city, approximately 68,000 persons, along the Little Miami River in the southwestern part of Ohio. The city has developed into a suburb of nearby Cincinnati. In 1989, the Milford Police Department (MPD) became the smallest police agency—16 officers—in North America to be accredited by the Commission on Accreditation for Law Enforcement Agencies (CALEA)—a significant achievement. The MPD's official Web site states "As a full service, value-driven police agency that's responsive to community needs, we are devoted to our core values and committed to asking ourselves" "*Am I doing the right thing, at the right time, in the right way, and for the right reason*" (www.milfordohio.org). Not all the officers were doing the right thing, at the right time, and in the right way.

In 2010, Milford, Ohio made national news because the female mayor and an on-duty police officer engaged in a sex tryst, without asking themselves the core values questions (DiPietrantonio, May 15, 2010).

Milford, OH has a city manager mayor-council form of government with the mayor elected for a two-year term and serving as the chair of the council. Council members, including the mayor, have no more control over city departments than any other council member. All executive power is vested in a city manager. In 2010, the Mayor was Amy Brewer, married but going through a divorce. Police Officer Russell Kenney, a full-time officer since 2007, was married but estranged from his wife. These two would become the major players in am alleged sex scandal that began with an unknown "whistle blower."

The Milford police chief received an anonymous complaint that Officer Kenney parked for long periods of time at night outside the residence of Mayor Brewer (Baker, May 13, 2010). The area was a low crime area, and the complainant believed Kenney and Brewer were having an affair with the mayor. The police chief began his investigation by examining the records from the GPS locator in Kenney's patrol car—*technical supervisory assist*. He discovered Kenney visited Brewer's condominium while on-duty six times between November 30, 2009, and January 7, 2010. Those stops lasted from 48 minutes to 1 hour and 53 minutes. Then, an audiotape of an in-car camera recording of an arrest Kenney made on January 13, 2010, revealed a risqué conversation between Kenney and a woman named Amy—*technical supervisory assist*. Amy's voice was not audible, but it was believed to be Mayor Amy Brewer. Kenney is heard saying, "Do you really think if you rode around with me, we'd probably just stop everywhere and screw." Later, he said, "I'd like to have your legs wrapped around my waist or my shoulders. It don't bother me" (Baker, May 13, 2010).

Officer Keeney when first confronted by the chief denied ever having sex with the mayor on duty and arrogantly asked for a disciplinary hearing. The chief presented the GPS records and the audiotapes, changing Kenney's attitude and demeanor. Kenney was offered a 15-day unpaid suspension for conduct unbecoming an officer, which he accepted and waived his right to a disciplinary hearing. The suspension was spread out over three months as requested by his union representative. The chief wanted to fire Kenney but decided the expense of a disciplinary hearing and arbitration was not worth it. The city law director said it would be likely that the police union contract would result in Kenney getting his job back and the city having to pay back salary. Union contracts are roadblocks in dealing with police misconduct and lead to *real and perceived low-risk* conditions in police agencies. Firing miscreant police officers, not charged with a crime, where union contracts are in force is an arduous time-consuming unsuccessful undertaking.

Mayor Brewer denied having sexual relations with Officer Kenney when first approached by the Chief. He presented the audiotapes and Kenney's admission. The mayor became visibly shaken and apologized for her behavior, the chief wrote in his investigative report. When the results of the investigation became public, the mayor declared "my personal life is just that, personal, and I am not going to comment on it further." She declared that she would not resign from her position as mayor. That changed. A week after the affair became public, the mayor called a council meeting. She resigned as mayor but retained her position as a member of the council, ending the scandal, and a return to business as usual (Baker, May 13, 2010).

## Grand Rapids, Michigan—Police Dispatcher Groupie

In 2007, the Grand Rapids, Michigan Police Department (GRPD) became embroiled in a sex scandal involving a police dispatcher and as many as ten police officers and a male dispatcher (AP, August 29, 2007). Six of the on-duty sexual encounters allegedly took place inside police headquarters in a bathroom. A "whistle blowers" complaint to the department's Internal Affairs started the investigation. Newspaper accounts identified the female dispatcher as the wife of a Grand Rapid's police officer. At the time, the sex scandal splashed across the newspapers, she and her husband were going through a contentious divorce.

The female dispatcher was, in her words, forced to resign. She claimed her forced resignation was a double standard because other similar incidents were handled quietly and discretely. She did not supply specific incidents. However, a police officer and the male dispatcher resigned before the investigation was complete. Four officers were fired for their alleged involvement in the sex scandal. The police union filed a complaint against the firing of the officers, claiming that even though they admitted wrongdoing, the punishment was too severe, using the boys will be boys defense—*union roadblock to police reform*. Four other officers allegedly had sex with the dispatcher off duty and were not subject to departmental discipline.

The city manager in his press release recognized that the fired officers had admitted their "egregious errors of judgment" and had clean personnel records with good performance records and numerous commendations. However, he emphasized that such conduct embarrasses themselves and their fellow officers and tarnishes the image of the police department and the city. He stressed that police officers are held to a higher standard of behavior. The personal judgment of police officers must be impeccable because they required to judge the behavior of others daily in their work duties (AP, August 29, 2007).

## Cleveland, Tennessee—Love Nest in a Storage Unit

A bizarre case of police consensual sex on duty occurred when the Chief of Police for the Cleveland, TN police department (CPD) and his sex partner the Executive Director of Mainstreet Cleveland, a non-profit organization dedicated to the revitalization and promotion of historic downtown Cleveland, Tennessee—were alleged to be involved in on duty sexual misconduct (Egan, December 12, 2013).

Cleveland, Tennessee is a city of approximately 42 thousand people located just of I-75 in southeastern Tennessee (www.facebook.com/Mainstreet-Cleveland).

The Cleveland, TN police department has 91 sworn officers and 11 full-time civilian employees and is accredited by the Commission on Accreditation for Law Enforcement Agencies (CALEA). CALEA nationally accredits police agencies based on national standards developed by law enforcement professionals. The state of Tennessee has also accredited CPD. On paper, the Cleveland, TN PD looks good and meets all the standards of professional police departments department, but there are warts on the facade.

The police department has seen its share of police misconduct incidents, including accusations of police pill misuse, brutality, sexual relations with inmates and the 2010, convictions of two officers for statutory rape (AP, August 29, 2007). The chief, a thirty-three veteran, ten years as chief, whose father was a CPD chief, had not been implicated in any of the past scandals. That changed when the owner of Rhodes Storage Management reported a tenant of one of his storage units was occupying the unit during business hours for 60–90 minutes at a time (Egan, December 12, 2013). The renter of the storage unit was the alleged chief's mistress.

Surveillance tapes reviewed by investigators showed the chief and his sex partner entering a storage unit at the Rhodes Climate Controlled Storage on numerous occasions. The two remained in the unit for 60–90 minutes at a time. The owner of the storage units let the police in the unit, and they found a "love nest," including an area rug, several blankets, pillows, a folding chair, baby wipes, paper towels, a handheld mirror, a hairbrush, and a half bottle of brandy. Confronted with this evidence several days later the chief submitted his retirement letter.

The married chief his single mistress appeared before a packed City Council meeting and offered their sincere apologies for their "poor judgment" and asked for forgiveness. Their apologies were greeted by loud applause from the packed room (Leach, December 10, 2013). The chief must have sensed that all was forgiven by his reception at the City Council meeting because two days before his retirement took effect he asked to take his retirement letter back. The city manager sent an emphatic NO.

## Conclusion

The examples reveal the inherent dangers of consensual on-duty sex to the participants, the police agencies, and the *policework* occupation. The examples show the effects of organization culture on the *real and perceived risk,* and the explicit and implicit coercion involved in a supposedly consensual act between persons of unequal power and authority. We see how the use of *technical supervisory assists* combined with a zero tolerance approach can monitor the behavior of police officers to control and punish police sexual aggressors. However, it appears that the use of body cameras is not the silver bullet for PSM—a point we return to in the last chapter.

# References

Ahern, J. (1972). *Police in trouble: Our frightening crisis in law enforcement.* New York: Hawthorne Books.

Anonymous. (2011, August 28). *The Streets are Watching.* http://getcopsofftheblock.blogspot.com.

Anonymous. (2014, January 24). Embattled Lakeland Police Chief Lisa Womack resigns. *Bay News.*

AP. (2007, August 29). *Report: 6 face firing in Michigan police sex scandal.* www.foxnew.com.

Baker, J. (2010, May 13). Milford cop suspended for sex with mayor. *Cincinnati.com.*

Barker, T. (2011). *Police ethics: Crisis in law enforcement* (3rd ed.). Springfield, IL: Charles C. Thomas.

Caulfield, P. (2013, June 26). They're Florida's horniest! Cops in Lakeland police department snagged in massive sex scandal: Report. *New York Daily News.*

City of Phoenix. (2011, June 15). Internal Investigation—PSB11-003.

Claim for Damages. (2010, July 30). Claim for damages, Government Code Sec. 910, ccet.sequ. *City of Rialto. City Clerk, City of Rialto.*

DiPietrantonio, S. (2010, May 15). Reaction to mayor-cop sex scandal. *Fox19.com.*

Dulaney, J. (2010, November 18). Rialto police end sex scandal investigation, restore four officers to duty. *Daily Bulletin.*

Egan, J. (2013, December 12). Tennessee police chief and mistress turned storage unit into "love nest." *The Storage Facilitator.*

Leach, P. (2013, December 10). Cleveland police chief, Main Street director, apologize after love nest found. *Times Free Press.*

Maready, J., Pleasant, M., & Rousos, R. (2013, June 26). Investigation uncovers allegations of sexual misconduct at the Lakeland Police Department. *The Ledger.*

Morris, A. (2013, February 28). Former deputy faces charges. *Greenville Journal.*

Press Association. (2017, December 14). Police sack sergeant who met woman for sex on duty during night shift. *Police Oracle.*

Rawlings, P. (2002). *Policing: A short history.* Portland, Oregon: William Publishing.

Raymond, K., & Kramer, B. (2005, July 3). Investigation to switch focus in Yukon polices sex scandal. *The Oklahoman.*

Smith, P. T. (1985). *Policing Victorian London: Political policing, public order, and the London Metropolitan Police.* Westport, CT: Greenwood Press.

Staff. (2011, October 8). Former Cherokee County Sheriff's deputy arrested. *GoUpstate.com.*

Taylor, J. (2012, August 2). Former deputy arrested; Relationship with informant alleged. *The Monitor.*

Toner, J. (2017, April 22). Devon and Cornwell officer sacked for repeatedly having sex on duty. *Police Oracle.*

Toner, J. (2017, August 8). 'Deviant' helicopter sex voyeur officer jailed. *Police Oracle.*

Winton, R. (2010, November 19). 2 Rialto police officers resign, 4 disciplined amid scandal investigation. *LA Times.*

# 8

# Type 6: Custodial Sexual Misconduct

## Introduction

Custodial and detention workers classified as Law enforcement officers work in detention facilities at all levels of government. Municipal police agencies have jails and lockups. Sheriffs and their deputies, jailors, and other detention staff are defined by statute as law enforcement officers. The federal government defines any government official engaged in detention duties as a law enforcement officer. Custodial and detention officers have arrest powers—narrow or general. Some states grant them arrest powers only within their institutional work setting—narrow. Other states grant general arrest powers, the same as any other law enforcement officer-general. The "on the job" sexual abuse by custodial officers occurs in a setting where the sexual aggressor has a captive pool of vulnerable victims with legally defined credibility issues. Potential victims can't slide the bars open and walk or run away. Sex abuse victims cry for help night and day in jails and prisons. Help never comes. And, who is going to believe an inmate against the word of his badge carrying guard. Sexual misconduct in custodial settings is a textbook example of the **PSM Causal Equation: inclination + opportunity + real or perceived low risk = PSM.**

© The Author(s) 2020
T. Barker, *Aggressors in Blue*,
https://doi.org/10.1007/978-3-030-28441-1_8

In all 50 states, any sexual contact between a custodial/detention officer and an inmate is illegal, even if both parties "supposedly" consent (Bell et al. 1999). However, the evidence suggests all types of police sexual misconduct, with the possible exception of sexual serial murders and sexual exploitation in joint school police and community-sponsored programs. The situational setting may be different, but the law enforcement and custodial victim offender relationships are similar. The relationship between a custodial staff member and an inmate is always an extortionate relationship; never on equal terms—an obvious disparity in coercive power (Winters, December 24, 2012). The inmate or detainee is in a captive setting not free to escape the sexual abuse. Case law is explicit in expressing that fear or coercion can be inferred by the disparity between the sexual aggressor and the victim (Smith and Loomis 2013). However, defendants use the consensual defense in an attempt to sway the jury or lessen the punishment.

In many instances, the predatory sexual behavior of custodial/detention officers is galling because their victims are in many cases accused but not convicted of any crime. The victims are in jail awaiting trial because they are poor minority members or a member of a marginalized class who cannot make bail. Once again, we see the tragic consequences of being poor, a minority group member, or marginalized person in an unequal system of justice. Only those with money can successfully play the justice game no matter what organizational model—rational goal model or the functional systems model—they follow (Feeley 1972). Both models require financial resources to achieve the end—due process.

We begin our discussion with one the most egregious example of custodial sexual abuse in US history that I am aware of.

\* \* \*

## Baltimore, Maryland—Prison Gang Criminal Enterprise and Correction Officer Sexual Misconduct

The Maryland Corrections Officers and inmates in this Illustrative Example engaged in their "consensual sexual acts" to further a criminal enterprise conspiracy directed by a prison gang (Barker 2015). The Black

Guerrilla Family (BGF) prison gang is a serious threat in the prisons/jails and the community in Baltimore. There is a history of collusion between corrupt prison officials and Black Guerilla Family members and associates in Maryland. That collusion includes sexual misconduct with corrections officers and contraband smuggling (Barker 2015).

Three black female corrections officers (CO's) and a prison kitchen work pleaded guilty in 2009 for their part in the smuggling of drugs and cell phones into numerous prison facilities in Maryland, including the Metropolitan Transition Center (MTC) in Baltimore (US Attorney's Office-District of Maryland, *Press Release*, November 12, 2009). DEA agents monitoring inmate contraband cell phones heard a CO discussing smuggling contraband into the MTC and alerted Maryland Corrections officials. They searched the female CO and found her smuggling two cell phones for delivery to an inmate with whom she was engaged in a sexual relationship. According to her plea bargain agreement, she admitted she and others had distributed heroin at the MTC from 2008 until April 2009 when she was arrested.

In 2013, the extent of the BGF control of a prison facility and collusion with corrupt prison staff became national news with the Federal indictment of 25 persons, including 13 black female corrections officers at the Baltimore City Detention Center (BCDC), for racketeering, drug trafficking, and money laundering charges involving the Black Guerilla Family inside the jail. It was alleged that the BGF with the aid of the correctional officers controlled the jail underground economy by smuggling and selling tobacco, marijuana, prescription drugs, and food. Seventy-five percent of the facilities six hundred and fifty correctional officers were females and one inmate witness testified that 60–75% of them were involved in contraband smuggling and having sexual relationships with inmates (Toobin 2014).

The leader of the Black Guerrilla Family in the BCDC, Tavon White, allegedly had sexual relationships with four guards and fathered five children by them. As of this writing, seven of the 15 female correctional officers have pleaded guilty. Tavon White, always the schemer, pleaded guilty and "ratted" out his codefendants. He received praise from the judge for his cooperation and was sentenced to 12 years in prison to run concurrently with a 20-year sentence he is already serving. He will be lucky to serve his sentence and be released before s BGF member kills him for being a rat.

# Custer County, Oklahoma—Custodial Sex in the Jail

Oklahoma Sheriff Mike Burgess allegedly ran a sex-slave operation from his jail and membership in a Drug Court Team. He is now serving a 79-year prison sentence among the sodomites. The backstory is bizarre.

Sheriff Burgess had been in office for twelve years when he was arrested in 2008 for thirty felony counts that alleged 14 counts of second-degree rape and seven counts of forcible oral sodomy (State of Oklahoma vs. Michael G. Burgess. Probable Cause Affidavit for Warrant of Arrest, April 16, 2008). He was accused of running a sex-slave operation at the county jail. He was also accused of repeatedly sexually harassing a female deputy during her 3-year employment at the Custer County Sheriff's Department. The sexual harassment allegations included unwanted touching, putting his hand inside her uniform pants and touching her bare buttocks, groping her legs, touching her breasts outside her clothing, and constantly making sexually suggestive statements.

The Washita/Custer County Drug Court Program—court-supervised treatment program for non-violent drug-related offenders—was part of the jail's programs for inmates. The program allegedly provided an available pool of vulnerable sexual abuse victims. As a voting member of the Drug Court Team, Sheriff Burgess had a vote in deciding who would enter or stay in the drug court program.

According to the arrest warrant affidavit, Sherriff Burgess allegedly had sexual intercourse and oral sodomy with inmates of the Custer County Jail and participants in the Washita/Custer County Drug Court Program in various "safe" locations. The encounters allegedly took place at the Biltmore Hotel in Oklahoma City, a private residence in Weatherford, Oklahoma, a private residence in Clinton, Oklahoma, a motel in Clinton, and his sheriff's vehicle. The sheriff was careful to avoid sex in the jail, except for his sexual harassment of the female deputy. These sexual acts, according to the indictment, took place two or three times a week from February 2006 to April 2007. He, again according to the indictment, would call his victims—not in jail—and have them meet him at the assignation sites or pick them up in his official vehicle and take them there. He promised each victim—12 at trial—that for sex he would get them in the drug court program and keep them from going to jail or prison.

Sheriff Burges's "sex-slave" scheme came to an end when one of his victims was called in for a drug screen that she failed. She was put in the county jail, and the sheriff did not secure her release. The "pissed-off" victim alleged that she had sex with Sheriff Burgess and he promised to protect her and keep her out of jail. The district attorney was notified, and he directed the Oklahoma State Bureau of Investigation (OSBI) to investigate. The sheriff's House of Cards tumbled down as a result of a scorned woman.

At a two-day preliminary hearing, several female offenders testified that the sheriff demanded sex in exchange for his help in getting them in or keeping them in the two-county drug court programs. The sheriff and his attorney questioned the credibility of the witnesses, drug offenders, and other criminal offenses, a common defense sometimes successful. Not this time, the sheriff was bound over for trial. At trial, the defense invoked the customary "my client forced no one to have sex" defense. Sex was consensual, and they are lying, the defense argued.

The trial was moved to another Custer County because of intense media coverage, and Texas County prosecutor's conflicts of interest. The trial testimony was devastating for the former sheriff; he resigned before trial. The former female deputy recounted the alleged groping and sexual harassment. A former inmate testified the sheriff promised to make her a trusty for sex. The cross-examination revealed she was bipolar and had, at times, hallucinated because of a crack cocaine habit, calling her credibility into question. Several female drug offenders testified they had sex with Sheriff Burgess because they feared he would send them to prison if they did not. One woman testified that she and Burgess had sex two or three times a week over a 14-month period. The defense pointed out that most of the women were convicted felons in an attempt to impeach their testimony.

The jury convicted the former sheriff of 13 felonies, including five counts of second-degree rape and three counts of bribery by a public official—accepting sex for influence is bribery. He was acquitted of 23 other felonies, including second-degree rape, forcible sodomy, and rape by instrumentation. The jury recommended a sentence of 94 years in prison. The judge reduced the jury's recommendation to 79 years at sentencing—a reduction without consequences. Fourteen of former Sheriff Burgess's victims filed a federal suit against the sheriff and the county and received a judgment of $10 million.

## Latimer County, Oklahoma—Custodial Sex

In 1998, a man, shooting a rifle, chased his recently divorced wife through a department store and into the street in Wilburton, Oklahoma—the county seat of Latimer County (http://mewsok. com/article/2623271-Archive ID: 732793). Shoppers and bystanders screamed and dove for cover. The former happily married couple and parents of two small children, 3 and 5, were going through a bitter child-custody battle. When the husband and wife reached the street, he shot her three times in the head with a .22 caliber rifle as she lay at his feet on the main street of this town of 3000 people. At that exact moment, Latimer County Sheriff Melvin Holly reached the scene. Sheriff Holly was immediately shot in the stomach. Although the bullets critically wounded the sheriff, nicking his liver and spleen, the sheriff returned fire, killing the gunman. He was still on his feet as he walked around saying, "I've been shot." "I've been shot." The brave hero was flown by medical helicopter to a Tulsa hospital about 100 miles northeast of Wilburton. When Sheriff Holly returned to Wilburton, he was greeted by an appreciative outpouring of thanks and recognition as a real hero. His hero status later came to an end.

In October 2005, three months after losing a reelection bid, former Sheriff Melvin Holly was arrested and accused of having sex with four inmates, having sexual contact with four others, and inappropriately touching three employees and the teenage daughter of an employee. His defense followed the usual line—inmate accusers were dope makers, dope sellers, and dope users with credibility issues. Holly and his defense team introduced a novel defense twist. Allegedly, Sheriff Holly could not have sexually abused anyone—medical issues made an erection impossible. Medication and the effects from his previous gunshot wounds were the cause of his impotency and erectile dysfunction. The prosecution countered by asking why Burgess never mentioned this problem in any of his 102 doctor's visits since 1998.

Holly's trial lasted five days, and thirty-two witnesses testified, including the defendant himself. Court documents revealed four acts of nonconsensual sex with inmates and one act where an inmate's resistance stopped the sheriff from having sex with her (US v. Melvin S. Holly, 1007). Victim 1 (V-1) testified that Holly took her from jail to his farm. He then told her to get in the backseat of his car and proceeded to rape her. V-1 said she didn't run because she was afraid he would shoot her. She claimed that he bragged about shooting people on other occasions. Victim 2 (V-2) said Holly raped her in his office after allowing her to make personal calls. Victim 3 (V-3) was allegedly raped in a trailer in a nearby town after Holly took her there from jail. Victim 4 (V-4) had numerous sexual encounters with the sheriff, according to her testimony. They all took place in his office, and she did not fight back because she was afraid of his reaction. Three of these women testified they had sex or flirted with Holly partially for the benefits and jail privileges they received. Victim 5 (V-5) was allegedly called to the sheriff's office on the pretext of her having a family emergency. The inmate testified that she screamed and physically fought the sheriff causing him to stop the assault and tell her to get back to her cell. The sheriff allegedly did not have sexual intercourse with this victim, but he did penetrate her vaginal area with his finger. The sheriff took the stand and denied that any sexual attacks took place, again citing his impotence problem.

Holly was convicted of fourteen criminal counts, including eight counts of misdemeanor deprivation of civil rights under color of law, five counts of felony deprivation of civil rights involving aggravated sexual abuse, and one count of tampering with a witness—threatening to kill an inmate if she told anyone. His appeal for a new trial was rejected, and the disgraced former lawman was sentenced to 25 years in federal prison.

# New York City—Custodial Sex—But We Love Each Other

People find love in the strangest places

The quote above comes from the lawyer of Nancy Gonzalez, a federal corrections officer at the Metropolitan Detention Center in Brooklyn, New York (Secret, February 5, 2013). Her lawyer's statement is a gross understatement of the nature of the alleged illicit affair between Gonzales and Ronell Wilson, a member of the Bloods street gang and convicted of the execution-style murder of two undercover NYPD police officers during a gun sting gone wrong. While awaiting trial for the two murders, the cop killer began to worry about his legacy and wrote to another inmate: "I just need a baby before thiiz pigz try to take my life, I need to have something behind [sic]." Correction Officer Nancy Gonzalez, according to court documents, decided to be the one to have his baby. She was recorded as saying: "I took a chance because I was so vulnerable and wanted to be loved and now I am carrying his child" (Secret, February 5, 2013). She told a New York Magazine, "Why not give him a child as far as giving him some kind of hope" (Vazifdar, February 5, 2013).

Their sordid behavior became known when several inmates at the detention center reported seeing them talking together and then disappearing behind closed doors. They were also seen kissing each other. Three inmates reported that the two "love birds" had been seen having sexual intercourse in Wilson's cell and in a vacant room next to his cell.

In a bizarre twist to an already bizarre illicit sexual relationship, Gonzales became romantically involved with another inmate after having Wilson's baby. Her new lover was in the Metropolitan Detention Center for shooting a man and violating his federal probation on drug-trafficking convictions. She allegedly promised her new paramour that she was finished with Wilson, and he promised to raise the baby. Gonzales was fired from her position at the detention center and lost custody of the child after being arrested for driving drunk with the baby in the car. The former female jail guard pleaded guilty to having sex with inmate Ronell Wilson and was sentenced to one year in prison. The last bizarre twist to this sordid affair occurred when cop killer Ronell Wilson requested to have access to the child as his confirmed father. A Suffolk Family Court judged the Bloods gangster and convicted cop killer to be "civilly dead" and denied him access (Alger, October 4, 2013).

## Worth County, Missouri—Custodial Sexual Groping and Voyeurism

In 2011, Neal Wayne "Bear" Groom, the sheriff of Worth County pleaded guilty to depriving eight women of their civil rights by coercing them to expose parts of their body to him (FBI, August 17, 2011).

In 2006 and 2007, this voyeur with a badge persuaded eight different women to expose their breasts or other parts of their body under the pretext of checking them—domestic violence victims or accident victims—for injuries or signs of drug use. The eight-year veteran lawman admitted to photographing some of his victims. He pleaded guilty in federal court to misdemeanor accounts of violating the civil rights of his eight victims and was sentenced to 18 months in prison.

## Orleans Parish, Louisiana—Custodial Sex—Sexual Rape of a Transvestite

A black male deputy, Juan Thomas, a guard at the Orleans Parish Prison, Louisiana, was arrested on September 2, 2011, and charged with rape, second-degree kidnapping, and sexual malfeasance in prison. The married guard with two years on the job, according to the official Orleans Parish Sheriff's Arrest Register (-7394-11), removed a male prisoner from his cell on the pretext of a sick call, handcuffed him, and took him to a closet. In the closet, Deputy Thomas allegedly removed the handcuffs and forced the male prisoner to perform oral sex. The inmate then told the investigating detectives he ran back to his cell and spat the guard's semen, secreted in his mouth, into a condom.

The inmate was a known transvestite. Newspaper accounts reveal that the inmate had two prior solicitations [for prostitution] arrests. Furthermore, when arrested this time for solicitation and drug charges, he was wearing a wig and appeared to be a female. The condoms in his cell were probably used for sex with other inmates on his tier. Deputy Thomas was probably correct in asserting that the oral sex was consensual, but he forgot one major detail—**IT IS ILLEGAL IN LOUISIANA.**

## Okfuskee, Oklahoma—Custodial Sex. Female Jailer—Oral Sex with an Inmate

On New Years Eve 2008, Okfuskee County, Oklahoma, female jailer, Billie Lee Pelley, allegedly entered the cell of a male prisoner awaiting trial for a felony bomb threat charge (Okfuskee County District Court. Affidavit for Probable Cause to Make Warrantless Custodial Arrest, January 17, 2008). Surveillance cameras recorded her entry into the cell but not what followed. During the investigation, Ms. Pelley told investigators that she and the inmate kissed for a while and then she proceeded to engage in oral sex with the inmate. Coming to her senses, she claimed she stopped and was sitting on the inmate's bed when a female dispatcher walked in the cell. Ms. Pelley was arrested and learned at arraignment that the oral sex act was "forcible sodomy" because in Oklahoma "an inmate can not legally consent to sexual relations, whether or not the act was consensual." Ms. Pelley pleaded guilty to sexual abuse of a person over 16 and is a registered sex offender.

## Orange County, California—Custodial Sex—Female Sex with Skinhead

A black female deputy, working at the Men's Central Jail in Santa Ana, California, was arrested and charged with having multiple sexual acts, possibly 20, with a white supremacist member of the OC Skins— Orange County Skinheads. The 30-year-old white supremacist was in jail for attacking a black man while yelling racial epithets during a robbery (Moxley, February 17, 2012). The 29-year-old five-year veteran deputy could not have missed the prominent White Power tattoos on the Skinheads face, "88" on his chin depicting Hiel Hitler, and the "1" under his right eye and the "4" under his left eye referencing the 14 Words pro-Nazi stressing racial purity. The OC Skins member claimed that his lover left him with an STD.

## Gwinnett County, Georgia—Custodial Sex—Transgender Sex

A black seven-year veteran of the Gwinnett County Sheriff's Department was in charge of a pod of 65–85 prisoners when he was arrested and fired from his position for having sex with a transgender inmate (Green, February 10, 2012). The 36-year-old transgender inmate claimed the gay assaults occurred repeatedly for a month. Although the deputy claimed the sexual acts were consensual, that is no defense because such acts between inmates and jail staff are illegal in Georgia.

## Paducah, Kentucky—Custodial Sexual Misconduct by Private Transportation/ Extradition Officers

The commodification of inmates during the explosion of incarceration in the United States has created a burgeoning new industry, private-for-profit corrections (Welch and Turner 2007–2008). Corrections Corporation of America (CCA), the largest private corrections company, operates correctional and detention facilities across the nation and receives prisoners from multiple states. A 2013 Grassroots Leadership Report found that 10,500 state prisoners were housed in private-for-profit prisons outside their home states. The same report found that states would spend an estimated $320 million incarcerating state prisoners in private prisons (Welch and Turner 2007–2008).

A new private business and occupation was developed to support the private corrections industry—prisoner transportation services. A private company can carry out a public function, such as extradition if the company has a contract with the government agency. The transportation of prisoners across state lines is a very profitable business. In 1996, TransCor America, a subsidiary of Corrections Corporation of America (CCA) that transports prisoners nationwide earned $10.6 million in gross revenues (Friedmann 1997). The new occupation led to a new designation of pseudo law enforcement officers, transportation/extradition officer, increasing the occupational opportunities for custodial sexual misconduct.

Members of the new occupational designation of transport/extradition officer were allegedly sexually abusing vulnerable female prisoners in transit soon after they came into being. In 1994, the co-founders of Fugitive One Transport Company were arrested and charged with raping a female prisoner they were transporting from Connecticut to Texas (Friedmann 1997). In 2009, 168 female prisoners from Hawaii were removed from the Otter Creek Correctional Center in Kentucky following charges of having sex with prisoners against five correctional staff members, including a chaplain, four were convicted.

A most disturbing case of alleged sexual misconduct by a "private" prisoner transportation officer occurred in 2010 in Kentucky. A magistrate court in Lincoln County, New Mexico, issued a warrant for a female, M.M., to appear in court (FBI, September 20, 2012). M.M. waived extradition and the judge directed the Lincoln County Sheriff to have Court Services Incorporated (CSI) transport M.M. from Murfreesboro, Tennessee, to New Mexico. Albert Preston Long, a CSI employee, was the driver of the transport vehicle. Long picked up M.M. and three male prisoners in Tennessee and transported them to Hopkinsville, Kentucky. At the jail in Kentucky, Long placed the male prisoners in the jail and claimed that the jail would not take the female so took her to a nearby motel. At the motel, he allegedly gave the female alcohol and Vicodin and forced her into sexual relations.

Long checked the male prisoners out of jail and continued his transport to Paducah, Kentucky, where he repeated his actions of the previous stop—males checked into jail and the female were taken to a motel. Once again, Long allegedly forced M.M. to have sex. The journey came to an end in Fort Smith, Arkansas, when Long tried to check the male inmates into the Sebastian County Detention Center, and a detention officer asked why the female prisoner listed on the manifest was not checked into the jail, a good question—Why didn't Kentucky detention officers ask this question? M.M. was removed from the transport van, and Long was arrested.

The investigation revealed that Long had two prior felony convictions making it illegal for him to possess a firearm and raising the question, Why was he hired to be an armed transport officer by CSI—*poor vetting*? Long pleaded guilty to traveling in interstate commerce for the purpose of engaging in any illicit sexual contact with a female arrestee, deprivation of rights under color of law, felon in possession of a firearm, and use of that firearm in furtherance of a crime.

## Conclusion

Custodial Sexual Misconduct is the exemplar of law enforcement sexual misconduct where sexually inclined LEOs are in charge of a vulnerable pool of potential victims—opportunity—without power to resist the sexual advances. All types but serial sex murders and sexual abuse in police-community-sponsored programs have been identified in custodial settings. The secure conditions in the custodial setting provide a real or perceived low-risk environment. Technical assists such as surveillance cameras can, and do, provide a means to prevent or punish malefactors. Supposedly "consensual" sex takes place in custodial settings, except all sexual contact is illegal in these settings. The alleged sexual misconductby pseudo LEOs in private corrections agencies is an area that needs to be examined thoroughly. Private correctional agencies have problems. Their loyalty and service are bought and paid for-not a part of public duty and an oath to serve and protect.

## References

Algar, S. (2013, October 4). Cop-killer Ronell Wilson 'civilly dead' has no right to see son. *New York Post.*

Barker, T. (2015). *North American criminal gangs* (2nd ed.). Durham, NC: Carolina Academic Press.

Bell, C., Coven, M., Cronan, J. P., Guggemus, J., Garza, C. A., & Storto, L. (1999). Rape and sexual misconduct in the prison system: Analyzing America's most "open" secret. *Yale Law & Policy Review, 18,* 195.

FBI. (2011, August 17). *Former worth county Sheriff pleads guilty to violating the civil rights of eight women in Missouri.* Office of Public Affairs: Press Release.

FBI. (2012, September 20). *Private prisoner transport employee pleads guilty to civil rights, traveling across state lines to engage in unlawful sexual activity, and firearms.* U.S. Attorney's Office: Western District of Kentucky.

Feeley, M. M. (1972). Two models of the criminal justice system: An organizational perspective. *Law & Society Review, 7*(3), 407–425.

Friedmann, A. (1997, November 1). US: Private transportation firms take prisoners for ride. *Prison Legal News.*

Green, J. (2012, February 10). Deputy jailed for alleged sex with inmate. *Gwinnett Daily Post.*

Moxley, R. S. (2012, February 17). Jennifer Tamara McClain is a prisoner of love. *OC Weekly News.*

Secret, M. (2013, February 5). Impregnated by prisoner, guard Now faces charges. *The New York Times.*

Smith, B. V., & Loomis, M. C. (2013). Sexual abuse in custody: A case law survey. *National PREA Resource Center.*

Toobin, J. (2014). This is my jail. *The New Yorker, 90*(8), 26–32.

Vazifdar, L. (2013, February 5). Guard pregnant by Cop Killer: Corrections officer Nancy Gonzales arrested for having sexual relations with inmate, Ronell Wilson. *Travelers Today.*

Welch, M., & Turner, F. (2007–2008). Private corrections: Financial infrastructure, and transportation: The new geo-economy of shipping prisoners. *Social Justice, 34*(3–4), 56.

Winters, R. (2012, December 24). Power relationships & sexual misconduct corrections. *Corretions.com.*

# 9

## Type 7: Harassment Discrimination in the Police Workplace

## Introduction

*Policework* is a highly bureaucratized traditional male-dominated occupation. This myopic description has changed somewhat in modern societies moving to a work world without strict gender categories. However, the introduction of females into the police workplace as equal partners has not been without controversy and the transition is not complete. Many police workers still see policing as a "man's" world and the culture of their police agency and the command structure aids and condone this worldview. This attitude leads to a legal and employment nightmare called sexual harassment not limited to one gender.

Sexual harassment occurs in police agencies throughout the world (see Box 9.1). A 2016 independent review of the Australian Federal Police (AFP) found that 46% of the females and 20% of the males reported being sexually harassed within the last five years (Anonymous, August 22, 2016). Females were 60% of the unsworn AFP workforce. Sexual harassment is a legal nightmare for US police agencies because "Sexual harassment is a form of sex discrimination that violates **Title**

© The Author(s) 2020
T. Barker, *Aggressors in Blue*,
https://doi.org/10.1007/978-3-030-28441-1_9

**VII of the Civil Rights Act of 1964** "(www.gov/eeoc/publications/ fs-sex.cfm)." As described in the EEOC report:

> Sexual harassment occurs in a variety of circumstances, included but not limited to the following:

- The victim as well as the harasser may be a woman or a man. The victim does not have to be of the opposite sex. (Collins [2004] in her seminal study of disciplinary measures taken against Florida LEO officers guilty of sexual harassment found two cases where both the harassers and the victims were men and two cases involved female police officers sexually harassing male officers.)
- The harasser can be the victim's supervisor, an agent of the employer, a supervisor in another area, a co-worker, or a non-employee.
- The victim does not have to be the person harassed but could be anyone affected by the offensive conduct.
- Unlawful sexual harassment may occur without economic injury to or discharge of the victim.
- The harasser's conduct must be unwelcome. (*Source* www.eeoc.gov/ eeoc/puublications)

---

**Box 9.1   RCMP Sexual Harassment Apology**

A class action lawsuit known as the Merlo-Davidson suit after the two women former RCMP officers—who filed it against the Royal Canadian Mounted Police—the largest federal police agency in Canada—alleged that "female regular members, civilian members and public service employees were subject to systematic discrimination, harassment, and bullying on the basis of gender and/or sexual orientation, and that the RCMP failed to protect the women from the treatment" (http://rcmpclass-actionsettlement.ca/faqs.html).

The lawsuit was settled in October 2018 with an unprecedented public apology from the RCMP Commissioner to current and former females who were subjected to bullying, discrimination, and harassment. He announced a $100 million dollar payout for all who filed substantiated claims from September 1974 (Bronskill, October 6, 2015). Each victim is eligible for a payout between $10,000 and $200,000. It was expected that 1000 victims would submit claims. Thus far, there have been 3131 claims.

---

\*   \*   \*

US police administrators have learned the costs of failure to adopt policies and take an aggressive and proactive stance against sexual harassment. Numerous lawsuits have resulted in compensatory and punitive damages and loss of employment for recalcitrant administrators. Sexual harassment incidents create work environments filled with tension and conflict. The media portrayal of sexual harassment incidents damages police-community relations and erodes the agency's public image. The effects on the victim are devastating, creating depression, fear, humiliation, and other psychological symptoms. The organization and the administrators are liable if they knew or should have known of its occurrence when it is openly practiced or well known. The failure to take immediate and appropriate corrective action when complaints are made is an invitation to disaster. What is sexual harassment?

In a nutshell, sexual harassment is unwanted and unasked for sexual attention coming from the opposite or same sex. Collins divided sexual harassment by police officers into three categories: gender harassment, unwanted sexual attention, and sexual coercion.

**Gender Harassment:** A broad range of verbal and nonverbal behaviors that convey insulting, hostile, and degrading attitudes about women [or males] solely because of their gender, for example, sexual epithets, slurs, taunts, the display of obscene or pornographic materials, and other threatening or hostile acts.

**Unwanted Sexual Attention:** Verbal and nonverbal behavior that is offensive, unwanted, and unreciprocated, being stared at, leered at, or ogled, being continuously asked for dates despite being told no, being touched, or being continuously asked to have sex.

**Sexual Coercion:** The classic form—quid pro quo—of sexual harassment is the extortion of sexual favors in return for job-related considerations such as getting or keeping employment benefits.

Our discussion begins with a rarely reported example of sexual harassment—female sexual harassment of males.

*   *   *

## Paso Robles, California Police Chief Lisa Solomon—Female Sexual Harassment

If the allegations presented against the first female chief of police of Paso Robles, California, Lisa Solomon are accurate, they represent a textbook case of sexual harassment of a female against a male. Lisa Solomon was a twenty-four-year veteran of the Paso Robles, California Police Department. Chief Solomon was a poster child for the integration of women into American police work. She moved up through the ranks as the first woman sergeant, lieutenant, and captain before being appointed chief in 2007.

In 2012, she was accused of sexually assaulting her male officers (Velie and Blackburn, January 26, 2012). The allegations included a laundry list of sexual assaults against male officers, many in front of witnesses, repeated affairs with subordinates, including one that resulted in a child out of wedlock. One officer claimed she grabbed his penis while he sat in her car. Another claimed he was making a bar check when the chief who was on the floor dancing came over and grabbed his head and pushed his face into her breasts. A room full of bar patrons observed this act. Officers said they did not report her behavior because "crossing Solomon is dangerous." She had the reputation of trumping up criminal charges on any officer who rebuffed her advances or questioned her management practices.

Following the claims, the city hired an investigator to examine the allegations. The officer who claimed his face was pushed into her breast told the investigator, "Her MO is to make criminal charges against anyone who crosses her. She will do whatever she can do with her power." It appears from published reports that her bizarre sexual harassment behaviors were well known. The 2012 allegations were not the first serious allegations of sexual harassment made against the chief.

In a 2008 article titled "Girl chief gone wild," the "former beauty queen-turned-lawman" was alleged to be giving lap dances to her officers (Velie and Blackburn, September 11, 2008). She was quoted as saying "I am an entertainer," when asked about her known habit about dancing in public places. She added, "As for inappropriate behavior, that is absolutely false. I have never given a lap dance or danced on a bar." People who had an ax to grind spread those stories, she claimed. During the 2008 Super Bowl, she allegedly called a team-building exercise at a lodge and required her command staff to attend. After the exercise, Chief Solomon allegedly ordered the men into the hot tub, where she said, "You want to see boobs" then removed her top and rubbed her breasts in a commander's face (Velie and Blackburn, September 11, 2008). According to reports, she then slid her hand into a sergeant's shorts and grabbed his penis. After this unwanted sexual assault, she allegedly groped another officer.

The bizarre sexual harassment case against Chief Solomon abruptly ended on March 21, 2012. On March 20, 2012, Chief Solomon submitted her letter of resignation and requested early retirement. The next day the City manager announced the city, and the chief had signed a separation and release agreement. Under the agreement, the city would allocate a payment of $250,000, and both parties would agree not to sue (Anonymous, March 21, 2012). The city would not confirm or deny that there was an investigation of the allegations.

## New Britain, Connecticut PD (NBPD)—A Pattern of Sexual Harassment

In 2011, a female NBPD police officer, Susan Keller, a nine-year veteran, filed suit against the police department. She alleged that Captain Anthony Paventi, the head of the NBPD Internal Affairs Unit, had engaged in numerous acts of sexual harassment and gender discrimination against her because she rejected his sexual advances. Keller alleged she was passed over for promotion, special assignments, and extra-duty jobs because she rebuffed Paventi's sexual advances. She alleged that the Chief of Police William Gagliardi and other supervisors knew about Paventi's behavior and took no action. There were previous sexual harassment and gender discrimination complaints against him and other NBPD supervisors, but no action was taken (Stacom, April 21, 2011).

According to the suit, repeated and offensive sexual comments and advances were part of "the routine culture of the New Britain Police Department," despite the city's "zero tolerance" policy. The 140-person police department had less than a dozen females; however, Officer Keller's suit was the fifth federal suit filed against Captain Paventi and the police department since 2009.

The 2009 federal civil suit by female officers Jennifer Raspardo, Needasabrina Russell, and Gina Spring outlined a list of allegations (Raspardo, Russell, Spring v. Carlone, Gagliardi, Steck, Panetta, City of New Britain, New Britain Police Department No. 9-CV-1321— Alvin Thompson Judge). All three women alleged their direct supervisor, NBPD Sergeant John Carlone, created a hostile work environment by sexually harassing them through inappropriate jokes, comments and engaging in unwanted physical contacts with Raspardo and Russell between early 2007 and early 2008. The other defendants created a hostile work environment by not investigating his behavior. Following an investigation, Carlone was demoted from sergeant to patrol officer and recommended for termination by the chief. He retired on January 31, 2009, to avoid termination.

While the federal suit was pending additional charges of sexual misconduct were raised against Captain Paventi. A woman came forward and testified at deposition that she and Paventi, when he was a patrol officer, had numerous sexual encounters while he was on duty. The acts allegedly included sex on the hood of his patrol car and in the bathroom of a school. She claimed she broke up with him when he wanted to have three-way sex with her and another woman in a motel (Stacom, August 20, 2011). The police department put Paventi on administrative leave while they investigated the complaints. In an attempt to tamp down the public scandal, Paventi and the police union negotiated a retirement agreement during the investigation. Paventi agreed to retire and cooperate in the civil suits, and the city would keep secret the findings of the investigation.

In July 2012, Chief William Gagliardi retired after 41 years with the New Britain PD, chief since 2007. Two months later, the city settled Officer Paula Keller's lawsuit with a $60,000 payout. In October 2012, the new police chief promoted five officers to sergeant, and Paula Keller was one of them. In April 2015, the city of New Britain voted to settle the remaining lawsuits with a payout of $153,000. The settlement agreement called for former Sgt. Carlone to pay an additional $65,000 directly to the plaintiffs.

# Queen Anne's County, Maryland Sheriff's Department—Federal Civil Right's Action Against a Law Enforcement Agency

"The Attorney General of the United States has certified that the underlying lawsuit presents a case of public importance to the United States" (DOJ 2013). Those twenty-three words signaled that the federal government believed Kristy Lynn Murphy-Taylor, a former Deputy Sheriff with the Queen Anne County, Maryland Sheriffs Department had her Civil Rights violated by the sheriff and five sheriff's department's employees. The alleged civil rights violations were a result of sexual harassment and sexual discrimination, resulting in a hostile work environment and her wrongful termination.

The Justice Department's Civil Rights Division can and does intervene, in such cases under an agreement the Department of Justice has with the US Equal Employment Opportunity Commission (EEOC) to take the lead in job discrimination litigation claims against state and local agencies. The allegations that formed the lawsuit's basis were disturbing. Murphy-Taylor claimed her sexual assaults began in 2006, with repeated attempts by John Hoffman, the Sheriff's brother, to touch her breasts in the office and in official vehicles (DOJ 2013). The sexual assaults continued.

In 2007, Murphy-Taylor claimed Hoffman sexually assaulted her in a hotel room while they attended an off-site training course. She claimed she reported these sexual assaults to the Sheriff Gary Hoffman, John Hoffman's brother, and the sheriff did not take corrective action to stop or prevent their occurrence. And, the allegations got worse. Deputy Murphy-Taylor claimed in 2009, the sheriff's brother, John, was driving a car in which Murphy-Taylor was a passenger when he reached over with his right hand and put it down her pants, touching her vagina area. He also felt her right breast. She told him to stop and pushed his hand away, but he overpowered her and continued to touch her breasts.

According to the lawsuit, other sheriff's department officers, a lieutenant and a detective, made derogatory and sexually explicit comments about her and another female detective, including insinuating the two female officers had sex at an off-site training session. Murphy-Taylor filed a written complaint with a captain complaining of sexual harassment by John Hoffman, the lieutenant and the detective, all three were her supervisors. While her complaint was investigated, she continued to work closely with and was supervised by the same three officers. Her complaints, after investigation, were substantiated; however, the three harassers remained in their positions and continued to supervise Murphy-Taylor. As a result, Murphy-Taylor claimed she was subjected to numerous acts of reprisal.

In February 2010, Murphy-Taylor filed a charge of discrimination with the EEOC, detailing the sexual assault by John Hoffman and the sexual harassment by him and her other male supervisors. Murphy-Taylor also listed her unsuccessful complaints to the management of the Sheriff's Office. On August 25, 2010, John Hoffman was arrested and charged with second-degree assault and fourth-degree sexual assault of Deputy Murphy-Taylor. He pleaded guilty on May 12, 2011, to second-degree assault of Murphy-Taylor that occurred in August 2009. The next day, May 13, 2011, Murphy-Taylor received a letter from the Sheriff's Office informing her she was terminated. During a worker's compensation hearing of her termination, the Sheriff offered to let her return to work in a demoted position and under John Hoffman's supervision; he was not removed after his conviction of second-degree assault. Murphy-Taylor declined the offer.

The Sheriff's brother, John, was retained as a sheriff's deputy in a supervisory position, even after his conviction for second-degree assault until December 2011. In November 2011, the Maryland Police Training Commission conducted a hearing to determine if he had the moral character to remain a Maryland police officer in light of his second-degree assault conviction. The Commission members voted 12–0 to decertify him and revoke his police license in December 2011. Queen Annie's County settled their suit with Murphy-Taylor in June 2014 for $620,000: $194,188.52 for back-pay and interest, $89,120.46 for back benefits, $74,364 for front-pay and $2277.02 for medical benefits, as well as $260,000 to plaintiff's attorney (Price, June 2, 2014).

The Justice Department entered into a consent decree with the state of Maryland and the Queen Anne's County Sheriff. Under the decree, the Sheriff's Office agreed to revise their sexual harassment policies and procedures for handling complaints of sexual harassment and retaliation. The Maryland State Police will provide oversight for the handling of complaints. Also, Murphy-Taylor will receive $250,000 in damages. Sheriff Gary Hoffman won reelection in 2014 and is in his third term.

## Philadelphia Police Department (PPD)—Sexual Harassment and Sex and Religious Discrimination

Captain Debra Frazier, a black female and a Muslim, had been on the PPD for 23 years when she filed a federal lawsuit against her supervisor Deputy Police Commissioner William Blackburn (Peacock, April 30, 2012; Gambacorta, May 1, 2012). Cpt. Frazier, the head of the Narcotics Unit, alleged that Blackburn engaged in a three year—2008–2011—pattern of treating her differently based on her race, gender, and religion. His behavior created a hostile work environment.

The allegations stated that Deputy Commissioner Blackburn sent her text messages demanding sex or female companionship for favorable treatment. She alleged that the Deputy Commissioner ogled and leered at her at a gym they attended, stalked her, and once threatened to run over her. She alleged Blackburn asked discriminatory questions about her Muslim faith and off-duty dress, asking why she wore Muslim garb off duty. Cpt. Frazier allegedly made informal and formal complaints about Blackburn's behavior, but the police commissioner said investigations did not support her claims because there were no witnesses. The police commissioner was quoted as saying, "I have full confidence in Deputy Commissioner Blackburn in terms of his abilities to lead and so forth," and he further stated, "We'll see what comes out of this litigation, but he has my support" (Gambacorta, May 1, 2012).

Testimony during the lawsuit provided support for Frazier's sexual harassment complaint. Blackburn's former aides testified Blackburn directed them to browse through the PPD personnel files for photos of female officers for him to select those he wanted to meet. One former aide said Blackburn would select the photos, find out where they worked and then "William Blackburn then would have me drive

[him] to meet the female officer." This occurred regularly, according to published accounts. In November of 2013, the police commissioner moved Deputy Commissioner Blackburn from Major Investigations—Homicide, Narcotics and Forensic units, and Homeland Security—to handle the administrative duties of Support Services. The move was supposedly due to a retirement and not the lawsuit. The city of Philadelphia paid a settlement of $45,000 to Captain Frazier.

## Nevada Capitol Police—Sexual Harassment and Age Discrimination

The Nevada Capitol Police Department (NCPD) is an example of a special district/jurisdiction police agency with full police powers. The Nevada Capitol Police Department is responsible for security in Nevada's Capital building. The capital building houses the offices of the governor, secretary of state, treasurer, and controller and their staffs. Included within their jurisdiction are the attorney general's and the Governor's Mansion. Every state and the nation's capital, Washington, D. C., have a capital police agency.

Alice Alverez filed a lawsuit in 2013 claiming she was the target of sexual harassment and age discrimination by at least five of her male colleagues, and her supervisors had done little to investigate or take action (Ryan, August 28, 2013). The suit alleged the five defendants suggested she could not do her job because she was a woman and one made a very derogatory comment about having sex with her. The same officer who made the sex comment allegedly rubbed up against her sexually. Her male colleagues allegedly made sexual comments and said she should have chosen another career such as being a "stay-at-home mom." The lawsuit said she feared retaliation and continued discrimination in a hostile work environment.

She alleged she was one of four women in the police department and one other female officer had also been sexually harassed. The Nevada Governor ordered an investigation. Several officers were placed on administrative leave while the investigation proceeded. A settlement was reached in February 2014. The state paid Miss Alverez $99,999, fired a sergeant, and four other officers received unspecified "lesser discipline."

## Hull, Massachusetts PD—Sexual Harassment in a Small Police Agency

The quiet tranquility of this seaside town of 10,000+ was turned upside down when an eight-year veteran of the Hull Police Department (HPD) filed a sexual harassment suit against the town's police chief and two commanding officers. The civil suit brought unwanted bad publicity and divided the town and police department into opposing camps. Officer Wendy Cope-Allen's attorney is quoted as saying "I have never seen a workplace environment so poisoned by misogyny" (Germano, September 28, 2011). Hyperbole is expected from attorneys describing their client's case, but the allegations provided a firm foundation for his statement.

Officer Wendy Cope-Allen alleged that Police Chief Richard Billings, Captain Robert Sawtelle, and Lieutenant Dale Shea engaged in a long-time pattern of sexual harassment, including telling others that she was promoted from dispatcher to police officer by being sexually promiscuous, and "that Cope-Allen was having sex with numerous male police officers and firefighters." She was, according to the lawsuit, subjected to sexual slurs and forced to mend uniforms off duty with no additional pay. Lt. Shea allegedly used sexually demeaning terms when giving her instructions and made crude remarks about her "tight pants." Captain Sawtelle allegedly engaged in sexually suggestive comments to her in front of others. When Wendy Cope-Allen complained about Sawtelle's behavior, he allegedly told her "Shut the [expletive] up, or you're not gonna have a paycheck, and you can start looking for another job" (Schworm, September 28, 2011).

Two longtime female dispatchers in supporting affidavits said they often saw the three supervisors display "outrageously misogynistic conduct" toward female employees and call Cope-Allen a slut and say, "she got her job because she is a little flirt." One female dispatcher said the supervisors often began roll call with "crude talk about pornography and sexually demeaning jokes about women." Another dispatcher said in an affidavit that Chief Billings referred to another female dispatcher almost daily as a "slut."

During the discovery phase lawsuit, it was discovered that Chief Billings had a prior incident—2001—of sexual harassment before becoming chief. Billings, then a sergeant was investigated for harassment and discrimination against a gay officer, found culpable and disciplined (Schiavone, December 18, 2011). The employee said Sgt. Billings would ask, "why don't you like girls" and were his feet sore from marching in the Gay Pride parade, and he makes other vulgar remarks. Billings admitted to making the statements and claimed they were in jest. This was a matter of public record and known, or should have been known, by the town council that appointed him chief—*improper vetting*. In November 2014, the gay officer, now a sergeant, filed suit against the department, Chief Billings, Captain Sawtelle, and Lt. Shea for being continuously harassed since 1998. He alleged that the three supervisors commonly used crude, derogatory terms for his sexual orientation, and tried to fire him because of his sexual orientation.

## Telford Borough, Pennsylvania—Sexual Harassment in Small Agencies

The Telford Borough Police Department (TBPD) is a small 5 man, no females, agency located 120 miles west of Harrisburg, the capital of Pennsylvania. They have no full-time female officers. The TBPD did have one full-time female police officer, Connie McGinnis, but she was fired in 2010 and subsequently sued the agency and the city for sexual harassment, intimidation, and wrongful termination (Reed, September 1, 2012). According to Miss McGinnis's suit, she was a five-year veteran with the department when Chief Randall Floyd fired her in retaliation for her complaints to him and other supervisors. The suit alleged that Chief Floyd made sexual advances to her, invited her to his home, a hotel, and his mountain house. McGinnis alleged Chief Floyd touched her inappropriately and constantly leaned up against her, smelling her hair and trying to kiss her. Other officers allegedly stalked her and made sexual comments to her, showed pornography, and made derogatory comments about women to her. One fellow officer allegedly asked her to perform a sex act on him. When she complained to the chief, he told her, "If you don't like it, just leave" and reduced her hours and overtime.

The suit alleged her desk was ransacked and personal belongings, including a bra and tampons, were taken. She complained to the chief and nothing was done. In the same time period, the chief allegedly made a sexual advance to her that she rebuffed. Several weeks later, she was fired for "failure to document a summary citation." In June 2012, her civil suit was settled with a payout of $14,000.

## Harassment in Small Police Agencies—Shannon Woolsey

Shannon Woolsey was a ten-year veteran officer of the Town and Country, Missouri Police Department. During those ten years, Woolsey claims she was subjected to continuous acts of sexual harassment including gender harassment, officers talking about sex, strippers, and pornography; being told to shut her "man pleaser" when talking; and unwanted sexual attention, suggestions that she meet her supervisor monthly for sex; sexual coercion-demands for sex in order to be promoted or get a good assignment (Bertacchi, March 27, 2012). She compared the 30-man "good ole boy" police department to a frat house. She finally had enough when a sergeant and a corporal called her off her shift into the department office and belittled her until she became physically ill. She resigned and sued the department for sexual harassment.

## Sexual Harassment in the UK

### Two Decades of Sexual Harassment by the Medical Advisor of the Norfolk Police Force

According to an official British government report, the sexual abuse and sexual harassment of female police officers by the medical adviser for the Norfolk Police force during their recruitment examinations was allowed to continue for two decades—1991 to 2003—*real or perceived low risk.* The primary reason for this continued pattern of sexual abuse was the "superficial investigation" of complaints. During that time period, at least 33 females alleged that the examining doctor had conducted a comprehensive full body check that included the examination of breasts, genitalia, and anus. He performed the examinations of the women alone—*an obvious abuse of accepted protocols.* He had free reign to grope and digitally probe his victims. The report said women who complained were told "to keep quiet" and were threatened to be sued if they slandered the examining doctor (Garrod, December 11, 2017).

The depth of this medical examiner's sexual depravations did not become public until 2013 when he pleaded guilty to indecently assaulting 13 "extremely vulnerable" women during his examinations. He also pleaded guilty to rape and sexual assault of two girls under 14. Six other officers were examined for possible misconduct for failure to properly handle the complaints. They were allowed to retire without disciplinary action. Case closed.

## Chief Constable for Avon and Somerset Police Forces

Chief Constable Nick Gargan was suspended for a year with full pay in 2014 after being charged with 10 counts of gross misconduct for making inappropriate sexual advances to junior female colleagues. Following a 2015 ten-day closed hearing, he was found guilty of misconduct and given eight written reprimands. He could not be dismissed because he was not found guilty of gross misconduct. He also could not be demoted. He was cleared to return to work. The scandal and the seemingly light discipline lead to an eruption of calls for him to resign. Twenty-four of the twenty-five senior officers in his police forces voted no confidence in him. Three months after the findings, he yielded to the pressure and resigned (Morris 2015).

# Conclusion

The Illustrative Examples show, once again, how Law Enforcement Sexual Misconduct can thrive in a work setting where LEOs with the *inclination* to commit forbidden sex acts—in these cases on their own colleagues—when the *opportunity* presents itself under a *real or low-risk* setting. We also saw the consequences that occur when the sexual aggressors misjudge the risk.

# References

Anonymous. (2012, March 21). Paso Robles police chief Lisa Solomon relieved of command. *The Tribune.*

Anonymous. (2016, August 22). Sexual harassment within Australian Federal Police almost twice the national average. *ABC News.*

Bertacchi, D. (2012, May 27). Female police officer speaks out against sexual harassment. *MO Patch.*

Bronskill, J. (2015, October 6). RCMP earmarks $100 million in compensation for sexual harassment against female Mounties. *The Canadian Press.*

Collins, S. C. (2004). Sexual harassment and police discipline: Who's policing the police? *Policing: An International Journal of Police Strategies & Management, 27*(4), 512–538.

DOJ. (2013). Plaintiff-intervenors complaint—Kristy Lynn Murphy-Taylor and United States of America v. The State of Maryland, Queen Anne's County Maryland and Sheriff Gery "Gary" Hoffman, Sheriff Queen Anne's County Case No. 1: 12-cv O2521-ELH.

Gambacorta, D. (2012, May 1). Deputy police commissioner faces sex-harassment suit. *Daily News.*

Garrod, S. (2017, December 11). Police officer's sexually assaulted 'badly let down by investigation.' *Police Oracle.*

Germano, B. (2011, September 28). Hull officer sues police chief, commanders for sexual harassment. *WBz-TV.*

Morris, S. (2015, October). Nick Garden resigns as Avon and Somerset chief Constable. *The Guardian.*

Peacock, W. (2012, April 30). Sexual harassment allegations amongst top cops. *Philadelphia Employment Law News.*

Price, A. (2014, June 2). County agrees to pay former deputy $620,000. *Queen Anne's County News.*

Reed, B. (2012, September 1). Ex-cop charges Telford Borough with sexual harassment. *The Philadelphia Inquirer.*

Ryan, C. (2013, August 28). State investigating conduct of Capitol Police officers. *Las Vegas Sun.*

Schiavone, C. (2011, December 18). Hull officer files second suit against department, town. *The Enterprise.*

Schworm, P. (2011, September 28). Female officer sues police force. *The Boston Globe.*

Stacom, D. (2011, April 21). New Britain police hit by another sexual harassment suit. *The Hartford Courant.*

Stacom, D. (2011, August 20). More allegations of police captain misconduct. *The Hartford Courant.*

Velie, K., & Blackburn, D. (2008). Girl chief gone wild? *Calcoastnews.com.*

Velie, K., & Blackburn, D. (2012, January 26). Police chief accused of sexually assaulting her officers. *Calcoastnews.com.*

# Part III

## Police Child Molesters & Pornographers

## Introduction

In the United States, a child or minor is defined by state statute. However, the Office of Juvenile Justice and Delinquency Prevention (OJJDP) defines child "as someone who has not yet reached his/ or her 18th birthday (OJJDP 2010: 13)." We will use this definition. Therefore, a police child molester is any law enforcement officer who engages in sexual activity with a child of any gender less than 18 years of age. The sexual abuse is always criminal activity no matter the nature of the act. There is no consensual sex with a minor.

The majority of reported police sexual activities with children occur off duty (Barker 2015). However, the off-duty law enforcement officer often misuses their power and authority to facilitate the sexual abuse. Sometimes this child abuse includes incest. A search of Google Alerts from 2009 to 2014 revealed 36 cases of incest reported against off-duty police officers (Barker 2015). One was the 4-year-old relative of a retired Maine State Police Chief and the most decorated police officer in Maine history. During the same period, there were 38 cases of police child molestation where the victims were under 12 years of age. We must distinguish child molesters from pedophiles.

## Police Child Molesters

The terms child molester and pedophile are often used interchangeably, but this is not accurate. Pedophilia, a sexual preference for children, is a psychiatric diagnosis with specific criteria and suggested treatment regimens. Pedophiles have a specific preference for children and have sexual fantasies and erotic imagery focusing on children (OJJDP 2010). Legally, pedophiles can indulge in their sexual fantasies by fantasizing and masturbating—not in public. When the pedophile acts on his/her sexual preferences and molests a child, they are child molesters subject to punishment, not treatment.

Once pedophiles cross the legal line, the criminal justice system exists to stop future child molestation and punish them for what they have done. Identifying and punishing police child molesters should be an objective of all law enforcement agencies. A police executive who denies police child molesters exist in their agency—when they do—or allows them to escape punishment or move to another agency makes an unforgivable mistake and adds to the Gypsy Cops problem.

## References

Barker, T. (2015, March). *Sleazy Blue Line: Police Sexual Misconduct.* Paper presented to the Annual Meeting of the Academy of Criminal Justice Sciences.

OJJDP. (2010). *Child molesters: A behavioral analysis: For professionals investigating the sexual exploitation of children.* Office of Juvenile Justice and Delinquency Prevention. National Center for Missing & Exploited Children.

# 10

## Type 8: Child Molestation

## Police On-Duty Child Molesters—Victim Contact

The sample of on-duty police child molesters presented is not all that was found in the research for this book. They represent Illustrative Examples of the most disturbing cases.

## Robert Lellock—Gay Pittsburg Police Officer—Child Molester, Multiple Victims

In July 2012, Pittsburg Public Schools Police Officer Robert Lellock was accused of molesting a 13-year-old boy in 1999. The boy at the time was a student at a middle school on Pittsburg's north side. The following sources are the basis for the narrative that follows: Brandolph and Boren, August 28, 2012; Ziatos, August 28, 2012; Brandolph, September 1, 2012; September 17, 2012; and Gurman, September 19, 2012. Although the sexual molestation allegation occurred in 1999, under the 1999 Pennsylvania statute of limitations a victim could file charges for up to five years after they turned 18.

© The Author(s) 2020
T. Barker, *Aggressors in Blue*,
https://doi.org/10.1007/978-3-030-28441-1_10

Officer Lellock was put on administrative leave with pay following the complaint. On September 19, 2012, Lellock submitted his resignation to the school board, and they voted 7–1 to accept it. The one member, voting "no" wanted to fire him, not let him resign. Following a three-week investigation, Lellock was arrested and charged with 23 offenses, including involuntary deviate sexual intercourse, corruption of minors, endangering the welfare of children and indecent assault. The 2012 criminal complaint listed 4 male victims, all about 13 years old at the time of victimization, dating back to 1998.

His 1998 victim told police he met Officer Lellock while making a familiarization tour of the school. Lellock, according to the allegations, made a comment about a stain on the boy's pants and his pants pocket. The boy confessed that he had a stolen credit card in the pocket. The tour continued, and Lellock allegedly grabbed the boy's crotch and told him to keep quiet about the stolen credit card, or he could go to jail. He did not see Lellock again until school started.

The young boy had been in school for a week when Lellock called him out of class. Lellock allegedly took the boy to a janitor's closet, pinched him through his pants, and reminded the boy of the stolen credit card and asked sexual questions. The sexual attacks increased after this incident to at least twenty similar assaults, according to the complaint. Each involved Lellock removing the boy from class, taking him to the janitor's closet, sexually assaulting him, and forcing the boy to perform oral sex acts. While the sexual assaults were occurring, Lellock allegedly told the victim he would kill him and his family if he ever told anyone. The victim became so afraid of Lellock that he began carrying a knife to school. The knife was found on the young victim, and he was expelled.

A second man came forward, and alleged Officer Lellock sexually assaulted him in 1999 when he was 13 or 14. He said Lellock would let him cut school and smoke marijuana. Lellock would pull him out of classes and take him to the janitor's room where Lellock allegedly sexually assaulted him. A third victim claimed Lellock would walk him around the school grounds when he was caught skipping classes. When they reached isolated hallways, Lellock "play wrestled" with him, touching his genitals. A fourth boy claimed Lellock encouraged him to cut school, and he met with the boy and his friends while they smoked marijuana that Lellock gave them.

Lellock's victims came from a target pool of vulnerable victims with credibility problems—a low-risk setting. The victims attended the school's "alternative classroom" program for problem students. At trial, the prosecutor described the victims, "The kids you're going to hear from are the down and out. They're juvenile delinquents. They're thieves. They're drug users. They're kids on in-school suspension. In other words, they're the perfect victims from a child molester's perspective (Ward, July 23, 2013)—PSM results from *inclination + opportunity coming together under a real or perceived low rusk setting.*"

The abuse could have been stopped at an earlier time with appropriate and called for action. In May of 1999, the school investigated an incident where Lellock pilled a student out of class and took him to the janitor's closet where they were discovered "play wrestling." The district director of employee relations classified the encounter as a "critical incident" and remarked that she "cannot stress how disturbing this case is to me and all those who have reviewed it" (Brandolph, August 28, 2012). She further stated "You pulled the student in question from class on at least one other occasion to go to the storage room and wrestle. In addition, the evidence reveals that you have gone to the storage room with other students under similar circumstances." The chief of the school's police wanted to terminate Lellock, but the district's chief human resources officer and an attorney told the chief that there was no reason to notify outside law enforcement agencies and no grounds to fire Lellock—*bureaucratic impression technique.* He was given a 20-day suspension. The child molestation continued for years.

In July 2013, Lellock took the stand in his own defense and denied molesting anyone. The trial lasted two days, and the jury deliberated for three hours before finding him guilty on 13 charges, including endangering the welfare of children, corrupting minors, and indecent assault. In October 2013, Lellock was sentenced to 32–64 years in prison.

## Long Beach, California—Officer Noe Yanez—Child Molester, Multiple Victims

Officer Noe Yanez was a nine-year veteran of the Long Beach Police Department (LBPD) when he was arrested on April 19, 2012, on suspicion of child pornography (Anonymous, February 22, 2013). Allegedly, he met a minor girl during his routine police duties and began texting her. During their series of text messages, he asked the young girl to send him nude pictures. The girl sent the pictures and told the School Resource Officer (SRO) at her high school. The SRO reported this to his supervisors, setting off an investigation that uncovered a serial police child molester who had been sexually molesting young girls from 2008 until his arrest in 2012.

Yanez was released on bail on April 20, 2012, and rearrested on May 7, 2012, after an extensive investigation revealed 13 more victims (Van Dyke, May 11, 2012). He was charged with 24 felonies and 15 misdemeanor charges. The felony charges included sexual penetration by a foreign object of a person under 18; oral copulation of a person under 18; unlawful sexual intercourse; using a minor for sex acts; possession of matter depicting a minor engaged in sexual conduct; meeting a minor for lewd purposes; false imprisonment by violence; and contact with a minor for a sexual offense. At his arraignment, Yanez was ordered to be held in jail until his trial.

In February 2013, Yanez pleaded guilty to six felony counts involving five minors. He was sentenced to 11 years and eight months in prison and to register as a sex offender. Forty-five other counts were dismissed.

## Pocahontas County West Virginia Deputy Sheriff—Child Molestation, Custodial Sex, and Sexual Harassment

The case of Pocahontas County Deputy Sheriff, Bradley C. Totten reads like bad fiction. The ten-year veteran officer was indicted twice in 2012 (Jenkins, November 7, 2013). The first indictment involved 19 alleged counts of sexual abuse of four children and one adult woman. According to the allegations set forth in the indictment, Totten, on duty and in uniform, forced two female juveniles to perform oral sex on him, forced another to allow him to perform oral sex on her, and fondled the fourth and had her fondle his penis. He was also indicted for allegedly forcing an adult woman in custody to have sex with him.

In August 2012, Totten was indicted again on 47 counts of alleged sexual abuse of women and girls from 1995 to 2010. The 66 charges linked him to approximately two-dozen women and girls over a 15-year period. He was also accused of sexual harassment in a civil suit (Smith, November 14, 2012).

The Special Prosecutor appointed to try this case offered Totten a plea deal instead of standing trial for all 66 charges. The rationale was that a plea deal would spare the victims from having to testify and balance the interest of the victims and the interest of the public. The plea bargain also prevented a public scandal that would be exposed at trial—*bureaucratic impression management.* Totten pleaded guilty to a single count of sexual abuse of a 17-year-old girl whose sexual abuse began when she was 15. Totten was sentenced to not less than 10 and no more than 20 years in prison and fined $5000.

## Wheeler Minnesota Police Department—Police Chief: One Man Department—Child Molester

In 2010, the small community of Wheeler, Minnesota, hired Gary Wayerski to be its part-time police chief and only police officer—a tragic mistake. A routine background investigation would have uncovered that Gary Wayerski was a Gypsy Cop and a known child molester (*State of Wisconsin v. Gary L. Wayerski.* Cir. Ct. NO. 2011CF186)—*improper vetting.* According to the investigation and court records, in 1986, a 16-year-old boy alleged that Wayerski put him in handcuffs and performed a sex act on him. This charge was later dropped. Then in 2007, while he was an on-duty deputy with the Pepin County Sheriff's, he watched pornographic computer images of boys. He resigned in lieu of being charged. In 2011, Chief Wayerski was arrested and charged with second-degree sexual assault of a child, exposing a child to harmful substances and misconduct in public office.

The felony charges alleged Chief Wayerski used his position as a law enforcement officer to exploit two teenage boys sexually. His initial contact with the boys came when he caught them breaking into a church. Wayerski persuaded the boys and their parents to allow him to enter into a mentoring relationship in order to help them. The mentoring consisted of a sexual grooming process that began with ride alongs in his patrol car and then invitations, both individually and together, to visit him in his apartment. The investigation revealed that he began to fondle and masturbate them while they watched pornography. Wayerski threatened them by saying he would "get them sent to Juvie or jail if they told on him." The sexual abuse took place numerous times from March to July 11, 2011.

His threats worked until July 11, 2011. The boys, after an overnight stay, couldn't take it anymore and left his apartment on foot. Wayerski tried to get them to return, but they would not, and one called his father and reported what had been going on.

County deputies executed search warrants on Wayerski residence and found hundreds of pornographic images of nude teenage boys. They also found a computer with its hard drive removed. He told the deputies he destroyed the hard drive because he knew it would be examined. He also told the deputies that he was a "porno addict" who was bisexual and into "all sorts of kinky stuff." Wayerski pleaded not guilty by reason of insanity. That defense did not work. He was found guilty of two counts of felony child enticement, two counts of causing a child to expose genitals or pubic region, two counts of causing a child to view or listen to sexual activity, and eight counts of felony sexual assault by a person who works or volunteers with children. He was sentenced 14 years in prison followed by 16 years of extended supervision.

## Flint, Michigan—Lawrence B. Woods—Decades of Child Sexual Abuse

Lawrence B. Woods, a retired Police Sergeant from the Flint, Michigan Police Department, was charged with 16 felony counts of first-degree sexual conduct in September 2014 (Mitchell, September 6, 2014). Six of those charges were for alleged rape of children under 13. The investigation into Wood's decades-long child sex abuse began when the retired officer was arrested for sexually assaulting two young girls who were the daughters of a woman he was in a relationship with. At the time of his arrest, law enforcement authorities speculated the retired sergeant had raped 50 women and children while on duty. This speculation was based on the large amount of child pornography found in his residence and places he stayed. According to the authorities, the time and date stamped Polaroid images showed sexual assaults inside the police department, in police vehicles, and on city property.

After the allegations became public, four more women have come forward alleging Woods sexually molesting them when they were minors. He is awaiting trial, and a psychiatric exam has been ordered to see if he is competent to stand trial.

## Alex Robinson—A Lifetime of Mentoring at-Risk Youths and Child Molestation

Alex Robinson is a retired Sergeant from the Wichita, Kansas Police Department (WPD). At the time of his arrest in January 2013, he was the Wichita School district school safety supervisor. A 24-year-old man came forward and alleged then Sergeant Robinson of the Wichita, Kansas Police Department, had molested him when he was 12 years old. The allegations were particularly shocking because Robinson spent most of his private life mentoring at-risk youths. He received presidential recognition—President Bush—for his volunteer work for the non-profit mentoring organization Real Men, Real Heroes, and the Boys and Girls Club of South Central Kansas (Leiker, March 13, 2014). Robinson allegedly used the children he met during his volunteer work as a pool of vulnerable victims.

While the police were conducting the investigation of the January 2013 allegation, they uncovered additional victims and charged Robinson with molesting three more male victims, who ranged in age from 11 to 14 at the time they were sexually molested. He was charged

with two counts of criminal sodomy, three counts of aggravated indecent liberties, one count of aggravated liberties with a child, and two
counts of indecent liberties with a child. In March 2014, Robinson was
charged in El Paso County, Colorado, with two counts of sexual assault
on a child by a person in a position of trust during a visit in the summer
of 1996 or 1997.

The Colorado charges grew out of the Wichita investigation. The
Wichita PD detective in charge of the case received a call from a man
who said Robinson had molested him "between 14 and 16 years ago."
The Wichita detective interviewed the man, and he said Robinson provided him with pornographic magazines and movies and they slept in the
same bed when Robinson visited Colorado. He alleged he and Robinson
played sex games together. At the time the victim was 14 or 15.

The investigation uncovered "red flags" suggesting Robinson was not
qualified to be a police officer. He was first hired by WPD as a police
officer on July 9, 1984. He was demoted to service officer on July 26,
1986, and terminated on December 31, 1989. There were no reasons
given for these disciplinary actions. Robinson was rehired as a Clerk II
on January 18, 1990, and promoted to police recruit officer on August
19, 1991—*improper vetting*. He was promoted to police officer on
December 21, 1991. The final word on the nature of his disciplinary
actions and the outcome of his trial will come later.

## Texas Alcohol Beverage Control Officer Joe Chavez: Child Molester with a Past

Joe Chavez, a seven-year veteran Texas Alcohol Beverage Control
(TABC) agent conducted undercover investigations of licensed estab-
lishments that sell alcohol, especially those suspected of selling alcohol
to minors. It was standard operating procedure to use underage teenagers in these sting operations. According to a Texas Attorney General's
Press Release, TABC Agent Chavez not only used a 16-year-old female
in his sting operation but also raped her in his state-issued vehicle after
the operation was completed (TABC Press Release, June 10, 2009).

A Bastrop County Grand Jury indicted Chavez on two counts of sexual assault of a child and one count each of online solicitation of a minor, abuse of official capacity and official oppression.

The 16-year-old female reported to authorities that after the sting operation, Chavez sent her a sexually explicit photograph of himself the day before the operation took place. She did not report this to anyone and went through with the operation. After the sting was completed, Chavez allegedly raped her in his state vehicle. She reported the rape and Chavez was suspended without pay, and he resigned.

Chavez was Gypsy Cop. Court documents, filed June 27, 2011, show Chavez had a history of prior sexual misconduct complaints (Chavez v. Texas, August 24, 2012). The allegations included sexually harassing two teens during TABC sting operations. Allegedly, he solicited sexually explicit photos from one of them in 2007. He was accused of having sexual encounters with two teens while working with the Cuero, Texas Police Department. One encounter was a sexual assault of a child, and the other was an "extramarital affair" on duty. He was fired from the Cuero Police Department in 1996 for causing a vehicle accident while intoxicated. The TABC knew or should have known that he should not be hired as an agent—*improper vetting.*

In August 2011, after a weeklong trial, Chavez was convicted of one count of sexually abusing a child and acquitted of a second count. He was sentenced to 20 years in prison (Anonymous, August 12, 2011). He was also convicted of online solicitation of a minor and sentenced to 10 years in prison on this charge. The TABC suspended the use of these stings, and when they were reinstated, all participating minors had to be transported by at least two officers.

## Haines City Florida PD—Child Molester and Under Age Sex Ring

The Winter Haven Florida PD was investigating a missing person case when they made a startling discovery. Paul Aaron of Hines City, Florida, a Polk County School Bus Attendant, was operating a prostitution business out of his home using juveniles as sex slaves (Pleasant, July 14, 2011). Two juvenile runaways, ages 14 and 15, were picked up by Aaron in July 2009 and had been forced into a life as prostitutes until they escaped in February 2010. The business run out of his residence was known as Genuine Quality Entertainment on social media. Aaron allegedly "pimped" out the girls at $20–$100 a trick approximately 100 times. One victim was allegedly forced to have sex with Aaron at least 50 times and the other 30 times. The investigation revealed Aaron kept the teenagers locked in a room and fed them only ramen noodles. Aaron kept all the money the girls made. He told them they had arrest warrants out on them, and if they caused any trouble, they would be arrested—*marginalized victims with credibility problems create a real or perceived low risk for PSM*. A black five-year veteran of the Hines City Florida Police Department, Demetrius Condry, backed up his threats of arrest.

Demetrius Condry frequented the residence and Genuine Quality Entertainment on duty and in uniform driving his marked police car. However, he did not pay for sex with the two girls. Instead, he was given oral sex in exchange for protection against busts. One girl told investigators she was forced to have oral sex with him at least 20 times (Pleasant, February 11, 2013). Condry was arrested for sexual battery by a law enforcement officer, lewd battery, and official misconduct. He resigned after his arrest. In February 2013, Condry pleaded guilty to lewd battery and official misconduct. The more serious charge of sexual battery by a law enforcement officer was dropped. He was sentenced to 10 years in prison.

## Jackson County, Missouri SO—Sexual Assault of Minor—The Department of Justice Steps In

Court testimony revealed that on July 24, 2007, Jackson County Deputy Sheriff Steven W. Burgess encountered a 15-year-old girl and her friends drinking in a park in Sibley, Missouri at 2 a.m. Burgess ordered the friends to leave and the young girl to stay. As soon as the friends were out of sight, he allegedly began fondling the breasts, buttocks, and vaginal area of the frightened young girl and then forced her to give him oral sex. He drove the teenager to her aunt's house and told her if she told anyone about the forced sex, he would tell about her drinking (DOJ, November 12, 2009). The girl went into the house and immediately told her relatives what had happened. Burgess was arrested, charged, and ordered to stand trial. Burgess resigned his position as deputy and pleaded guilty to felony statutory sodomy and deviate sexual assault in Jackson County Circuit Court in 2008.

The case would have ended when Burgess was sentenced to 14 years in prison; however, the Jackson County judge suspended the prison sentence and gave him five years probation. This enraged the family and many in the community. The family sought relief from the Department of Justice.

The US District Attorney for the Western District of Missouri charged former Deputy Sheriff Steven Burgess with violating the 15-year-old girl's constitutional rights by sexually assaulting her while she was in his custody. The violation occurred while Burgess was on duty and in uniform (DOJ, April 9, 2009). Burgess pleaded guilty and was sentenced to 14 years in federal prison without parole. The young girl also filed a federal suit against Burgess, the sheriff's department, the sheriff, and several supervisors. She claimed the sheriff's department condoned a "culture of sexual misconduct" in the department that was a cause of her sexual assault. She cited as proof the following: A sergeant had received a three day suspension for sending sexually explicit jokes and cartoons from department computers; another sergeant received 5-days suspension for sending and receiving sexually explicit emails on department computers; and the department had reassigned an officer to be a high-school School Resource Officer (SRO) for telling an inappropriate sexual joke to a female officer. The reassigned SRO was still in his position after several complaints from parents. In 2013, a US District Judge ordered Burgess to pay $2 million in damages to the girl. The likelihood of her collecting any of this settlement is probably zero, but Jackson County has already paid her $400,000 to settle her claim.

## Catoosa County, Georgia Sheriff's Department— Deputy William S. Crossen—Child Molester

The parents of a 16-year-old girl went to the Georgia Bureau of Investigation (GBI) and reported that Deputy Crossen, a five-year veteran of the Catoosa County SO, had been having inappropriate sexual relationships with their daughter (Cook, July 12, 2013). Complicating the complaint is the age of consent in Georgia is 16. A brief investigation was conducted by the GBI and revealed that Deputy Crossen had, while on duty and in uniform, enticed the girl into a sexual relationship and, during a period in February 2012, engaged in oral sex with the 16-year-old girl, took nude photos of her and distributed those photos.

Georgia law allows consensual sex between a 16-year-old girl and an adult, but it does not allow someone to possess nude pictures of the 16-year-old girl or distribute those photos and engage in oral sex with her. He was immediately fired from the sheriff's department for rules violations and charged with sexual exploitation of a child [use of a child under 18 for sexual gratification by an adult is sexual abuse in GA], sodomy, and distribution of pornography.

In March 2013, William S. Crossen pleaded guilty to sexual exploitation of a child, dissemination of computer pornography, interference with custody, and sodomy. He sentenced to five years in prison.

## Ocala, Florida Police Officer—Sexual Misconduct with a Runaway Prostitute

Forty-one-year-old Bennie Wilson, the married father of three children, joined the Ocala Florida Police Department in September 2012 (Anonymous, October 31, 2014). He brought a wealth of police experience and glowing references to his new job, 18 years with the Albany, Georgia police department. He also had one year of service with the Sumter County Florida Sheriff's office.

In October 2014, the Ocala Police Department received an anonymous complaint that one of their officers was having sex with an underage prostitute (Anonymous, October 31, 2014). A sergeant from Internal Affairs was assigned to investigate the complaint. The sergeant found the young girl. The 16-year-old had run away from home and was engaged in prostitution. She admitted to having sex with at least 20 men a day to support her drug habit. She said she had sexual encounters at least twice with an Ocala officer, once where he fondled her breasts and then oral sex and sexual intercourse on another occasion. The girl was able to describe the officer, his vehicle, and the time of day where the incidents occurred.

The young girl said when they first met the conversation turned sexual and the officer asked if he could touch her. She agreed, and he fondled her breasts through her clothing. According to her, the officer asked if he needed to wait until her 18th birthday. Two weeks later they met again, and he asked if they could go somewhere to be alone. She agreed but said she had to smoke her crack cocaine pipe first. Twenty minutes later, the officer picked her up in his patrol car, and they drove behind a business and got out. She performed oral sex on him. They then had sex after he put on a condom. He gave her $20 afterward.

It did not take the investigators long to identify the officer Bennie Wilson, and they brought him in for an interview. Wilson admitted having sex with the teenager and knowing she was under 18. He denied this later. He was arrested and charged with two counts of unlawful sex with a minor and fired. He was set to go to trial on December 11, 2015, but minutes before the trial started he decided to plead guilty. He pleaded guilty to one count of unlawful sexual activity with a minor, contact with a minor, oral sex, and sexual intercourse. In spite of pleas for leniency and the minor's willingness, the judge sentenced him to 12 years in prison and three years subsequent probation. He also must register as a sex offender.

## British Police Child Sexual Molesters

Police sexual abuse exists to some extent in all police agencies. Police sexual misconduct is an example of deviance in a sexual abuse-prone occupation. Although I am not aware of any scholarly studies of PSM in the UK, there is anecdotal evidence. My Google alert search found examples and a qualitative search of 2017 and 2018 newspaper articles listed on the *Police Oracle* Web site—www.policeoracle.com, London, UK—found others.

A former police superintendent—police chief—who worked in Wrexham in North Wales was convicted of historical sex offenses against male victims who were 14 or 15 at the time of their sexual abuse (Hurst, October 21, 2016). The police superintendent was in charge of center for delinquent boys convicted of petty crimes. They received military style "shock" treatment. He allegedly forced the young boys to exercise naked and watched them in the showers before sexually abusing them. He was convicted of indecent assault of several boys who came forward as grown men to testify against him. He died of natural causes six weeks into his prison sentence.

A 31-year veteran of the West Midlands Police Force was charged and convicted of the sexual assaults of 17 young boys—the youngest was eight—between 1976 and 2013. He was a police constable and a scoutmaster. The sexual assaults took place at scout camps, swimming pools, police stations, and other locations. His depravations were reported several times but not acted on because it was felt that there was not enough evidence for conviction.

An undercover investigation caught a North Wales Police Constable officer trying to arrange sex with a child. He was also charged with distributing and possessing child pornography. The police constable received a 28-month sentence.

A Borough of Ealing police constable was charged with raping a child under 15. He was driving the child, a rape victim, home from a meeting she had with child health services. During the drive, the rape victim allegedly performed oral sex on him. He then drove her to his flat where they had intercourse. He was sentenced to four years in prison.

## West Midlands Police (United Kingdom)—Sergeant Allan Richards—A Life Time Sexual Predator

"It's abundantly clear to me you have been a sexual predator all your adult life," sentencing Judge Francis Laird—November 2016.

Disgraced former West Midlands Police Sergeant Allan Richards was sentenced to 22 years in prison for forty sexual assaults of seventeen young men, some as young as eight between 1976 and 2013. The charges included sexual activity with a child, serious sexual assault, three charges of gross indecency, and seven counts of sexual activity of a child. He kept photos of the naked boys (Anonymous, October 21, 2016).

The attacks allegedly took place at a police station, Boy Scout camps, and swimming pools. He abused his first young victim when he was with a football team as a Scout leader in the 1970 s. The child molester kept a coded diary and a computer record of his victims. The evidence at trial revealed that he could have been stopped and prosecuted in 2000 or 2004 when the allegations first surfaced. Instead, he was removed from public contact and allowed to remain in the police service until he retired in 2011—*bureaucratic impression technique.* The Independent Police Complaints Commission (IPCC) apologized to the victims and promised to investigate the entire affair.

The 2017 to 2018 *Police Oracle* search found additional instances of British police child molestations. A Cumbria Police Constable admitted to three attempts to entice a child to engage in sexual activity. He was suspended and remanded for trial (Toner, January 24, 2017). A Constable with the London Metropolitan Police force pleaded guilty to three counts of attempting to engage in sexual activity in the presence of a child and one charge of causing or inciting a child to engage in sexual activity. He had a 14-year-old girl perform sex acts during Skype calls (Press Association, February 3, 2017). During a South Wales Pedophile Online Investigation, the police discovered one of their own engaging in child sexual assaults (Hutber, August 8, 2018). He was sentenced to 12 years in prison after admitting to one count of rape and five indecent assaults. A twenty-year veteran of West Yorkshire Police agency was fired after sending "inappropriate and unprofessional" sexual messages to a 14-year-old girl in a children's home (Press Association, August 2, 2018). The officer had received a missing person's report at the home and engaged in a conversation with the young girl, receiving her contact information. A Leicestershire Police Officer was sentenced to seven years in prison for abusing a 17-year-old girl (Hudson, August 30, 2018).

# Conclusion

Several disturbing patterns are present in the known Illustrative Examples in this chapter. First, the serial nature—multiple victims— and long history of law enforcement child molesters are disturbing. Second, the known number of police sexual aggressors who molest children. One can only speculate on the number of secret LEO child molesters. More research on this is needed. This chapter provides a sad segue into the next pattern of LEO sexual misconduct.

# References

Anonymous. (2011, August 12). Former TABC agent gets a 20-year sentence for sex assault of 16-year-old girl. *Lubbock Avalanche-Journal.*

Anonymous. (2013, February 22). Former long beach police officer sentenced to 14 years for sex crimes involving minors. *CBS Local.*

Anonymous. (2014, October 31). Ocala police officer arrested for sex with a minor. *Ocala Post.*

Anonymous. (2016, October 21). Ex-police officer found guilty of 40 sex offenses against children. *The Guardian.*

Brandolph, A. (2012, August 28). Handling of sex abuse allegations raises flags. *Pittsburg Tribune-Review.*

Brandolph, A. (2012, September 1). Dad asks son to be removed from accused man's home. *Tribune-Review.*

Brandolph, A. (2012, September 17). Accused officer to resign job. *Tribune-Review.*

Brandolph, A., & Boren, J. (2012, August 28). Handling of sex abuse allegations raises flags. *Tribune-Review.*

Chavez v. Texas. (2012, August 24). No. 1300-98. Court of Criminal Appeals.

Cook, A. (2013, July 12). Former Catoosa County deputy's jail sentence reduced from seven to five years. Northwestgeorgianews.com.

DOJ. (2009, November 12). Former Missouri Sheriff's Deputy Pleads Guilty to Sexually Abusing a Teenage Girl While She Was Detained. Department of Justice.

Gurman, S. (2012, September 19). Former Pittsburg School Resource Officer Faces Sex Charges. *Pittsburg Tribune-Review.*

Hagen, E. (2014, May 13). Former Minneapolis police officer sentenced for child sex crimes. *ABC Newspapers*.

Hudson, N. (2018, August 30). Officer's sexual abuse of teenager ends in dismissal. *Police Oracle*.

Hurst, P. (2016, October 21). Retired police superintendent found guilty of sexually abusing boys in his care. *Wales Online*.

Hutber, J. J. (2018, August 8). Ex-PC jailed for raping "very young" child. *Police Oracle*.

Jenkins, J. (2013, November 7). Former deputy faces prison time. *Metro News*.

Leiker, A. R. (2014, March 13). Wichita school district safety supervisor charged with multiple child sex crimes. *The Wichita Eagle*.

Mitchell, A. (2014, September 6). Retired flint police officer faces 16 counts of sexually assaulting children on duty. *Inquisitr*.

Pleasant, M. (2011, July 14). Haines city police officer, school employee arrested on sex-crimes charges. *The Ledger*.

Pleasant, M. (2013, February 11). Ex-Haines city officer guilty in sex case, sentenced to 10 years. *The Ledger*.

Press Association. (2017, February 3). PC admits getting girl, 14, to perform sex act on Skype. *Police Oracle*.

Press Association. (2018, August 2). PC dismissed after sending inappropriate Messages to 14-year-old. *Police Oracle*.

Smith, L. (2012, November 14). Additional claims of sexual misconduct leveled Against Totten in second civil rights suit. *The West Virginia Record*.

TABC Press Release. (2009, June 10). Bastrop County Grand Jury Returns Felony Indictments Against Former TABC Officer. *Texas Attorney General*.

Toner, J. (2017, January 24). Officer admits attempted sexual assault of a child. *Police Oracle*.

Van Dyke, J. (2012, May 11). Update: LBPD officer rearrested for more offenses. *Gazettes.com*.

Ward, P. R. (2013, July 23). Former Rooney Middle School student testifies that ex-schools cop sexually abused him. *Pittsburg Post Gazette*.

Ziatos, B. (2012, August 28). Public school officer suspended. *Tribune-Review*.

# 11

# Type 9: Child Pornography

## Introduction

The viewing, possessing, producing, or transmitting of sexually pornographic material by a law enforcement officers is of two types—adult and child. Viewing adult pornography while on duty, either through electronic means on personal or departmental owned devices, or possessing adult pornographic material while on duty (magazines, photos, etc.) is typically not a crime. However, it is usually a violation of agency policies, procedures, and rules. Therefore, it is subject to administrative sanction, including dismissal. On the other hand, the possession of child pornography by any person is a criminal offense and subject to criminal and administrative penalties. Therefore, the production, possession, transmission, or viewing of child pornography by a law enforcement officer on or off duty is a serious crime.

The production of child pornography requires perpetrator victim contact and is a violent crime. On the other hand, viewing, possessing, and transporting already produced child pornography does not require victim–sex aggressor contact. Therefore, this heinous police sexual misconduct is not a violent crime. If fact, that is used as a not successful

© The Author(s) 2020
T. Barker, *Aggressors in Blue*,
https://doi.org/10.1007/978-3-030-28441-1_11

rationalization in many instances. The examples presented show that LEOs at all levels of government engage in the viewing, production, possession, and transportation of child pornography. Child pornography is charged and prosecuted by both state and federal agencies.

# Federal Prosecution of Law Enforcement Officers

## Anthony V. Mangione—Head, US Immigration and Customs Enforcement (ICE) for South Florida

"This case reveals the disturbing truth that child predators will go to great lengths to sexually exploit minors," federal law enforcement officer Anthony Mangione said in a 2008 news release, after a Martin County [Florida] man was sentenced to 10 years in prison for using the Internet to entice a minor into sexual activity. "ICE is committed to identifying and arresting these individuals who seek to victimize children and help ensure that justice is served," he added (Franceschina et al., September 28, 2011).

The lofty words were emblematic of the public position on "child predators" that shared pornographic images of children over the Internet expressed by Anthony Mangione, a secret child pornographer. Mangione hid his sexual perversion behind a mask of respectability. The 27-year veteran federal law enforcement officer (LEO) was married and the father of three and since 2007 was the chief law enforcement officer for ICE in the South Florida region. As chief LEO for ICE, he supervised 450 agents in nine counties as they investigated drug smuggling, money laundering and financial crime, commercial fraud, national security, and cybercrimes that included the transportation, receipt, and possession of child pornography as part of the federal government's efforts for Project Safe Childhood. While he railed against child pornography in public, Mangione collected child pornography and transported it to other collectors.

According to a September 28, 2011, FBI Press Release, Mangione transported and received visual depictions of minors engaged in sexually explicit conduct from March 2010 to September 2010. He also possessed electronically stored messages that contained images of child pornography (FBI, September 28, 2011). Mangione allegedly used the Internet provider AOL to send and receive child pornography. That is what led to his exposure.

AOL's sophisticated software to detect potential pornography flagged files being sent from Mangione's email account and shut down the account while preserving the information. The retrieved pictures were sent to the National Center for Missing and Exploited Children. From there, the files were forwarded to the appropriate law enforcement agency as outlined in Project Safe Children. Once the Broward County Sheriff's Office (BSO) and the FBI received the information, they executed search warrants on Mangione's house and ICE office.

The searches of Mangione's home computer revealed his AOL accounts were regularly used to send nude and pornographic pictures of children. In one instance, in September 2010, Mangione sent sexually explicit images of boys under 10 and one of a girl under 12 to an unidentified recipient. Later court documents revealed 150 child pornographic images on his laptop with some of the victims as young as three. He allegedly was part of Internet chat groups with other child pornography owners, sending pictures to a man in Delaware who reportedly had 700 child porn images.

At first, Mangione pleaded not guilty and delayed his trial while a defense expert examined the computer images. Then, he reached a plea deal with federal prosecutors and admitted using two different email handles to send 16 emails containing child pornography to a single email address. He was sentenced to 70 months in prison followed by an additional 20 years on supervised release.

## FBI Special Agent Donald J. Sachtleben—Child Pornographer and Secret Deviant

Donald Sachtleben during his 25-year distinguished career with the FBI was a member of the FBI's terrorist squad and a bomb expert. He served as the team leader at the bombings of the 1993 World Trades Center, the 1995 bombing of the Alfred R. Murrah Federal Building, the 1998 bombing of the US Embassy in Kenya, and the 2000 bombing of the USS Cole. He coordinated the search and arrest of the Unabomber Ted Kaczynski. In 2008, Sachtleben retired as an FBI Special Agent and went to work as an FBI technician working as a bomb analysis and government contractor. Sachtleben was an admired patriotic federal agent, but his public persona had a dark and secret deviant side.

Investigators with the Illinois Internet Crimes Against Children Task Force—Project Safe Childhood, while searching the computers of a man in Roscoe, Illinois discovered child pornography being exchanged between the man and an IP address belonging to Donald Sachtleben in Carmel, Indiana. On May 11, 2012, FBI agents and officers with the Indiana State Police served a search warrant on Sachtleben to search his computers and residence for child pornography (Kno, May 11, 2012). They found 30 images and video files of child pornography featuring girls under the age of 12. Sachtleben allegedly traded these images and videos with others on the Internet. An FBI agent swore in an affidavit that Sachtleben sent 220 images of child pornography on one night in September 2010. He was charged with possession of child pornography and distribution of child pornography. As bad as Sachtleben's legal problem were they became decidedly worse. Sachtleben was charged with leaking classified CIA information (West, July 112, 2014).

Sachtleben still worked for the FBI as a contractor and retained his top-secret security clearance. On May 7, 2012, four days before his arrest for child pornography, the *AP* published a story that US intelligence learned that Al-Quida's Yemen branch had built a new, nearly undetectable bomb and had plans to put the bomb on a US-bound plane around the anniversary of Osama bin Laden's death. The story attributed to unnamed government sources reported the FBI had the bomb in their possession. The story ignited a firestorm of criticism against leaking of classified national defense information and a frantic effort to identify the leak's source.

A year later, the Justice Department informed *AP* that the government agency had secretly obtained two months of call records from 20 telephone lines used by *AP* reporters and editors in an attempt to discover the source of the leak. The Justice Department identified Sachtleben as the possible source and secured a search warrant for

Sachtleben's electronic devices. The federal government already had his cell phone, computer, and other electronic media devices in their possession as a result of the child pornography investigation. A search of these devices revealed him as the alleged source of the leak and in possession of classified information. Sachtleben was charged with leaking classified information and distributing child pornography.

Sachtleben entered into a plea agreement and received a sentence of three years, seven months on the national security charge and eight years, one month for child pornography—a sad ending to a long and distinguished public career.

## Captain David Bourque—Granby, Connecticut Police Department—Child Pornographer—Largest Collection in Connecticut History

Captain David Bourque was with the 15-person Granby Police Department for only 18 months when he was arrested on federal child pornography charges. The arrest and forensic investigation of two laptops—one personal and one police department issued—two external hard drives, and a media card found approximately 22,282 images and 4084 videos of child pornography. The recovered images depicted the sexual abuse of prepubescent boys, including toddlers and infants. It was the largest collection of child pornography in Connecticut history (FBI, February 10, 2012). Bourque's background gave no indication of his secret perversions.

Bourque was hired at Granby PD with the rank of captain after thirty years with the Suffield, Connecticut Police Department—a 15-person department. He was hired because of his known computer skills. The rigorous background check included a polygraph examination, psychological examination, computer arrest examination, and a lengthy interview. No "dings" were found in his background, and he was hired over four other candidates for the position. His arrest for child pornography shocked his friends and colleagues.

The investigation and arrest of Captain Bourque were conducted as a part of the DOJ's Project Safe Childhood and Connecticut's "Operation

Constant Vigilance" aimed at protecting children from sexual exploitation. According to the FBI press release cited above, in March 2011, a Connecticut State Police trooper assigned to the Connecticut State Police Computer Crimes Unit logged into a publicly available Internet file-sharing program and downloaded images of child pornography. The State Police traced the IP address back to Bourque's home address. Connecticut State Police (CSP) executed search warrants on Bourque's office and residence.

Bourque met with CSP investigators and FBI agents and explained how he had encrypted the hard drives to conceal his child porn collection and provided them with passwords to access his accounts. He admitted using his law enforcement background to help hide his illegal activity. Specifically, he mentioned attending an FBI seminar on child pornography investigations and asking the presenters how they investigated chat rooms and pedophile Web sites. Bourque was placed on administrative leave and resigned from the police department.

In July 2011, Bourque pleaded guilty, admitting that from August 2010 to April 2011 he "received and exchanged visual depictions of minors engaging in sexually explicit conduct on my computer." Before his sentencing, Bourque asked for a lenient sentence because he had post-traumatic stress disorder that impaired his judgment. The judge not impressed with his leniency plea and sentenced him to 10 years in prison.

## Trooper Randy Quinn, South Carolina Highway Patrol—Child Pornographer—Operation Predator

The US Department of Homeland Security (DHS) and its investigative agency Homeland Security Investigative (HSI) conduct national and international efforts against the sexual exploitation of children. The HSI through its Child Exploitation Unit supports programs such as Operation Predator, a global initiative to identify, investigate, and charge child predators who: possess, trade and produce child pornography, travel overseas for sex with minors, and engage in sex trafficking of children (www.ice.gove/predator). The trooper was discovered in one of the routine investigations.

Immigration and Customs Agents (ICE) were conducting online Internet investigations to identify individuals possessing and sharing child pornography when they discovered a computer sharing 49 files with names that indicated child pornography. The agents downloaded an IP address that led them to Trooper Quinn's home address in South Carolina.

On June 7, 2011, ICE agents executed a search warrant on Quinn's residence and seized a laptop, desktop, and other disks with thousands of images of child pornography. They discovered that Quinn was a three-year veteran of the South Carolina Highway Patrol with previous experience as a Gaffney, South Carolina Police Department officer. Quinn was fired the same day. He was indicted on two alleged counts of child pornography—possession and distribution. He pleaded guilty and was sentenced to three years in prison.

## Richard Chandler—Kingsport, Tennessee Police Department—Child Pornographer—Operation Delego

Operation Delego was, at the time it was launched in 2009, the largest international investigation of a pedophile ring dedicated to the sexual abuse of children and the creation and distribution of child pornography (DOJ, August 3, 2011). Those arrested came from five continents and 15 countries. Seventy-two individuals were arrested worldwide, including 55 in the US One of those arrested, tried, and convicted was a Kingsport, Tennessee Police Officer Richard Chandler.

The targets of the massive operation were members of a pedophile ring operating through an invitation-only Internet site named Dreamboard. Dreamboard members allegedly traded graphic images and videos of adults molesting children of 12 years old and under, including infants, often violently. Dreamboard members allegedly created a massive private library of child sexual abuse. Homeland Security Secretary Janet Napolitano said the amount of child pornography swapped by participants was equivalent to 16,000 DVDs (Anonymous, August 3, 2011).

Membership in the pedophile ring was tightly controlled. Prospective members had to upload child pornography portraying children 12 years old or younger when applying for membership. When they became a member, they had to continually upload images of child sexual abuse or be expelled. The members were divided into groups based on their involvement in child sexual abuse and the supplied uploads of pictures documenting their sick perversions. *Super VIP* was the highest level of membership. These child molesters allegedly created new images of child pornography and shared the pictures with the five Dreamboard administrators. *VIP* rank was next, and the lowest level of membership was simply Members. Members allegedly moved up the ranks by producing child abuse images and providing a large number of images or uploading images never seen before. A particularly violent and sought after category of images were known as *Super Hardcore.* These images involved adults having violent sexual intercourse with "very young kids," sometimes infants, who were obviously in distress and or crying. The members allegedly could view all the pornographic postings at their level and the levels below them.

Court documents indicated Chandler joined Dreamboard in 2010 while he was a police officer. He made 117 posts to the Dreamboard site, twice while he was on duty. The majority of the posts were children from 8 to 14 who posed or engaged in sexual acts with adults. At the time of his arrest, Chandler was at the *VIP* level of membership—the second-lowest level of membership. He was charged with (1) engaging in a child exploitation enterprise; (2) conspiring to advertise the distribution of child pornography; and (3) conspiring to distribute child pornography. In April 2012, Chandler pleaded guilty to engaging in a child exploitation enterprise and sentenced to 35 years in prison. The other charges were dismissed.

## NYPD Sergeant Alberto Randazzo—Child Molester and Child Pornographer

NYPD Sergeant Alberto Randazzo, a 15-year police veteran, worked out of the Midtown North Precinct of Manhattan. In February 2013, the NYPD Internal Affairs Unit was investigating complaints that Sgt. Randazzo allegedly had child pornography in his possession (Keshner, April 19, 2017). They executed search warrants on his computers and found a cache of illegal videos. There were twenty-three still images and videos depicting sex acts with children, some as young as 1 and 2 years old.

The discoveries of the pornographic videos led to allegations that Randazzo directed 11 different child porn videos. Some of the videos, dating back to 2010, showed a woman fondling newborn infants and engaging in oral sex on a boy and a girl. The NYPD sergeant was arrested and charged with the state crimes of using a child in a sexual performance, promoting the sexual performance by a child and possession of a sexual performance by a child. He was suspended without pay and jailed with a $40,000 bond (Chinese and Thomas, February 19, 2013).

Randazzo was out on bail when he was arrested a second time in February 2014 on federal charges of child pornography. Homeland Security Investigation agents accused him of downloading 30 video files depicting child pornography. Federal prosecutors took over the prosecution of his earlier crimes from the state crimes because his offenses involved interstate transactions. The woman in the videos with the infants was discovered to be in Colorado when they were made. Federal authorities indicted a 52-year-old Massachusetts grandmother for conspiring with Randazzo to produce pornographic videos while he was out on bail. She allegedly drugged an eight-year-old boy and sexually abused him while she chatted with Randazzo. The mother of the infants in the earlier videos is in jail and awaiting trial along with Randazzo.

Randazzo and the two women faced mandatory minimum of 15 years in prison if convicted. In 2017, he was sentenced to 28 years in prison (Keshner, April 19, 2017). The HSI agents discovered 28 new pornographic videos after they traced them to an IP address associated with Randazzo. He and 70 other pedophiles, including two more police officers, were identified during **Operation Caireen**.

## Operation Caireen Identifies Two New York Officers—Child Pornographers

Operation Caireen was the largest operation by Homeland Security Investigation (HSI) ever conducted in New York (ICE, May 5, 2014). From April 4 to May 15, 2014, HSI special agents, NYPD detectives, and other law enforcement partners surreptitiously infiltrated peer-to-peer file-sharing networks to identify individuals in the New York City metropolitan area engaged in child pornography. The operation identified 150 distinct Internet addresses involved in the trading of sexually explicit images of children. NYPD Sgt. Randazza's Internet address was one of those identified. The law enforcement investigators identified files using words traditionally associated with child pornography and connected to those IP addresses and browsed the files shared at that address. Then, they obtained search warrants and seized the computers and electronic devices at the addresses and made an arrest.

Seventy-one subjects were arrested, and nearly 87 search warrants were executed, resulting in the seizure of 600 computing devices—desktops, laptops, tablets, smartphones, and thumb drives. Several of those arrested held positions of public trust such as police officers. Two New York police officers, Chief Brian Fanelli of the Mount Pleasant Police Department and NYPD Officer Yong Wu, were arrested.

## Chief of Police Brian Fanelli—Town of Mount Pleasant, New York—Operation Caireen

The Town of Mount Pleasant, NY is located in Westchester County approximately thirty miles north of New York City. Brian Fanelli had been with the Mount Pleasant Police Department (MPPD), 39-person department, since 1981 and their Chief of Police since October 2013, one month before he became a target of Operation Caireen. The suburban community and his family and friends reacted in utter disbelief when the new chief, who taught sex abuse awareness classes to children, was arrested and charged with downloading child pornography on January 23, 2014. Chief Fanelli told the investigators that he began viewing child pornography a year before his arrest as part of the research for his sex awareness classes and then started downloading it for his personal interest (Remizowski and Brown, January 24, 2014).

One hundred and twenty pornographic files were found on two computers in Fanelli's home. The files contained photos and videos of girls, some as young as seven years old. The children were engaged in sex acts with adults and other children. He shared those files with others, including undercover federal agents. While he was engaging in this behavior, Chief Fanelli was a volunteer catechism teacher at a Catholic school and spoke to hundreds of children at St. Elizabeth Ann Seton Parish School about the dangers of sexual abuse. He was immediately prohibited from the school after his arrest.

The disgraced former police chief pled guilty to one count of possession of child pornography. The charge carries a maximum sentence of 10 years in prison, but Fanelli was sentenced to 18 months in prison. His sentence also included five years of supervised release.

## NYPD Officer—Yong Wu—Child Pornographer—Operation Caireen

Investigators discovered that NYPD Officer Yong Wu had downloaded at least sixty files of "investigative interest." The first video clip examined was five minutes long and showed an underage girl performing a sex act on herself. A short time later, Yong Wu allegedly downloaded another clip of a 13-year-old girl having sex with an adult man. When his home was raided, law enforcement agents found five more video clips on his desktop showing girls as young as 8-year-old having sex with adult men. The NYPD officer was arrested for seven counts of promoting a sexual performance of a child and possession of a sexual performance by a child and is awaiting trial.

## Waltham, Massachusetts Police Officer Paul Charles Manganelli—Child Pornographer—Project Safe Childhood

In 2013, the Queensland, Australia police arrested a man for distributing child pornography and identified email accounts of suspected child pornographers around the world. One hundred and eleven of those accounts were based in the United States. One of those identified was a

20-year veteran of the Waltham, Massachusetts Police Department, Paul Manganelli, known as the "millionaire cop" for winning a 1 million dollar lottery in 2011.

US federal authorities discovered Manganelli used his Yahoo email address to send and receive child pornography from his home to individuals outside of Massachusetts (DOJ, March 26, 2013). Those individuals included suspected pornographers in Australia and Britain. The search of his computers revealed he traded child pornography via email from December 2011 through March 2013 and had more than 850 images and 40 videos containing child pornography. He claimed he was researching to identify online sex predators. His department countered by pointing out he had never been assigned to conduct such investigations, and he had never reported a child pornographer. He later admitted that he lied.

In May of 2014, Manganelli entered into a plea agreement with the federal authorities. He pleaded guilty to one charge of possession of child pornography and the government dropped the charge of receipt of child pornography. He was sentenced to five years in prison followed by five years of supervised release. He will register as a sex offender when he is released from prison.

## McHenry County, Illinois Sheriff's Department—Sgt. Gregory M. Pyle—Child Molester (Incest) and Child Pornographer

> While Pyle lived a seemingly law-abiding life as a police officer, he was a horrible person who did despicable things. (US District Judge Frederick Kapala quoted in Marrazzo, September 17, 2014)

The words of Judge Kapala came during the sentencing of former McHenry County, Illinois Deputy Sheriff for the repeated sexual abuse of a child related to him from 2006 to 2010—incest. The alleged sexual abuse began when the victim was 8 years old and was videotaped and shared with other child molesters online. The effects on the young victim were devastating. His mother testified her son is angry and depressed and has been hospitalized twice for suicide thoughts.

Pyle's secret life came to an end when federal investigators searched a home in downstate Illinois as part of a child pornography sharing investigation. The subject at the residence told them he traded child pornography with a person using names Scouts_Out_888 and Trucid012. The investigators traced the usernames to Pyle, a ten-year veteran of the McHenry County Sheriff's Department. Pyle was a law enforcement officer with specialized training in computer forensics and had once been the sheriff's department's lead investigator for child pornography as a member of the Internet Crimes Against Children Task Force. Once, they identified Pyle the investigators soon identified his young victim.

The boy told investigators Pyle had repeatedly sexually abused him from the time he was eight until he was 10. The abuse allegedly took place at Pyle's home and on trips to a hotel in Wisconsin. One or more of the sexual assaults in Wisconsin were filmed and shared online. Pyle pleaded guilty to aggravated sexual abuse of a child, crossing a state line to engage in a sexual act with a child under the age of 12, and was sentenced to 50 years in prison.

## Richmond City, Virginia Sheriff's Office Deputy Robert A. Thompson—Child Pornographer

A Richmond, Virginia police officer assigned to the Southern Virginia Internet Crimes Against Children Task Force was conducting an undercover investigation of peer-to-peer networks exchanging child pornography when he identified Deputy Thompson, a ten-year veteran deputy sheriff as a possible suspect. Thompson was arrested and charged with possessing child pornography and possession with intent to distribute. He was fired after an investigation by the sheriff's office and prosecuted by the Virginia Attorney General's Office. Thompson pleaded guilty to eight counts of child pornography possession and was sentenced to three years and 10 months in prison (Times-Dispatch Staff, September 22, 2011).

# Combined State/Federal Prosecutions

## US Drug Enforcement Administration—Administrative Agent—Scott Whitcomb—Child Molester and Child Pornographer

Scott Whitcomb was a DEA administrative agent, not involved in criminal investigations, from 2007 to his arrest on December 22, 2010. During his law enforcement career, Agent Whitcomb had been a US Air Marshal and a prison guard. During his service as a DEA Agent, Whitcomb allegedly coerced three young boys into sexually explicit acts and recorded them. His secret was first discovered by an officer from the Minneapolis Police Department (MPD) conducting an online investigation into P2P—peer-to-peer—file sharing of child pornography (FBI, December 23, 2010). The MPD officer identified suspicious activity connected to a particular IP address and downloaded an explicit video depicting child pornography and viewed two other child pornography videos.

The MPD officer shared his information with the Sherburne County Sheriff's Office (SCSO), and they conducted a state search warrant at Whitcomb's residence. The SCSO officers seized a desktop and laptop computer and performed a forensic examination of the seized computers. The investigators positively identified a 15-year-old boy involved in the pornographic videos. Whitcomb was arrested and charged with four state charges.

After Whitcomb's arrest, investigators learned the 15-year-old boy had a younger 12-year-old brother. The investigation revealed Whitcomb had allegedly "groomed" both boys and engaged in numerous sexual acts with them over the past three years. The process of "grooming" common among child molesters involved eroding their defenses and revulsion by repeatedly showing them pornographic videos and magazines and giving them Xbox games to play (Walsh, July 28, 2011). Whitcomb "groomed" the parents also by convincing them his association with their children was safe because his long law enforcement career demonstrated he was "someone who could be trusted."

The identification of multiple victims led to FBI agents contacting the county authorities to ask for federal complaints against Whitcomb.

On December 22, 2010, federal charges were placed against Whitcomb. He was arrested and appeared in US District Court on December 23, 2010, charged with possession and distribution of child pornography and ordered held for trial without bond. In July 2011, Whitcomb pleaded guilty and admitted he made pornographic videos of three boys between 2007 and 2010 and was sentenced to 25 years in prison.

## Louisiana State Trooper Jay Sandifer—Child Molester and Child Pornographer

Another case where state charges led to federal prosecution is the bizarre case of Trooper Jay Sandifer (Anonymous, March 11, 2012). Sandifer, a 15-year veteran, was indicted in May 2010 on three state charges of indecent behavior with a juvenile. According to newspaper accounts, the investigation that led to his arrest began when a hospital called and reported a child a doctor examined and observed the possible signs of sexual conduct attributed to a state trooper. Then a woman in LaSalle Parish complained that Trooper Jay Sandifer had engaged in inappropriate behavior with her five-year-old girl during an overnight stay. He allegedly took a bath with the girl and slept nude with her. The investigation uncovered evidence Sandifer engaged in sexual contact from 1998 to his arrest in 2010 with three girls ages 5–13. He also had an alleged sexual relationship with a 16-year-old female. This juvenile babysat for Sandifer and had sexual intercourse with him up to five times.

Following his indictment on the state charges, an examination of Sandifer's work and personal computers found 90 images of child pornography. The photos showed the genitalia of girls' ages 10–12 with some engaged in sexual contact with adult males. Sandifer allegedly found the child porn Web sites with Internet searches.

State authorities anticipating a lengthy federal prison sentence and sparing the young victims having to appear in court agreed to allow federal authorities to take over the case and try Sandifer in federal court on the child pornography counts. Sandifer pleaded guilty to one count of receipt of child pornography and received a sentence of nine years in prison.

## Pennsville Township, New Jersey Officer Robert Waterman—Child Molester and Pornographer

Pennsville Township, New Jersey, is a small community with a police department of 22 sworn members. In March 2010, Officer Robert Waterman, a four-year veteran, was suspended from the force for possessing child pornography. Waterman at the time of his suspension was the Pennsville Middle School District's School Resource Officer (SRO) and taught the Drug Abuse Resistance Education (D.A.R.E.) to middle and elementary schools. These duties involved contact with minor and young children and made his child pornography allegations more serious and disturbing.

The FBI notified Waterman he was being investigated for an allegation of child pornography. Waterman admitted in court that following the FBI interview, he went home and retrieved a hard drive from his garage and drove to the police station and broke the hard drive into small pieces and threw them away (FBI, September 6, 2013). He pleaded guilty to obstructing a child pornography investigation and was sentenced to 15 months in prison and three years of supervised release.

# Police Child Pornography in the UK

## 2002 Operation Ore—UK "Pay for View Child Pornography."

In 2002, the FBI conducted a worldwide operation against "pay-per-view" child pornography sites worldwide. The global operation identified 7000 users in Britain. The British effort against those 7000 users was known as Operation Ore and resulted in the arrest of 1300 suspected pedophiles. Fifty of those arrested were police officers (Burrell, December 12, 2002). The Chief Constable at the National Crime Squad was quoted in the newspaper that they were not hiding that police officers were involved. He added that eight of the police officers had been charged, and the rest were given bail pending further investigation.

## 2017–2018 Incidents Reported on Police Oracle

A 14-year Sussex Police Constable was dismissed for sharing pornographic images with fellow officers while on duty (Hickey, February 20, 2017). He even shared them with his female supervisor—sexual harassment. A Metropolitan Police officer assigned to the Kingston borough pleaded guilty to downloading 65,000 indecent images of children. The child pornography was found in search of his home. He was sentenced to 20 months imprisonment that was suspended for two years (Weinfass, March 28, 2017). A Met officer who was based in Parliamentary and Diplomatic Protection admitted to possessing 1700 pornographic images, including graphic images of children (Hutber, November 20, 2017). Police officers from the Online Child Exploitation Team arrested a West Midlands police officer for making indecent images of children as young as two (Press Association, December 15, 2017). A Police Constable with the Roads and Transport Police was arrested for making inappropriate online messages with a 15-year-old girl. A search of his residence after the arrest found five images of child pornography on his computer (Hutber, January 12, 2018). A Met officer was arrested on suspicion of making, uploading, and distributing pornographic images of children. He was convicted of making pornographic photographs of children (Garrod, February 27, 2018). A West Midlands police officer pleaded guilty to making five pornographic images of a child and two counts of distributing pornographic photos of a child (Hudson, August 16, 2018).

# Conclusion

This pattern of LEO sexual misconduct—the viewing, possessing, distribution, and production of child pornography—like the pattern of child sexual molesters can occur on or off duty. Child sexual molesters are violent criminals and would fit in the earlier definitions of Police Sexual Violence (PSV); however, only the production of child pornography requires victim contact. However, they like all the patterns in our taxonomy fit into the **PSM Causal Equation—Inclination + Opportu nity + Real of Perceived Risk = Police Sexual Misconduct**. We see in the Illustrative Examples presented the anonymity of the Internet and other social media outlets are often not as secure as some would believe. The last example from the United States of a School Resource Officer— SRO-brings us to the last pattern in the *PSM Taxonomy*.

# References

Anonymous. (2011, August 03). Operation Delego: Dreamboard child sex ring bust nets 72 Arrests in U.S., Canada, France, Germany. *Huffington Post.*

Anonymous. (2012, March 11). Trooper Sandifer to serve nine years in child porn case. *Natchez Democrat.*

Burrell, I. (2002, December 18). Raids on paedophile suspects net 50 police officers. *Independent.*

Chinese, V., & Thomas, T. (2013, February 19). NYPD sergeant busted with child porn Caught on video instructing woman to fondle and "talk dirty" to newborn baby. *New York Daily News.*

Cook, A. J. (2011, September 27). Former deputy gets 30 years on child porn charges. *Rapid City Journal.*

DOJ. (2011, August 3). Attorney General and DHS Secretary announces largest U.S. Prosecution of international criminal network organized to sexually exploit children. *Department of Justice Press Release.*

DOJ. (2013, March 26). Waltham police officer arrested on child pornography charges. *U.S. Attorney's Office: District of Massachusetts-Press Release.*

FBI. (2010, December 23). Zimmerman man charged with one count of possession and distribution of child pornography. *FBI Press Release— Minneapolis Division.*

FBI. (2011, September 28). Florida Man Indicted for Transporting, Receipt, and Possession of Child Pornography. *FBI Press Release—Miami Division.*

FBI. (2012, February 10). Former Connecticut Police Captain sentenced to 10 years in prison for trading child pornography. *FBI Press Release—New Haven Division.*

FBI. (2013, September 6). Former Pennsville police officer sentenced to prison for obstructing child pornography investigation. *FBI Press Release— Philadelphia Division.*

Franceschina, F., Trischitta, L., & Burstein, J. (2011, September 28). Leader of ICE in South Florida pleads not guilty to child porn charges. *Sun-Sentinel.*

Franceschina, T. & Burstein, J. (2011, October 6). New details emerge in federal agent's child porn arrest. *Sun-Sentinel.*

Garrod, S. (2018, February 27). PC convicted of making indecent images of children dismissed. *Police Oracle.*

Hickey, H. (2017, February 20). PC dismissed for sharing porn on duty is ordered out of force for the second time. *Police Oracle.*

ICE. (2014, May 5). Operation caireen: Department of homeland security. *Press Release.*

Hudson, N. (2018, August 16). Inspector admits in court making indecent child images. *Police Oracle.*

Hutber, J. J. (2017, November 20). Mt Police officer pleads guilty to possessing hundreds of indecent images of children. *Police Oracle.*

Hutber, J. J. (2018, January 12). Met officer dismissed for possessing indecent images of children. *Police Oracle.*

Keshner, A. (2017, April 19). Ex-NYPD sergeant gets 28 years for persuading women to sexually abuse infants and children. *New York Daily News.*

Kno, L. (2012, May 11). Former FBI agent charged with child pornography. *Reuters.*

Marrazzo, A. (2014, September 17). Ex-sheriff's deputy gets 50 years in child sex abuse case. *Chicago Tribune.*

Press Association. (2017, December 15). Former West Midlands PC pleads guilty to making indecent images of children. *Police Oracle.*

Remizowski, L. & Brown, P. (2014, January 24). Police chief of New York town arrested on child pornography charges. *CNN.*

Times-Dispatch Staff. (2011, September 22). Former Richmond Sheriff's deputy sentenced to prison. *Richmond Times-Dispatch.*

Walsh, J. (2011, July 28). Child porn plea draws 25 years in prison. *Star Tribune.*

Weinfass, I. (2017, March 28). Met officer downloaded 65.000 indecent images of children. *Police Oracle.*

West, E. (2014, July 11). Explosive charges: The Donald Sachtleben case. *Indianapolis Monthly.*

# 12

# Type 10: Sexual Exploitation in Joint School Police and Community-Sponsored Programs

## Introduction

### "New Patterns of Police Abuse"

Police sexual abuse of women includes a disturbing pattern of police officer exploitation of teenage girls. The majority of these cases, moreover, involve girls enrolled in police-sponsored Explorer programs designed to give teens an understanding of police work.

> Walker, S. & Tribeck, D. (June 2013). *Police Sexual Abuse of Teenage Girls: A 2003 Update on "Driving While Female."*
> The University of Nebraska at Omaha Department of Criminal Justice.

The report brought national attention to police sexual abuse occurring in police/community-sponsored programs. However, the betrayal of trust exemplified by the police actions was not new, and the victims and police sexual aggressors came from all genders. The victims in this PSM type are both males and females, and male and female police sexual aggressors officers are the sexual predators. And, police sexual abuse in police/community-sponsored programs is not confined to Police Explorer Programs. The programs developed under the umbrella of

© The Author(s) 2020
T. Barker, *Aggressors in Blue*,
https://doi.org/10.1007/978-3-030-28441-1_12

"community policing" have been hijacked by a minority of police sexual aggressors. Saying that it is a minority offers little solace to the victims and their families.

My examination of newspaper articles from 2009 to 2015 found 72 cases of police sexual abuse involving teenage girls and boys in these community policing endeavors, thirty-one of the cases involved teenagers in the Police Explorer Program. The co-ed program in this type offers a variety of worksite-based educational programs for young people between the ages of 14 and 20 and is designed to prepare them for responsible and productive adult lives.

The programs are sponsored by local, state, and federal law enforcement agencies throughout the United States. The programs provide experience in police-related activities such as criminal investigation, firearms, and traffic control and community service. Ride-alongs are a part of most Police Explorer Programs. The goal is for young adults to obtain a personal awareness of the criminal justice system through training; practical experience, competition, and other Criminal Justice related activities—a laudable goal. Unfortunately, there is a darker and tragic side to these programs that expands the vulnerable victim's pool for police sexual aggressors, in effect putting the *Fox in the Henhouse*, a police child molester loose among their prey. It is beyond time to reexamine the use of police officers in public schools and recognize the problems involved and take steps to remediate the problems or end the programs.

## Police in Public Schools

An unknown number of sexual aggressors with the inclination to molest children choose police work for the known opportunities for sexual abuse. The previous two chapters made that clear. Some seek assignments to positions in schools. Public sworn police officers have always responded to calls for service and emergencies in schools. They make arrests on school property; provide traffic and security services during sporting events and other large events. However, in recent years, several events combined to increase the number, nature, and responsibilities of public sworn officers in schools. Those events include media-sensationalized school shootings, school safety as a political issue, criminalization of school discipline, and a zero-tolerance policy of weapons, alcohol, and drugs in schools. The events led to increased federal funding for public police in schools, providing the stimulus for more police assignments in schools. However, armed LEOs create the possibility of the civil rights violations of students by poorly vetted and poorly trained LEOs with the inclination for sexual misconduct and introduce more minors into the juvenile justice pipeline (Theriot and Cuellar 2016). Public sworn officers are now assigned to schools on a more permanent basis, and many public school districts from elementary to college/university have established separate police departments.

In addition to public paid police officers, private security officers are employed by elementary, middle, and high schools, particularly in urban areas, to oversee or monitor the access and egress school patterns. They perform tasks inside the schools once performed by student monitors and teachers. Private security guards provide protection and traffic responsibilities at sporting events and other functions as assigned by the school. These private employees are without general arrest powers and are armed with non-lethal weapons. On occasion, they are non-sworn members of a school police department. For example, the second largest US school police department, Los Angeles (CA) United School District Police Department, has 410 sworn police officers and 101 non-sworn school safety officers. The sworn police officers are assigned to the school's campus and patrol the surrounding area. The school safety officers are assigned to the school campus and parking enforcement.

Most of the nations' school police departments evolved from safety or security school agencies without sworn officers. School safety is a big industry. In 2008, there were 250 police departments operated by public school districts in the United States (DOJ, July 2011). These special district police departments employed nearly 5000 sworn law enforcement officers. The largest public school district police department is the Philadelphia School District Police Department with 450 sworn officers.

Special district police as sworn public law enforcement officers and experience the same opportunities for police sexual abuse as all law enforcement officers do, just in a different setting. Public school police have become more militarized, mimicking a development in other US police departments. According to an *AP* report appearing in the *Guardian*, twenty-six US school districts participated in the free military surplus gear program and acquired mine-resistant armored [sic] vehicles, grenade launchers, and M16 rifles. Several school police spokespersons quoted in the article said the military equipment was needed in the event of a school shooting. Maybe? However, school shootings, contrary to media presentations and politicians are rare events, and school violence has dropped dramatically since 1993 (Theriot and Cuellar 2016). The increase of police in schools flies in the face of the available evidence that suggests that the largest threat of law enforcement sexual misconduct with minors comes from School Resource Officers and other officers assigned to schools or joint police/community-sponsored programs.

## School Resource Officers—SROs

In addition to the increase in special district school police departments, there has been an exponential increase in School Resource Officers (SROs) from the local police or sheriff's agencies assigned to elementary, middle, and high schools. An SRO is a sworn law enforcement officer with general arrest powers assigned to an elementary, middle, or high school as their primary duties during the school year. As defined in the 1968 Omnibus Crime Bill, a SRO is "a career law enforcement officer with sworn authority deployed in *community-oriented policing*, and assigned by the employing police department or agency to work in collaboration with school and *community-based* organizations" (Theriot and Cuellar 2016: 365—emphasis added). These sworn officers are, in theory, assigned the goal of improving the safety of students and school personnel. They are employed by the law enforcement agency, not the school. However, there are inherent problems with this arrangement.

The assignment to the school with its bureaucratic administrative structure and employment by a law enforcement agency with its bureaucratic administrative structure is problematic for the officer, the school principal, and the agency chief or sheriff. SROs exist in two worlds, employed by a law enforcement agency and a part of the school's working staff under the immediate supervision of the school principal. Among the problems created by this arrangement are that the SRO and the school administrator often do not have a clear understanding of their roles, and the success of the relationship is determined by how the local police agency defines the "job" (Theriot and Cuellar 2016).

Furthermore, police officers typically see themselves as crime fighters, not "babysitters." This complicates the assignment and creates a punishment orientation to acts once considered a minor child or teenage peccadillos. Even more problematic, the agency or the police officers may not view the SRO assignment as a desirable assignment, leading to assignment as an SRO as punishment and placing the police slacker in a *real or perceived low-risk* setting with an especially *vulnerable population* (personal experience and interviews with working and former police officers). Specialized units in police agencies have always been used as a garbage can for officers who do not function well on patrol work. In order to be successful, SROs must receive specialized training preparing them to work with children in schools effectively. Oftentimes, this does not happen. And, there must be adequate funding for SRO programs. Most programs in existence today rely on federal grants that last for three years. Many SRO programs disappear after federal dollars are cut back.

Even more troubling are questions about the success of SROs in increasing safety and security in the school. Putting SROs in schools has unintended consequences. Studies suggest SROs increase the risk of student resistance to authority and antisocial behavior and erode the personal relationships between students and teachers, conceding power to SROs erects barriers to classroom relationships (Theriot and Cuellar 2016).

## How Successful Are School Resource Officer Programs?

Police officers in schools are a part of the increased interest in the latest buzzword in police operations—community-oriented policing. The COP movement began in the 1950s but did not take hold in American public schools until the social media furor surrounding the school shootings of the 1990s, culminating with the Columbine Massacre on April 20, 1999. Then, in December 2012, the deadliest school shooting in US history occurred in Sandy Hook Elementary School when one assassin killed 20 young children and a security guard before killing himself. In response, the Office of Community Policing Services (COPS) awarded nearly 45 million dollars to hire 356 SROs for the 2013 fiscal year. SRO programs are crisis-driven and perceived to be common-sense solutions to increasing school safety and reducing school violence, leading to the question: How successful are they? The answer to that question is not forthcoming.

Thompson and Alvarez (2012) report that in Colorado the year before the Columbine Massacre in 1999, the reported rates of violent student crime fell drastically. Following the massacre and the infusion of federal monies for the hiring of SROs, the national student to School Resource Officer rate rose dramatically as did the violent school crime rate until 2003. In 2003, budget cuts increased the student to School Resource Officer ratio, and the student crime rate dropped. They concluded there was no evidence that the presence of resource officers contributed to the decline in student reported crime. They also reported that a national longitudinal study compared the levels of student crime in 470 schools matching schools with SROs and those without SROs. The study found no measurable decline in student crime or improvements in student behavior between the schools with SROs and those without SROs.

Thompson and Alvarez (2012) reported some disturbing findings. Their evidence suggests that the presence of SROs might harm students and interfere with schooling. They suggested that SROs spend the majority of their time needlessly applying law enforcement solutions to what are traditional school discipline issues (swearing, fighting, disorderly conduct). They also found teachers and administrators relegate school discipline issues to School Resource Officers. The disturbing incidents of police sexual misconduct by SROs must also be considered in any examination of the program's success.

## SRO Sexual Misconduct

There is no official data collected on sexual misconduct in joint police/community-sponsored programs. The Learning for Life or the Boy Scouts of America—sponsors—does not collect data on Police Explorers sexual abuse. Neither does the National Center for Missing and Exploited Children. The National Association of School Resources Officers does not collect data on SRO sexual abuse.

There is a dearth of scientific research on police sexual misconduct in the school setting. However, Stinson and Watkins (2013), in their study of SROs arrested for criminal offenses, found the nature of police misconduct by school and non-school police officers is dissimilar. Non-school police officers were significantly more likely to be arrested for violence-related offenses, whereas SROs were more likely to be arrested for sex-related offenses. Sixty-two percent of the SROs crimes were sex-related. The SRO victims were most likely to be teenage girls enrolled in the schools the SROs were assigned to or patrolled—56%. The offenses ranged from making sexually explicit remarks to direct sexual contact.

The available evidence demonstrates that the problem of police sexual abuse in law enforcement assignments and other police/community-sponsored programs is more complex and varied than previously identified. Contrary to what the National Association of School Resource Officers (NASRO, 2012) states "Child welfare on campus is not compromised by school resource officers, but at risk without them," it appears that an unknown number of students are put at risk of sexual exploitation by School Resource Officers and other police-community-sponsored programs involving minors. The Illustrative Examples that follow demonstrate the need for a reexamination of these programs.

\* \* \*

## LAPD Deputy Chief David Kalish—Police Explorers Supervisor

In 2000, David Kalish, the openly gay, former board member of the Los Angeles Gay and Lesbian Center, and LAPD officer with 25 years on the job was appointed to deputy chief in charge of the LAPD's Operations-West Bureau. According to Police Chief Bernard Parks, Kalish was "specifically selected for the critical position because of his intellect, wisdom, experience, and his incredibly high level of integrity" (LAPD News Release, September 12, 2000). His "incredibly high level of integrity" would be put in jeopardy from accusations of on- and off-duty sexual molestation of young boys in the LAPD's Police Explorer Program. The alleged secrets in his past became public when he applied for the vacant chief of police position.

Deputy Chief David Kalish was a semifinalist for the position of LAPD Chief of Police after LAPD Police Chief Bernard Parks was forced from office. Kalish was not selected, but the publicity triggered the memory of sexual abuse in one of his victims and compelled him to register a complaint. The allegation was severe but old. In October 2002, a Santa Clara, California man claimed Kalish harassed and sexually assaulted him when he was in the 1970s LAPD Police Explorer's Program (Winton and Blankstein, March 26, 2003). Then in July 2003, a second complaint alleged that when Kalish was the supervisor of the department's Police Explorer program he had "sexually molested, harassed, assaulted, fondled and coerced" a male youth in the Explorer's program from 1974 to 1979 (Winton and Blankstein, July 4, 2003). Before the investigation ended, a third complainant would come forward with additional allegations of sexual abuse. The newly appointed LAPD Chief of Police was forced to take action.

William Bratton, the former NYPD Police Commissioner, was selected for the chief's position. One of Bratton's first actions was to place Kalish on paid leave, following a 5-month investigation into allegations he molested a youth in the Police Explorer program in the 1970s. The department investigation launched by Chief Bratton found substance to the allegations and was forwarded to the prosecutor's office for possible criminal charges. The length of time between the alleged acts and the filing of complaints raised serious legal questions.

The possibility of criminal prosecution for these alleged acts of sexual abuse of minors was barred by a US Supreme Court decision declaring a California law that allowed prosecutors to file new charges on old incidents of sexual abuse unconstitutional. The allegations against Kalish occurred in the 1970s, but the California law extended the 20-year statute of limitations in cases where there were serious sexual misconduct and corroborating evidence. The Los Angeles District Attorney's Office demurred on filing charges while soliciting legal advice.

The possible criminal prosecution of LAPD Deputy Chief David Kalish sputtered to an inglorious ending on November 7, 2003. The Los Angeles District Attorney's Office issued a three-page memorandum saying there was sufficient evidence to charge Kalish with molesting two Police Explorers but the legal deadlines for prosecution had passed (Winton and Blankstein, November 7, 2003). In effect, Kalish was believed guilty, but the prosecutor was unable to charge. The District Attorney's Office did not stop there. It added damaging support for the allegations. The memo gave brief descriptions of the incidents. The memo reported "Kalish engaged in oral copulation and masturbation with an Explorer Scout in the LAPD Devonshire Division Explorer program when the victim aged 15-17."

Furthermore, he engaged in sexual acts on a second Explorer from 1977 to 1979. Their findings, according to the memo, were based on reports and witness statements from the LAPD Internal Affairs Division and testimony before a Los Angeles County Grand Jury. Disappointed at the lack of criminal charges, the two victims filed civil suits against the city, but the California Supreme Court held that they had waited too long to file suit. Kalish retired from the LAPD with full benefits, nearly $10,000 a month, and retaining the right to carry a concealed weapon, police identification card, and a retirement badge.

## San Bernardino County, California Sheriff's Office—Two Police Explorer Supervisors-One a Former Police Explorer

> The most evil bastard ever to wear a badge....What you really are, Nathan Gastineau is a predator of the worst kind. A predator with a badge. (Fowler, March 21, 2014)

The words of the father of a 16-year-old female victim to former San Bernardino Deputy Sheriff (SBSO) Nathan Gastineau after he was found guilty of 16 counts relating to having sexual intercourse as well as performing lewd acts with a minor. He was also found guilty of one count of possessing child pornography—videos of the sexual encounters. His actions are particularly disturbing because the 10-year veteran deputy sheriff had been a Police Explorer with the SBSO before he became a deputy (Tenorio, January 5, 2012).

Deputy Gastineau was the supervisor of the minor's Highland-based Police Explorer post when he allegedly began having on- and off-duty sex with the minor. The sex molestation charges became known when the SBSO, responded to a complaint, source not identified, that Deputy Gastineau was having sex with a girl in the Police Explorer program he supervised. At one point an investigator, using the girl's cell phone sent Gastineau text messages and received confirmation of the illicit affair. He was called in for an interview. Gastineau, at first, said the girl was lying. When presented with the evidence—text messages—he admitted the sexual relationship, adding that it was consensual. There is only one encounter, he insisted. The girl gave contradictory information, saying that the two had sex, beginning in November 2010, six times before she was 16 years old and continued at least twice a week until mid-April 2011. She said Gastineau had oral sex with her at least once in his patrol car on a ride-along. The police executed search warrants on his home and work locker and found videos of the two having sex, confirming the deputy had, indeed, had sex with the girl when she was 15 years old.

In January 2014, former Deputy Nathan Gastineau went on trial in San Bernardino Superior Court. At the end of the three-week trial, the jury took three hours to find him guilty of sixteen counts of unlawful sex with the teenaged Explorer and one count of possessing child pornography. He received the maximum sentence of 16 years in prison. The Gastineau complaints were not the only the problems the San Bernardino Sheriff's Office had with their Explorer program.

Two weeks after Deputy Gastineau's arrest another SBSO Police Explorer supervisor was arrested for allegedly having sex with a female in the Explorer post he supervised. San Bernardino Deputy Anthony Benjamin, a five-year veteran of the SBSO, was charged with two counts of oral copulation with an underage girl (Tenorio, June 10, 2011). The 17-year-old female was in Deputy Benjamin's Victorville Police Explorer's post. His arrest came hours after an anonymous tip. Following the second arrest, Sheriff Rod Hoops declared it was a "sad day for the department" and suspended the Police Explorer program for 60 days to conduct a thorough review of the program. The sheriff added that the Explorer program was a key component of the department's outreach agenda with 245 Explorers at 15 stations. Many current officers, including Deputy Gastineau, used the program as a springboard into careers in law enforcement. However, the Sheriff's department acknowledged it needs to see if "there's something we need to change to prevent this from happening and that the kids involved in the program are protected."

Former deputy Benjamin accepted a plea deal and pleaded no contest to two felony counts of oral copulation of a person under 16. He was sentenced to 270 days in jail but did not have to register as a sex offender. After serving his sentence, he would serve three years of probation.

The sheriff's department still has problems with the Police Explorer's Program. In 2016, the coordinator of the Explorer program was accused of sexual misconduct with an underage girl participating in the program (Peleg, December 31, 2016). The accused had received the Commander's Award for his role in the Explorer's program in 2015.

## Caldwell, Idaho Ruben Delgadillo—School Resource Officer (SRO)

Caldwell, Idaho is the county seat of Canyon County, Idaho and is considered to be part of the Boise metropolitan area. The police department has 43 officers serving a population of around 46 thousand persons. Officer Ruben Delgadillo was a member of the Caldwell Police Department (CPD) from 2005 until his resignation in late 2008. He resigned after being charged with lewd conduct with a child and sexual battery of a minor child under 16 or 17 years of age. Delgadillo's victim was a 15-year-old boy he met and mentored while serving as the CPD's School Resource Officer at a local high school.

According to court documents (Complaint—Nicholson V. Ruben Delgadillo et al. Case No. 12-470 U.S. District Court for the District of Idaho September 13, 2012), Delgadillo met his victim while serving as a member of the high school's suspension board. The troubled freshman appeared before the board as a result of a school rule's violation. After the hearing, Delgadillo met with the mother of the young boy and convinced her he could mentor the boy and change his disruptive behavior. The mother trusted Delgadillo because he was a police officer and an SRO assigned to work with children. Allegedly, the mentoring process consisted of "grooming" the victim into sexual encounters.

The "grooming" allegedly consisted of daily contact where the SRO would take the boy jogging or on ride-alongs in his police cruiser. Then, he would have the young victim spend the nights at his house and sleep in his bed. According to the Complaint, Delgadillo would sexually fondle the boy. The fondling allegedly progressed to sexual intercourse. This sexual abuse occurred dozens of times over a period of months, according to the Complaint. The abuse continued for months until the young victim reported it to the Idaho State Police, leading to Delgadillo's arrest.

Delgadillo, at first, said the sex was consensual until the judge pointed out that sex with a minor is not legally possible. He pleaded guilty to felony injury to a child and was sentenced to 3–10 years in prison.

## Tampa, Florida Brian Morales—School Resource Officer

Very disappointed in this officer because ... "he was entrusted to be a positive influence in those [high school] individual lives." (Tampa Police Chief Jane Castor quoted in Girona, December 19, 2013)

The Tampa, Florida Police Department (TPD) has over 1000 police officers, 24 of them are School Resource Officers with three supervisors. One of them, Officer Brian Morales, was arrested and fired in 2013 for allegedly having sex with a 17-year-old student at the high school where he was a School Resource Officer. According to the chief, SRO's are tasked with "protecting the school and being a positive influence. The officers—male and female—ask to join the SRO program, and then they are carefully vetted" (Phillips, April 17, 2015). The chief said the department examines their background, experience, maturity, interest, and aptitude. There was nothing in Officer Brian Morales's past to indicate that he was not suited to be a School Resource Officer. The veteran officer, married, and the father of four children had no disciplinary actions in his past. Why he ended up committing such a "disgusting act" (chief's words) and becoming an embarrassment to the police agency cannot be explained, she said. The claim that the officer and his young victim had strong feelings is no excuse; a minor cannot legally consent to sex with an adult, the chief emphasized.

Although there are conflicting accounts of how the illicit relationship was discovered, it appears that the young victim went to the doctor and was diagnosed with a sexually transmitted disease (STD). She was forced to reveal her affair to her mother, and the mother called the girl's softball coach who called the police (Phillips, April 17, 2015).

Detectives went to the girl's home and Morales's home the day after they received the report. Morales was arrested for eight counts of felony sexual activity with a minor and fired. He had to be confined to a mental facility for several days because he threatened to hurt himself if the affair became public. The affair allegedly began on October 24, 2013, when the young girl checked herself out of school and went to Morales's home where they had sex. They allegedly had sex at least eight times, at his home, her home and in his personal car, according to published reports (Phillips, April 17, 2015).

In April 2015, Brian Morales pleaded guilty and was sentenced to six years in prison. His prison sentence was to be followed by two years of house arrest and three years of probation.

## Searcy, Arkansas PD, Hamilton Riley—School Resource Officer

He was a predator, and he was at the worst place of all. At a junior high school covered with a uniform, wearing a gun, and wearing a badge. It was a horrible situation. (Raff prosecuting attorney, March 2, 2011)

Prosecutor Raff was describing the actions of School Resource Officer Hamilton Riley of the Searcy, Arkansas Police Department. Riley was a seven-year veteran, 3 years as an SRO when the Arkansas State Police caught him climbing through the bedroom window of a 16-year-old female student (Anonymous, February 24, 2010). The student was from the high school where he was assigned. According to a published report, the girl and Riley had a longtime relationship, exchanging text messages since she was in the 8th grade.

The police acted quickly when the Complaint was made. The police department received a complaint that Riley was maintaining an inappropriate relationship with the young girl on a Monday and the State Police were notified. At 1 a.m. Tuesday, special agents from the state police were waiting for him in the girl's bedroom when he climbed in the window. He was arrested for sexual contact with a 16-year-old and resigned at 7 a.m. the same day.

Riley pleaded guilty without comment in March 2011 and was sentenced to 15 years in prison. The sentencing judge said that he committed a heinous offense against a vulnerable child.

## Bedford County, Virginia Sheriff's Department-Deputy Earnest William Grubbs—School Resource Officer

The Bedford County Department of Social Services notified the sheriff's office of allegations concerning Deputy Earnest William "E.W" Grubbs, the sheriff's department's School Resource Officer. The allegations consisted of an inappropriate relationship with a 16-year-old girl, a sophomore at the high school where SRO Grubbs worked. Deputy Grubbs had been with the sheriff's department for eleven years and a School Resource Officer for seven years. The investigation by the Virginia State Police resulted in Grubbs's arrest on October 19, 2011, for twelve counts of "taking indecent liberties with a child by a person in a custodial relationship" (Anonymous, October 20, 2011). Then, what was a strange case turned bizarre?

On Monday, November 7, 2011, the alleged 16-year-old victim was reported missing and in danger (Harvey, November 8, 2011). The Virginia State Police reported she could be with the now-fired SRO E.W. Grubbs. A BOLO was put out on the former officer, the missing teenager, and the Jeep Wrangler he was driving. Two days later, Grubbs used his debit card to purchase gas at a service station near Rush, Kentucky. Court records reveal the service station owner called the Kentucky State Police (KSP) and reported the purchase and gave a description of the car and occupants along with the tag number. The nervous attendant stayed on the line and reported Grubbs's car would not start, and Grubb's was looking for someone to jump him off. A KSP lieutenant started on his way in an unmarked car. Before the KSP lieutenant arrived, someone gave Grubbs a jump, and he left the station. The lieutenant saw the Jeep leaving and called for backup. A few miles down the road, the troopers made a "felony stop," and the bizarre odyssey was over.

Grubbs waived extradition back to Virginia to stand trial. The bizarre case had an odd ending. Following a plea negotiation, Grubbs pleaded guilty to five counts of taking indecent liberties with a minor

(Thompson, December 21, 2012). He was not charged with the abduction of the girl. He was sentenced to 10 years, but the sentence was suspended, and he was free to go. The prosecutor said there were evidentiary problems with the case, and this was the best way to handle it. The father of the young girl upset with the disposition filed a civil suit against Grubbs and the sheriff's office.

## Dumfries, Virginia Joseph Ruhren—School Resource Officer

Former Dumfries, Virginia Police Officer Joseph Ruhren left police work and opened up a business—ice cream shop. He thought he was safe from the consequences of past sexual abuse behavior while he was a School Resource Officer. He was wrong (Anonymous, March 14, 2012).

Joseph Ruhren was a Dumfries, VA police officer from 1996 to 2004. He was also a volunteer wrestling coach and School Resource Officer for a Middle School from 1996 to 2001. In 2004, he resigned from the police department in good standing, according to the Town Manager. The ice cream shop, JoJos Original Soft Serve, became a spot where young people congregated. The small business owner became a self-proclaimed child advocate and hired mostly 15- and 16-year-old boys. He gave away free ice cream to honor roll students and hosted bully-free zones for the middle schools. His outward appearance and demeanor masked that he was a dangerous child molester. While he was in jail on prescription fraud charges, claiming addiction to sleeping pills, a 27-year-old man told the police and the FBI that Ruhren had sexually assaulted him when he was a child—12- to 16-year-old. These assaults allegedly occurred from 1996 to 2001 while Ruhrem was a School Resource Officer at his school.

Ruhrem was charged with 12 counts of forcible sodomy, four counts of indecent liberties, two counts of crimes against nature and one count of aggravated sexual battery. While Ruhrem was awaiting trial, a second victim came forward and claimed Officer Ruhren had sexually abused him from 1996 to 1998, allegedly beginning when he was 12 years old.

Ruhrem was arrested on these charges, and his trial was postponed. A third victim reported that Ruhrem sexually assaulted him at his house between 1999 and 2002 when he was between 14 and seventeen years old. The final victim tally would go up to five before Ruhrem was put on trial.

In August 2014, Ruhrem was convicted of four counts of carnal knowledge of a minor, two counts of indecent liberties with a minor, one count of aggravated sexual assault and one count of forcible sodomy. The jury recommended a sentence of 74 years. The next month, September 2014, a jury found him guilty of six counts of taking liberties with a minor and four counts of forcible sodomy. The jury recommended four life sentences plus thirty years.

## Conclusion

As the Illustrative Examples make clear law enforcement sexual misconduct in joint police and community-sponsored programs fits into the taxonomy of police sexual misconduct and is a serious problem. The rational choice model explains the LEO deviant behavior—**PSM Causal Equation—Inclination + Opportunity + Real or Perceived Risk = Police Sexual Misconduct.** The I.E.s also demonstrate that there is a need to reexamine the use of armed LEOs in the school setting. School safety is an important social issue, but so are child civil rights and the right to be free of sexual exploitation by a law enforcement officer. Clear memorandums of understandings between the school and the police organization are necessary, as are the proper selection, vetting, and training of the law enforcement officers. Finally, there must be a zero-tolerance policy against any sexual contact between the students and the LEO.

## References

Anonymous. (2010, February 24). Searcy police officer arrested in teen's bedroom. *Thecabin.net*.

Anonymous. (2011, October 20). Sheriff's deputy arrested. *Bedford Bulletin*.

Anonymous. (2012, March 14). Ice cream shop loses customers after owner is arrested for child sex abuse. *CBS DC.*

AP. (2012, February 29). Cop-cadet sex case has precedents. *Associated Press.*

DOJ. (2011, July). Public School Police Districts. Department of Justice.

Fowler, L. (2014, March 21). Former deputy Nathan Gastineau sentenced to 13 years in prison. *San Bernardino Sun.*

Girona, J. P. (2013, December 19). Tampa police: Officer fired for having sex with teen. *The Tampa Tribune.*

Harvey, N. (2011, November 8). Runaway Bedford deputy caught with 16-year-old Audrey in Kentucky. *The Roanoke Times.*

NASRO. (2012). *To protect & serve: The school resource officer and the prevention of violence in schools.* National Association of School Resource Officers.

Parks, B. (2000, September 12). *LAPD Press Release.*

Peleg, O. (2016, December 31). San Bernardino County deputy arrested for alleged sex with minor. *Laist.*

Phillips, A. M. (2015, April 17). Former Tampa school resource officer gets six years for having sex with underage student. *Tampa Bay Times.*

Raff, C. (2011, March 2). Former police officer gets prison for sexual contact with girl. *Newport Television LLC.*

Stinson, P. M., & Watkins, A. M. (2013). The nature of crime by school resource officers: Implications for SRO programs. *Criminal Justice Faculty Publications* (Paper 11).

Tenorio, G. (2011, June 10). Deputy formally charged in sex with minor case. *CA Patch.*

Tenorio, G. (2012, January 5). Former deputy accused of sexual misconduct faces more legal woes. *CA Patch.*

Theriot, M. T., & Cuellar, M. J. (2016). School resource and students' rights. *Contemporary Justice Review, 19*(3), 363–379.

Thompson, D. (2012, December 21). Former Bedford County deputy sentenced to time served. *Newsadvance.com.*

Thompson, A. M., & Alvarez, M. E. (2012, July). Considerations for integrating school resource officers into school mental health model. *Children in Schools, 31*(3), 131–137.

Winton, R., & Blankstein, A. (2003, March 26). LAPD's Kalish relieved of duty. *Los Angeles Times.*

Winton, R., & Blankstein, A. (2003, July 4). New allegations against LAPD officer. *Los Angeles Times.*

Winton, R., & Blankstein, A. (2003, November 7). Deputy Chief won't be tried. *Los Angeles Times.*

# 13

# Final Thoughts

## Introduction

*Policework* is a morally dangerous occupation and one of several abuse prone occupations. Police sexual misconduct is but one of many deviant behaviors engaged in by police workers, to include police abuse of authority, police violence, and corruption (Barker 2011). However, it should be clear that police sexual misconduct is not confined to the United States. PSM is an occupational deviance problem that occurs in all police agencies worldwide. Admittedly, the examples provided were predominately from the UK, the United States, and other English-speaking countries; however, we supplied examples from other countries when we found them in English. The purpose of this book was to identify a typology of Law Enforcement Officer Sexual Misconduct (PSM) based on real-life examples. We divided PSM into ten types or categories and described each according to known characteristics of victims and offenders, violence or non-violent acts, and real or perceived risk to the offender. The typology should be useful to those who research the issue in the manner proposed first by the late Carl Klockers and continued by his colleagues. We provided select, not exhaustive, Illustrative Examples of each type.

© The Author(s) 2020
T. Barker, *Aggressors in Blue*,
https://doi.org/10.1007/978-3-030-28441-1_13

We provided a **PSM CAUSAL EQUATION Inclination + Opportunity + Real or Perceived Risk = PSM** to explain the occurrence of any PSM type. Police sexual misconduct occurs in an unsupervised work setting where sexually charged law enforcement sexual aggressors with the **inclination,** comes into contact with a pool of vulnerable victims who present the **opportunity** for a sexual encounter. The encounter takes place when the sexual predator "believes" the encounter it to be a **safe** risk situation with a small chance of detection or punishment. However, as the Illustrative Examples, we examined made clear, often the deviant acts are not as safe as the sexual aggressor perceives. However, there is an unknown number of "safe" encounters. Police sexual misconduct is hidden deviance. The perpetrators hide it, the law enforcement peer group and the law enforcement organization knows it occurs but hides it.

There is no way of knowing the actual number of "safe" acts, but we "assume" the most serious forms—sexual homicides, rapists in blue, pedophiles, or child molesters—numbers are small. Previous research studies confirm this assumption. However, that "small" number is a significant social issue. Maher, a former police officer and academic, points out that if only 3% of the approximately six hundred thousand US police officers are engaging in "very serious sexual misconduct" that amounts to an estimated 60,000 police officers, a huge and disturbing number.

A "small" reported numbers do not lessen our efforts to call attention to all types of police sexual abuse and make a concerted effort to prevent what can be deterred and hold the law enforcement professional community and its agencies accountable for punishing errant officers whenever they are identified. This includes proactive and reactive responses.

# Proactive and Reactive Responses to Police Sexual Misconduct

Proactive and reactive approaches are necessary because police sexual abuse is a pattern-prone form of police deviance that receives structural and organizational support from fellow officers who do not engage in that behavior. Proactive approaches come in improved vetting practices and identifying problem officers. No police officer should be hired without a thorough background check. Gypsy cops must become a thing of the past. Based on victimization surveys that indicate that 60–70% of rapes go unreported, former officer Maher opines that 80–90% of police rapes go unreported. One research study confirms the organizational support for a small number of easily identifiable problem officers who are responsible for a disproportionate amount of the deviant acts (Rabe-Hemp and Braithwaite 2012). The purpose of their study was to identify problem-prone officers who had been found guilty of engaging in police sexual misconduct and had been accused of "police sexual misconduct" in the past.

The identified recidivists are part of the "officer shuffle" aka "passing the trash" from one department to another after acts of misconduct. The study examined newspaper accounts of police sexual misconduct from 1996 to 2006 and found that 62 repeat offenders were responsible for 72% of the total victims. These recidivist offenders ranged from 2 to 21 previous allegations of police sexual abuse before the present offense for which they were found guilty. The repeat offenders were more likely to victimize a juvenile than a non-recidivist offender. Fourteen percent of the repeat offenders were allowed to resign from a previous department and resumed police employment at another department. Low rates of investigation and agency punishment were found in the police departments that allowed offending officers to move on, often with glowing recommendations. The practice was known as the NOCO Shuffle among police officers in the St. Louis area, where discredited officers moved from one agency in an area known as North County (Shockley-Elkes 2011). Departments in NOCO with high crime rates and excessive violence that offered little benefits and low salaries hired whoever was available—Gypsy Cops.

Missouri at the time of the study had a system of decertification of police officers for arrest and conviction of certain offenses, and most departments would not hire an officer who was fired from another department, but according to the study, most NOCO agencies avoided this because they were allowed to resign in lieu of charges.

This practice has a long tradition in American police work. In the police department, I worked, every officer who was fired or allowed to resign instead of termination, if they wanted to continue in police work, found a police position, usually in the same county. Some became the police chief or a ranking officer in the smaller city. A number of them repeated their bad conduct in their "second chance" department. We "passed our trash" and were glad they were gone.

## Consequences of Passing the Trash

A police department "passes their trash" to avoid publicity or criticism. The results can be horrific. A serial killer with a badge, Gerald Schaffer, continued his killing spree because his prior misconduct was kept secret. Florida Highway Patrol Trooper-Timothy Scott Harris was not suited for police work. His record at previous departments demonstrated that if someone had reported his behavior or the employing agency had conducted a better background check a six-year-old child would not have lost her mother. The crimes and misconduct of Gypsy Cops are a real legal and liability problem for their departments, and they spread fear and damage to vulnerable victims. However, the havoc caused by Gypsy Cops and the practice of "passing the trash" extends beyond police sexual misconduct.

Some Gypsy Cops are real Rogue Cops—considered an aberration even among "bad" cops. One racist Texas undercover narcotics officer, Tom Coleman, in one day in 1999 arrested 13% of the black population of Tulia, Texas, a city of 5000 people (Blakeslee 2005). In spite of the fact, that no drugs, cash, or firearms were recovered the defendants received a total of 750 years in prison and Coleman was named "Texas Lawman of the Year" by the Texas Attorney General. At trial, all the defendants were convicted based on his uncorroborated testimony. His House of Cards came down when appeals court judges examined his checkered background. It was revealed that Coleman left several Texas law enforcement agencies under suspicious circumstances and had been indicted once for theft. One appeals judge said his testimony was "absolutely riddled with perjury" and he was "the most devious, nonresponsive law enforcement witness this court has witnessed in 25 years on the bench" (*CBS News*, July 4, 2004).

There were consequences for the exposed revelations. Texas Governor Rick Perry pardoned all those convicted. The Tulia defendants shared a $6 million settlement of their civil suits. Texas passed the "Tulia Law" requiring corroborations in undercover investigations. Texas now requires a form (F-5) to be sent to the Texas Commission on Law Enforcement Officers Standards and Education on all officers who leave their department for whatever reason. All Texas agencies, before hiring an officer, must call the Commission and ask for the F-5s from previous employees. This action reduces, but does not eliminate the possibility that a Texas officer with a problem background will not become a Gypsy Cop in another Texas police department, but what if the problem officer applies for a police position in another state?

There are ways to address both issues—interstate and intrastate decertification—problem police officers. Uniform certification and decertification standards among the states would reduce the number of Gypsy Cops and morally unqualified officers. In the United States, all states must promulgate revocations procedures with standardized criteria among and between states. Six states—Massachusetts, New York, New Jersey, Rhode Island, California, and Hawaii employ 26% of the nations police officers but do not have the power to revoke certification for misconduct. This must stop. There must be a national database for all police officers decertified by the individual states. The practice of "passing the trash" must end.

This is especially true when the aberrant behavior is reduced or handled as a misdemeanor or policy violation. A deal is struck between the agency and the offending officer—resign or retire—and no charges or damaging publicity. Often, the agency is prohibited by law or department rules and regulations from divulging any information about "the real scoop" of why the employee left. That would require revealing information from the personnel file. However, some states do allow chiefs of police or sheriffs to disclose information about a former employee to a prospective law enforcement or jail employer.

The UK has created a Police Barred List to prevent police forces in England and Wales from employing officers who have been dismissed for conduct or performance matters (see Box 13.1).

---

**Box 13.1    UK Police Barred List**

1.1 The police barred list is a statutory-sponsored list which acts as a bar on working within policing and certain law enforcement bodies. The list intends to ensure that those who do not meet the high standards required of the police service are not able to continue to work within policing...

1.3 Any person who is dismissed from a position within policing becomes a barred person and is included on the barred list as a result of their dismissal...

**Version 5—Revised December 2017**

---

\* \* \*

There is a separate Police Advisory List that contains the names of officers who resign or retire while under investigation. Employing police forces must use the barred and advisory list during the vetting process. The College of Policing, according to its Web site, was established in 2012 as the "professional body for everyone who works for the police service of England and Wales" (www.college.police.uk). The purpose of the College of Policing is "provide those working in policing with the skills and knowledge necessary to prevent crime, protect the public, and secure public trust." The College sets standards in professional development, including codes of practice and regulation for the 43 police forces in England and Wales. In keeping with this mandate, the College of Policing is responsible for the database of the names of dismissed police officers in England and Wales. The Police Barred List began on December 15, 2017. Any police force dismissing an officer must notify the College within five days. There is a publicly searchable database of officers dismissed, or accused and retired or resigned, of gross misconduct. As of October 2018, there were 100 police officers, special constables, or police staff on the Police Barred List (Garrod, October 18, 2018).

Under the fragmented US police system of local, county, state, special district, and federal system, there is no one body that could legally or practically maintain a Police Barred List or anything similar. However, as pointed out in Chapter 1, forty-one states have some decertification process. It is within the realm of possibility for individual states and some combination/combine of states to develop a Police Barred List/s. The list should be publically searchable.

## Police Accountability

In addition to Police Barred Lists to prevent Gypsy Cops or "passing the trash," the police must become more transparent and accountable. The well-known organizational culture of police agencies that directly and indirectly supports police sexual misconduct through a false sense of "Brotherhood" and the "Blue Code of Silence" must change. The "Blue Code of Silence" leads to limited access to the day-to-day activities of those who are our protectors of individual and civil rights. It is a barrier between our publicly paid protectors and citizens. It shields the American police from true accountability, a necessity in a free society. American police agencies must become transparent and that means honesty and not public relations. Improved data collection and learning from past mistakes are a must for American police agencies at all levels. Voluntary police misconduct self-reporting is the norm in police work, leading to information withheld for impression management purposes. That must be changed.

Self-policing by American police agencies has a long history of failure. We, as a society of democratic citizens, must hold the police and their supervisors responsible for the decisions they make, especially when it comes to known or knowable sexual misconduct.

A public law enforcement agency must release the number and type of complaints alleging police misconduct and their disposition as well as the number and disposition of internal complaints? Public police are accountable to the public. The mere knowledge that police complaint files and disposition records could be reviewed would improve the handling of complaints. Police agencies should explain disciplinary outcomes to outside watchdogs. Why? Sexual predators are often well known in departments, so are violent men, and those "on the take." Why? Someone in the police agency should explain why a small group of officers receive numerous misconduct complaints and are continually sued. The public has a right to know, contrary to what police unions may say. Accountability of public agencies is a basic tenet of democracy. Police sexual misconduct will not survive in a law enforcement agency with a zero tolerance for sexual abuse and disciplinary system determined to be fully accountable for getting to the bottom or all complaints.

Accountability implies that the police agency makes a valid effort to proactively identify instances of police misconduct, including police sexual misconduct—an audit system. Using a system based on the Compstat system, the agency should collect data on police misconduct complaints and record the complaints by the officer and the incident location (Dunn and Caceres 2010). Surveys of persons who have had contact with officers—arrest, ticket, service calls, and other interactions—should be routine, not just when there have been complaints. This will also act as a deterrent to raise the risk level.

Police agencies should make public policies, procedures, and rules concerning police misconduct, including police sexual abuse. If policing policies call for an aggressive patrol strategy—stop and frisk, quality of life, zero tolerance—the public has a right to determine if the strategy leads to discriminatory practices, a quota system, and police sexual abuse. The public must have input into the policies and their implementation. The police and the citizens are partners in police work outcomes. This means more than lip service to something called Community Policing.

## Professionalism Not Profession

The US police community should continue to pursue professionalism—adjective—and leave the discussion of American police work as a profession—noun—to some later time in the future when they have accomplished needed changes in the organizational culture? Why? At a minimum, according to the Merriman-Webster Dictionary a profession, as a noun is "a type of job that requires special education, training, or skill" (www.merrain-webster.com). Local police agencies are unlikely to achieve this level in the near future. For local law enforcement agencies, the "minimum" standards of admission are age 19–21, high school diploma or G.E.D, driver's license, and no serious criminal record—no convictions, guilty/no contest pleas to felonies. Some states add pre-employment drug screening and psychological testing. Forty-eight states—Hawaii, New York and Washington, D.C. do not—have an agency that certifies police officers after completion of the basic training-not specialized education-and examination. This hodgepodge of agencies requires a range of requirement for decertification, and several states do not certify officers at the state level. Also, the basic minimum training varies by type of American police agency and level of government-local, county state federal and special district. By definition, a profession requires a specialized body of knowledge and prolonged-not basic—training.

A code of ethics guides professions and the behavior of its "certified" members. The International Association of Chiefs of Police (IACP) states that law enforcement is a profession "guided by a code of ethics (IACP, 1981)." Unfortunately, this is more rhetoric than reality. The Law Enforcement Code of ethics is a six-paragraph series of rhetorical and laudatory statements given in support of the Law Enforcement Profession. However, the "Code" lacks substance and does not prescribe "ways of acting" when faced with real-life problems. The "Code" must be changed, updated, or become a part of American police history. The cases examined are evidence that the American *policework* occupation needs a real "Code of Ethics." Furthermore, as a practical matter, no American occupational group has ever been accepted as a profession without requiring the minimum standard of a baccalaureate degree.

Should the American *policework* occupation continue to pursue "professionalism" as an adjective describing the behavior of members? Absolutely. There has been remarkable progress made in American policing in the last fifty years in some departments, states, and regions of the country. Some departments have more educated officers, including PhDs. Some departments provide more training than ever before in our nation's history. Minority groups—women, blacks,

Latinos, and others—have joined some police departments and risen to the highest ranks. Some of these minorities are included in the cadre of well-qualified and experienced police administrators who move from department to department as change/reform agents. These change agents attempt to bring about a change in the behavior of the agency and its members. They accept the idea that **all members of the police occupation can attain professional behavior** if they take pride in their work and follow a code of ethical behavior. The leaders and professional associations of the *policework* occupation must commit to developing a managerial system to identify prevention of all forms of police misconduct—abuse of power, corruption, and sexual misconduct—and a real and enforceable code of ethics. Part of that system of control would stop the practice of "passing the trash."

## A Concluding Note of Hope

The sordid cases examined demonstrate, on occasion, police sexual predators make the wrong assessment and choose the wrong victim and face the consequences of their deviant activities. There is hope that police sexual misconduct can be managed, controlled, and prevented. We must hire police officers that are guided by good personal morals and values and ensure that the police peer group reinforces these in the occupational socialization process. The law enforcement community can provide police, rules, and regulations addressing police sexual misconduct, and assure that the subject is taught in the police academy and in-service training and a part of field training. The opportunity structure built into the police work occupation will make it impossible to eliminate all forms of police sexual abuse, but we can lessen the opportunity with supervision and technical assists such as body and dash cameras and better data collection. We can improve the selection process and eliminate the scourge of Gypsy Cops and secret sexual deviants. Finally, when we identify sexual predators, the punishment—administrative, criminal, and civil—must be such that it convinces like-minded persons to avoid the *policework* occupation.

# References

Barker, T. (2011). *Police ethics: Crisis in law enforcement.* Springfield, IL: Charles C. Thomas.

Blakeslee, N. (2005). *Tulia: Race, cocaine, and corruption in a small Texas town.* New York: Public Affairs.

*CBS News.* (2004, July 4). Targeted in Tulia, Texas? Former undercover drug agent tells his story on 60 minutes.

Dunn, A., & Caceres, P. J. (2010, Spring). Constructing a better estimate of police misconduct. *Policy Matters Journal,* 10–16.

Garrod, S. (2018, October 18). College of Policing releases barred list figures. *Police Oracle.*

Rabe-Hemp, C. E., & Braithwaite, J. (2012). An exploration of recidivism and the officer shuffle in police sexual violence. *Police Quarterly, 16*(2), 127–147.

Schockey-Eckles, M. L. (2011, August). Police culture and the perpetuation of the officer shuffle: The paradox of life behind, "the blue wall." *Humanity & Society, 25,* 290–309.

# Index